McGraw-Hill's

CSET

Multiple Subjects

McGraw-Hill's

CSET

Multiple Subjects

Cynthia Johnson

New York   Chicago   San Francisco   Athens   London   Madrid
Mexico City   Milan   New Delhi   Singapore   Sydney   Toronto

1 2 3 4 5 6 7 8 9 10 11 12 13 14 15 16 17   QVR/QVR   1 0 9 8 7 6 5 4 3

ISBN   978-0-07-178175-6
MHID   0-07-178175-7

e-ISBN 978-0-07-178176-3
e-MHID   0-07-178176-5

Library of Congress Control Number 2012938277

CSET is a registered trademark of the California Commission on Teacher
Credentialing and is administered by Evaluation Systems (Pearson Education),
neither of which was involved in the production of, nor endorses, this product.

Interior design by Think Book Works
Illustrations by Cenveo

McGraw-Hill Education products are available at special quantity discounts to use as
premiums and sales promotions or for use in corporate training programs. To contact
a representative, please e-mail us at bulksales@mcgraw-hill.com.

This book is printed on acid-free paper.

CONTENTS

McGraw-Hill's
CSET
Multiple Subjects

PART 1

Introduction

The Exams

The California Subject Examinations for Teachers (CSET): Multiple Subjects exam is a computer-based test designed to measure subject matter knowledge for those wishing to teach in California's public school system. The Multiple Subject Teaching Credential allows the teacher to instruct all subjects in a self-contained classroom for kindergarten through twelfth grade, although it is generally used to teach in elementary schools, kindergarten through grade six.

The CSET: Multiple Subjects exam was developed by the California Commission on Teacher Credentialing (CTC) based on textbooks, the state's curriculum frameworks and standards, teacher education curriculum, and program standards of the CTC. The test contains three subtests, each of which includes multiple-choice and constructed-response questions. The subtests include the following subjects:

▶ Subtest I: Reading, Language, and Literature; History and Social Science
▶ Subtest II: Science, Mathematics
▶ Subtest III: Physical Education, Human Development, and Visual and Performing Arts

You may choose to take each subtest separately or take all three in a single session. The testing times for each subtest are shown in the following list. An additional 15 minutes will be given to complete a nondisclosure agreement and an on-screen tutorial prior to the test.

Subtest I . . . . 3 hours
Subtest II . . . . 3 hours
Subtest III . . . . 2 hours, 15 minutes
Subtests I, II, and III . . 5 hours

Questions

Each subtest will contain multiple-choice and constructed-response questions. The multiple-choice questions will have four answer choices, labeled A, B, C, and D. These items will include either a question or an incomplete statement that can be completed by one of the answer choices. The items may also include a passage or visual aid, such as an illustration, chart, or table. After reading the material, question, or incomplete statement, you must select the one best response for each item. Many of the multiple-choice items involve higher-order thinking skills, as opposed to simple recall. These questions may require you to analyze or apply information, compare it with other information, or make a judgment.

The constructed-response items will include a paragraph, scenario, quote, or visual aid, followed by a related prompt or assignment requiring you to interpret, evaluate, correct, explain, or compare the information. You will then provide a short essay-type response.

How many of each type of question will be on each of the subtests? Let's find out.

Subtest I

Subtest I will include a total of 52 multiple-choice questions and 4 constructed-response questions, divided evenly between the two domains:

▶ Reading, Language, and Literature: 26 multiple-choice and 2 constructed-response items
▶ History and Social Science: 26 multiple-choice and 2 constructed-response items

Subtest II

Subtest II will include a total of 52 multiple-choice questions and 4 constructed-response questions, divided evenly between the two domains:

▶ Science: 26 multiple-choice and 2 constructed-response items
▶ Mathematics: 26 multiple-choice and 2 constructed-response items

Subtest III

Subtest III will include a total of 39 multiple-choice questions and 3 constructed-response questions, divided evenly among the three domains:

▶ Physical Education: 13 multiple-choice and 1 constructed-response item
▶ Human Development: 13 multiple-choice and 1 constructed-response item
▶ Visual and Performing Arts: 13 multiple-choice and 1 constructed-response item

Writing Skills

The CSET: Writing Skills test is separate from the CSET: Multiple Subjects test. However, it can be taken only in conjunction with the Multiple Subjects test. The Writing Skills test is composed of two essay questions.

Using the Computer

The CSET: Multiple Subjects exam will be given on a computer. Although paper-and-pencil options are available for some of the other CSET exams, they are not offered for the Multiple Subjects exam. Before the test begins, you will be given a 10-minute on-screen tutorial, which introduces the features of a computer-based assessment and shows how to navigate through the test and make answer choice selections.

Before the tutorial begins, a nondisclosure agreement will be presented on the screen. You will be given five minutes to read and accept the agreement. Not responding within the time limit will end the test session. Once the agreement has been accepted, the tutorial will begin.

Since each subtest of the exam is timed, a timer will be visible in the top right corner of the computer screen at all times. This will indicate how much time remains for that particular test. Below the timer will be numbers that indicate which question or screen you are currently working on, such as 10 of 30. These reminders can be minimized by clicking on them. They can be restored at any point by clicking on the icons. A window will appear to indicate when 30 minutes are remaining in the test, and then the timer will appear automatically to indicate when 5 minutes remain.

Navigating the Screens

Throughout the test, three buttons will be visible at the bottom of the screen. These buttons have the following functions:

▶ **Previous** returns to the previous screen.
▶ **Next** moves to the screen that follows.
▶ **Navigator** allows you to move to any question or screen on the test.

To press these buttons, you may click on them using the mouse or navigate to them using the computer's keyboard. To use the keyboard, press the Tab key to move through the choices. Then, when the cursor appears over your choice, press the space bar to select it.

By using the Navigator button, located in the lower right corner of the screen, you can select any section of the test to complete first or answer any question at any time. In other words, you do not have to complete the test questions in order. After you click on this button, a Navigator screen appears. That screen indicates the name of the test section, lists question numbers, and labels each question as complete, incomplete, or unseen. A question is labeled as *complete* if it is a multiple-choice question for which an answer has been chosen or a constructed-response question for which even a single letter has been typed in the answer box. The Navigator screen also shows which questions, if any, you have flagged for review. We'll talk more about this option in the next section, on answering questions.

To choose a question or section you would like to move to, simply click on the question number or the section directions. To move out of the Navigator screen, click on the Close button in the bottom right corner.

Answering Questions

The vast majority of the test questions will be multiple-choice questions. For these questions, to indicate which answer you have selected, either use the keyboard to enter the letter of the option (A, B, C, or D), use the mouse to click on the bubble located at the beginning of your choice on the screen, or use the Tab key to move through the options and press the space bar when the cursor is over the answer you want to select. Once you have chosen an answer, you can change it by selecting a different option. You will have an opportunity to practice making multiple-choice answer selections during the tutorial prior to the test.

For each constructed-response question, the screen will present an assignment or prompt. Below it, you will see a large, empty box in which you will type your answer. At the top of the box are icons you may select to cut, copy, paste, undo, or redo typing. At the bottom of the box is a word counter.

As you work through the test, you may find questions you wish to return to later. No problem! At the top right corner of the screen is a button labeled *Flag for Review*. To flag the question currently displayed, either use the mouse to left-click on this button, use the Tab key to move through the options and select the button with the space bar, or hold down the Alt key while pressing the F key. A flag icon will be highlighted, and the question will be highlighted on

the Navigator screen. Questions can be flagged for review regardless of whether they have been answered. If time allows, you can go back to review questions at a later point during the test. If you decide to unflag a question, simply click on the *Flag for Review* button a second time, which will cause the highlighted flag to disappear.

Ending the Test

To end the testing session and exit the test, you will click on the Next button on the final question of the test. If you would like to review any of the questions or your responses, you must do this before exiting the test. Once you have exited the test, you will not be able to go back to any questions.

After you have clicked on Next on the last test question, a box will appear, telling how many of the questions, if any, are incomplete. It will then ask if you are sure you want to end the test. Clicking on Yes exits the test. Clicking on No allows you to review and change the answers to any of the questions you would like to see one final time.

Scoring

The CSET is a criterion-referenced test. That means your score is based on your knowledge and skills in relation to given standards, and not based on a comparison of your responses to those of other test takers.

To pass the CSET: Multiple Subjects exam, you must pass each of the subtests. Each subtest is scored based on the number of points earned on the multiple-choice and constructed-response sections. For the multiple-choice questions, you will earn points for each correct response but will not be penalized for incorrect answers; you simply will not earn a point for any questions that are not answered or are answered incorrectly. Constructed-response questions will be scored holistically by highly qualified California educators. The responses will be judged on overall effectiveness in respect to given performance characteristics and will be given a score based on a scoring scale. Points earned on each of these sections are then weighted to provide a score between 100 and 330. The minimum passing score is 220.

What happens if you pass some, but not all, of the subtests? You will not have to retake any subtests you passed, as long as you are able to use the score to earn certification within five years of the test date. In other words, you have five years to pass all three subtests and become certified, but you do not have to pass all the subtests on the same day. However, passing scores may be used indefinitely to satisfy the basic skills requirement. There is no time limit on the subtest scores in this case.

If, by chance, you need to retake one or more of the subtests, you may do so as many times as needed to achieve a passing score. You will need to re-register each time and wait a minimum of 45 days before retaking the test.

CHAPTER 2

Test-Taking Strategies

Generally, teachers are much more accustomed to giving tests than taking tests. However, they also recognize the importance of being prepared for these tests. That being said, you may have already begun to study the material that will be assessed on the CSET: Multiple Subjects exam, you are probably already planning to complete the practice questions in this book, and you are likely to wake up on test day with the confidence that you are ready to ace the exam. Good for you!

In this chapter, we'll review a few test-taking strategies that can help you do your best on the CSET, or any other test, for that matter. You may already be familiar with some of these strategies, but a quick refresher may help you remember them on test day.

Preparing for the Test

As you know, preparation is the key to doing well on any test. And it is always best to start studying early. Allow plenty of time to review all of the material, and try to avoid cramming in the few days before the CSET is scheduled. As you prepare, keep the following tips in mind.

Become Familiar with the Format

Answering practice questions, such as the ones in the coming chapters, is a great way to become familiar with the types of questions that will be on the CSET. Not only will you know what to expect when the test begins, but you also will be more comfortable with the test format.

Find Out What You Know

Use the practice questions in this book to find out your strengths and weaknesses related to the test material. This valuable information can guide your study time. Were you able to breeze through the history questions easily? That's great! You will not need to spend as much time reviewing that subject. Were the literature questions a little more challenging? Don't be discouraged. Now you know what to study.

What types of questions did you find most difficult? Rather than worrying that something was a challenge, focus on mastering it. For example, if you were not completely comfortable with constructed-response questions, practice writing short answers to a variety of prompts. If you are not sure where to find practice prompts, use any of the multiple-choice questions in this book, and respond to them as if they were constructed-response questions by writing a paragraph to explain your answer, rather than selecting A, B, C, or D.

Learn About Yourself

If someone were to ask you about your teaching style, you could probably answer quite easily. But what if someone asked about your test-taking style? Are you someone who works meticulously, or do you tend to get nervous and rush through test questions? Do you comprehend information best by skimming a passage and then reading it carefully a second time? Is it helpful for you to read the questions first, then the material? As you prepare for the test, figure out what strategies work best for you. Use this information to make a plan of attack for doing your best on test day.

Make a Plan

On test day, you can answer the questions in any order you choose. Think about which types of questions you want to answer first, so you can tackle them right away when the test begins. You might consider starting with the questions you find easiest in order to gain confidence early. Or you might want to start with the questions you find most challenging to get them out of the way. The choice is yours.

Also, pay attention to how much time it takes to answer the practice questions in the book, and figure out how much time you want to spend on each multiple-choice or constructed-response question during the test. Knowing which questions to answer first and how much time to spend on each will prepare you to hit the ground running on test day.

The Day Before the Test

By the time test day approaches, you will have spent plenty of time preparing for the exam. On the day before the test, focus on these things:

▶ **Take a break!** Try not to study much, if at all, on the day before the test. Instead, go for a walk, read a book, or call a friend. It is important to make sure you go into test day being relaxed.

▶ **Check the time.** Double-check the appointment time listed on your CSET confirmation to make sure you know exactly when to arrive at the test. Anyone arriving 15 or more minutes late may be required to reschedule the test, without refund. It is important to know when you need to be there, and plan accordingly.

▶ **Pack your bags.** Have all of your supplies and required materials ready to go ahead of time. Be sure to bring your signed photo identification, such as a driver's license or passport, and any other materials listed on your admission ticket. You will not be allowed to eat in the testing room, but you may want a snack between sessions. Bring something with you

in case there is not a convenient place to grab something during your break.

▶ **Get some rest.** Make sure you get plenty of sleep on the night before the test. Consider getting up early on the day before the test, so you will be ready to go to bed a little earlier than usual, too. That way, you will wake up refreshed and ready after a good night's sleep.

Tips for Test Day

The big day has arrived! Once you have studied and are well prepared for the test, what can you do on test day to make sure everything runs as smoothly as possible? Let's find out.

Give Yourself Some Time

Consider setting the clock early enough to give yourself a few extra minutes to get ready. That way, you will not feel the need to rush, and you can walk into the testing center feeling calm and relaxed. Also, an unplanned obstacle, such as heavy traffic, won't throw you off your game. There will be time to deal with the unexpected and still get to the test without feeling frazzled.

Begin with Breakfast

By now, you know the importance of eating a healthy breakfast. Test day is no different. The last thing you want is to be interrupted during the test by the sound of your stomach growling. Even if you don't feel like having a four-course meal, at least grab some toast with peanut butter, yogurt with granola, or a piece of fruit and a glass of milk. Regardless of whether you have scheduled one, two, or all three subtests for the day, you are definitely going to need energy to do your best.

Dress for Success

Wear something that is comfortable and gives you confidence. Since you do not know what the temperature of the testing room will be, consider dressing in layers or bringing a lightweight sweater.

Be Aware of the Rules

When registering for the CSET, you will have to agree to follow all testing center rules. As you might expect, these include not smoking, not bringing relatives or guests with you to the test, and not carrying any weapons. You must also agree not to bring a cell phone; electronic communication device such as an MP3 player, PDA, or calculator watch; calculator; printed materials or notes; packages or bags, including backpacks and briefcases; hats; food, drink, or gum; aids such as rulers, highlighters, or translation devices; and unauthorized medical devices including inhalers, EpiPens, or insulin injections, unless prior permission has been granted.

During the Test

All of your hard work and preparation come down to one thing: passing the CSET. So what can you do during the test to be sure you earn the best possible score? Let's go over a few helpful strategies.

Stay Calm

By now, you have studied, you have completed the practice tests, you have a test-taking plan in place, and you know what to expect. Don't let nerves get in the way of doing your best. If you begin to feel anxious, recognize that this is completely normal. Then take a few deep breaths, remind yourself that you are ready to take on the CSET, and focus on doing the great job you are capable of.

Follow Directions

Pay close attention to any directions given by the test proctor or provided on the computer. You may find directions related to specific questions or sections, as well as directions that relate to the overall test. If any directions are unclear, be sure to ask for clarification.

Read Everything

Make sure you read everything carefully. This includes all directions, passages, visual aids, labels, captions, questions, and answer choices. The information given is there for a reason. Consider all of it before attempting to answer any question. Also, reading quickly may cause you to overlook key ideas. A simple word such as *not* or *except* can completely change the meaning of a question.

With that in mind, some people find it helpful to read the questions first, then the passage. That way, they know what information to be on the lookout for as they read. If that strategy works well for you, use it. If you are not sure, try it as you work through this book. Figure out what helps you, and use this information on test day.

Also, some of the constructed-response items may include two steps, such as *analyze* and *compare*. Make sure you have read the question carefully enough to understand exactly what is expected. A complete response will need to address all of the given tasks.

Do Not Read More than Is Written

It can be tempting to read more into a question that what is written. You may wonder, "What is this question *really* asking?" Believe it or not, trick questions are not part of the CSET. Simply answer the question that is being asked, no more and no less.

Don't Read the Answer Choices . . . Yet

After reading a multiple-choice question, try to answer it without reading the answer choices. If you are unsure of the correct response, reread the information, and try again. Once you have figured out the answer to the question, look for your response among the answer choices.

Now Read Every Answer Choice

As you work through the multiple-choice questions, there may be times when answer choice A looks great. Before you select it, make sure you read all of the other answer choices as well. Several of the choices may be tempting. There may even be more than one option that is partially correct. But there is only one *best* answer. Carefully read all of the choices before determining which one is best.

One approach that can help you decide whether your answer choice is the best one is to explain to yourself *why* it is better than the others. This can help you focus on the important details that cause this option to address the question more completely.

Read the Question Again

Once you have selected the best answer choice, take another look at the question. Make sure that your answer completely and correctly responds to what is being asked. This works with constructed-response answers as well as multiple-choice.

Pace Yourself

As you know, the CSET: Multiple Subjects exam is timed, and it will be up to you to know how much time remains in each session. The good news is that the timer on the screen will be visible. Pay attention to it, and be aware of how much time is left, but do not focus on it.

Before the test begins, have an idea of how long you want to spend on the multiple-choice questions and the constructed-response questions, and budget the available time accordingly. Let's use Subtest I as an example. This is a three-hour test containing 52 multiple-choice and 4 constructed-response questions. Suppose, after completing the practice questions in this book, you expect to need 15 minutes to answer each constructed-response item. That's a total of one hour for those items, which leaves two hours to answer the multiple-choice questions. That equates to 26 multiple-choice questions per hour. If you spend about two minutes on each question, you will be able to complete the test and still have a few extra minutes at the end to review your work or go back to any flagged questions.

Does this mean you need to watch the clock to make sure you only spend two minutes on each question? Not at all! Just know that at the end of the first half hour, you should have answered about 13 multiple-choice questions. If you are behind that point, try working a little more quickly. If you are a little bit ahead, take a deep breath and know that you are on the right track to finishing the test with a few minutes to spare.

Don't Rush

You know the importance of pacing yourself and working quickly. But trying to move too quickly can lead to mistakes. Keep your eye on the timer, and work at a pace that allows you to still read carefully enough to do your best.

Answer Every Question

No matter what, be sure to answer every single question. Even if this means just clicking on one of the choices, make sure no question is left blank.

As you know, you will earn points for each multiple-choice question you answered correctly. That means there is no penalty for guessing. If you get an answer right, you get points. If you get it wrong, you get no points. If you skip it, you get no points. Skipping a question is the same as getting it wrong. So take your best guess. At least there will be a chance of earning the points if an answer is selected.

If you find that time is about to run out and you have not quite finished the test, quickly navigate through the remaining screens, and mark an answer for any questions that are left. This way, you will at least have a shot at possibly earning a few points on questions that otherwise would have been left blank.

Make Your Best Guess

How do you make your best guess?

▸ First, eliminate any answer choice that you know is wrong. The more choices you can eliminate, the better your odds of selecting the correct answer.
▸ Next, look for two answer choices that are similar, with the exception of a few words. Chances are, one of these two is correct. Forget about the other answers, and choose between the two similar options.
▸ Also, look for answers that are opposites. Obviously, they cannot both be correct, so at least one can be eliminated. Keep in mind that they may both be wrong, so take a look at the other answer choices before automatically selecting one of the opposites.

▶ After that, look for absolutes such as *always*, *never*, and *every*. Very few things *always* happen, *never* happen, or happen *every* time. There is a good chance you could eliminate inflexible answers that contain absolutes such as these.

▶ Then eliminate any choices that stand out from the others. For example, if the answer choices are 7, 70, 700, and 9,136, it is easy to see which one of these does not belong.

Why try to eliminate answer choices before guessing? Well, it all comes down to simple probability. When randomly choosing one of four answer choices, there is a 25 percent chance of selecting the correct one. Eliminating one answer choice improves those odds to one in three, or 33 percent. Eliminating two choices gives you a fifty-fifty chance of getting the question right. So it pays to eliminate as many incorrect answers as possible. Then choose between the ones that remain.

Is guessing the best way to take a test? No. Is it better than getting an answer wrong by not marking anything? Absolutely!

Keep Moving

Try not to spend too much time on any single question. If something is a little tricky, flag it and come back to it later. The correct answer may seem much clearer when you look at it with fresh eyes. Or a different part of the test might include information that offers a helpful clue for answering this question correctly.

The big concern is that you do not want to waste time pondering a single item. This could cause you to run out of time to answer a really simple question later in the test.

Keep in mind that a skipped question is the same as a wrong answer. Before flagging an item to come back to later, mark something, anything, just in case time runs out before you have a chance to give it a second look.

Check Your Work

At the end of the test, use any remaining time to check your work. Go back to any flagged items, and take a second look. Reread your constructed-response answers to make sure that what you wrote fully addresses the question. Take a second look at any multiple-choice questions that you were not sure of. Make the most of all of the time allotted.

Trust Your Instincts

Suppose you go back to check your work and are unsure of whether or not the answer you previously marked is correct. If you carefully read the information and reviewed each answer choice, there's a good chance that your original answer is the correct one. Research has shown that your first answer is usually correct. Unless you find that you overlooked a piece of information, remember something that did not come to mind earlier, or made an error in calculation, stick with the answer you chose originally.

Getting Started

Now you know a little bit about the CSET: Multiple Subjects exam. You also have a few tricks up your sleeve for doing well on the test. So there's only one thing left to do. Let's get started on reviewing the information on the test. Good luck!

PART 2

Diagnostic CSET

CHAPTER 3

Diagnostic Test

This diagnostic test is an abbreviated version of the CSET subtests, consisting entirely of multiple-choice questions. (You'll find critical-response assignments similar to those in the CSET in the book's two complete practice tests.) Before each subtest, you'll find an answer sheet that you can tear out of the book and mark your answers on. After completing the diagnostic test, you'll be able to check your answers on the Domain Results Worksheet.

Test Directions

Each of the multiple-choice questions in this diagnostic test has four answer choices. After reading each question carefully, choose the single best answer. Record your answers on the answer sheet provided before each subtest. You may work on the questions in the three diagnostic subtests in whichever order you choose.

SUBTEST I

READING, LANGUAGE, AND LITERATURE; HISTORY AND SOCIAL SCIENCE

Multiple-Choice Answer Sheet

Reading, Language, and Literature

QUESTION NUMBER	YOUR RESPONSE
1	
2	
3	
4	
5	
6	
7	
8	
9	
10	
11	
12	
13	

History and Social Science

QUESTION NUMBER	YOUR RESPONSE
14	
15	
16	
17	
18	
19	
20	
21	
22	
23	
24	
25	
26	

Multiple-Choice Questions

1. Some common vowel patterns are associated with more than one pronunciation (e.g., the *oo* in *moon* and *book*). Which of the following nonsense words illustrates a vowel pattern that is highly consistent in its pronunciation?

    A. Hain

    B. Flead

    C. Sough

    D. Trow

2. Which is of the following terms means the study of the way sounds function in a particular language?

    A. Syntax

    B. Phonology

    C. Morphology

    D. Semantics

3. Which of the following is the best example of Noam Chomsky's theory of universal grammar, as reflected in a child's linguistic error?

    A. "Me like you."

    B. "I not never want to play cards."

    C. "This ain't what it looks like."

    D. "I goed to school today."

4. Holophrastic speech is typical of which age group?

    A. 18 months to 30 months

    B. One to two years

    C. Two to five years

    D. Five to seven years

5. What verb form is the word *waiting* in the sentence "She was waiting for the results of the test"?

    A. A participle

    B. An infinitive

    C. An adverbial

    D. A gerund

6. In which of the following sentences is the italicized word used correctly?

    A. The state legislature was divided into two *discrete* parts.

    B. Each sales representative in the company has a *discreet* territory that he covers.

    C. The crowd thought that the politician was *discrete* in his comments about his opponent.

    D. It is possible to remain *discrete* even during a crisis.

7. Which of the following sentences contains an adverb clause?

    A. Jed felt confident as long as he was in charge.

    B. The picnic that our class had planned was canceled due to rain.

    C. After the conference on marketing concluded, the participants went to lunch.

    D. The president of our class and vice president both spoke at the school assembly.

Read the following passage; then answer the two questions that come after it.

(1) Oaxaca in southern Mexico has a long history. (2) Some of it is set down in codices, picture books without words which describe the lives of the people and rulers of that area. (3) The story of Fight-Deer, an important leader of the Mixtec people, is recorded, from 1030 until his death, in seven of these beautifully colored codices. (4) Each of these seven codices tells of Fight-Deer's rules, from the time he became chieftain in 1030, when he was 19, until his death at the age of 52. (5) After each victory (he won every battle until his defeat in 1063), he killed the opposing leaders, married their wives, and adopted their children. (6) Fight-Deer fought many battles against the neighboring people. (7) In this way, he acquired a huge family of wives and endless numbers of children.

8. Which of the following changes could best improve the logical organization of the passage?

   A. Move sentence 6 so that it follows sentence 1.

   B. Move sentence 6 so that it follows sentence 4.

   C. Move sentence 7 so that it follows sentence 1.

   D. Move sentence 7 so that it follows sentence 3.

9. Which of the following revisions would improve the style of sentence 3?

   A. The story of Fight-Deer, an important leader of the Mixtec people from 1030 until his death, is recorded in seven of these beautifully colored codices.

   B. An important leader of the Mixtec people, is recorded in seven of these beautifully colored codices, the story of Fight-Deer, from 1030 until his death.

   C. From 1030 until his death, the story of Fight-Deer, an important leader of the Mixtec people, is recorded in seven of these beautifully colored codices.

   D. The story of Fight-Deer is recorded in seven of these beautifully colored codices, an important leader of the Mixtec people from 1040 until his death.

10. Which of the following presentation components would be most important to a dramatic reading?

    A. Relaxation and pacing

    B. Volume and organization

    C. Pacing and volume

    D. Enunciation and gesture

11. Which of the following does a legend generally include?

    A. A story of a national hero, based on fact and fiction

    B. A story that takes place in the future

    C. An explanation of the earth's beginnings

    D. A humorous story with blatant exaggerations

Read the following poem, "Invictus" by William Ernest Henley; then answer the two questions that come after it.

Out of the night that covers me,
Black as the pit from pole to pole,
I thank whatever gods may be
For my unconquerable soul.

In the fell clutch of circumstance
I have not winced nor cried aloud.
Under the bludgeonings of chance
My head is bloody, but unbowed.

Beyond this place of wrath and tears
Looms but the Horror of the shade,
And yet the menace of the years
Finds and shall find me unafraid.

It matters not how strait the gate,
How charged with punishments the scroll.
I am the master of my fate:
I am the captain of my soul.

12. The images used in the poem help to reinforce ____.

    A. the difficulties encountered in life

    B. the complexities of feelings

    C. the anxiety of being lost

    D. the pain of separation

13. The narrator of the poem most likely thinks ____.

    A. that he will fail at his task

    B. that he has talents few know about

    C. that he is an artist at heart

    D. that he will be able to surmount his challenges

"If anyone steal cattle or sheep . . . if it belong to a god or the court, the thief shall pay thirtyfold therefore."

14. This quote is taken from which of the following sources?

    A. Rosetta stone

    B. Gettysburg Address

    C. Hammurabi's Code

    D. Mayflower Compact

15. The name Krishna is associated with which of the following beliefs?

    A. Buddhism

    B. Taoism

    C. Islam

    D. Hinduism

16. On which of the following dates did the Visigoths attack Rome?

    A. 44 BCE

    B. 410 CE

    C. 753 BCE

    D. 70 CE

17. Which of the following people came to power by uniting nomadic tribes in northeast Asia?

    A. Vasco da Gama

    B. Genghis Khan

    C. Alexander the Great

    D. Hadrian

Use the following list to answer the question that comes after it.

> ▶ Its name derives from a Latin root word meaning "universal."
> ▶ It imposed and collected taxes and also accepted gifts of all kinds.
> ▶ It had its own laws and its own lands.
> ▶ It controlled philosophy, the arts, and all education.

18. The list of facts best describes which of the following in the Middle Ages?

   A. Bulgarian Empire

   B. Knights Templar

   C. Roman Catholic Church

   D. Magna Carta

19. All of the following explorers were looking for a route to Asia. Which one was the first European to set foot in what is now Florida?

   A. Juan Ponce de León

   B. Amerigo Vespucci

   C. Samuel de Champlain

   D. Sir Humphrey Gilbert

Use the following map to answer the question that comes after it.

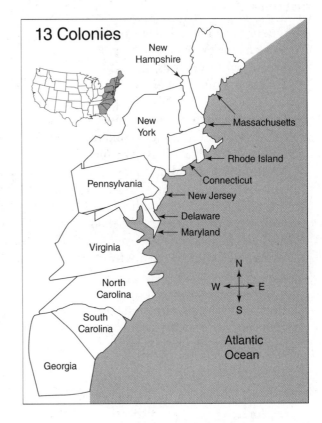

20. What information from the map supports the conclusion that farming in New England would be more difficult than in the other colonies?

   A. The New England colonies were the farthest north.

   B. The southern colonies were the largest in area.

   C. The middle colonies had larger farms.

   D. The New England colonies were the smallest in area.

Use the following excerpt to answer the question that appears after it.

"The period for a new election of a citizen to administer the Executive Government of the United States being not far distant . . . it appears to me proper, especially as it may conduce to a more distinct expression of the public voice, that I should now apprise you of the resolution I have formed to decline being considered among the number of those out of whom a choice is to be made."

21. From which of the following sources is the quoted passage excerpted?

 A. Articles of Confederation

 B. Washington's Farewell Address

 C. *Marbury v. Madison*

 D. Monroe Doctrine

22. Which of the following statements best describes the Northern Securities Company of 1904?

 A. It was a network of secret routes and safe houses by which African American slaves could escape to free states.

 B. It successfully broadcast the first transatlantic radio signal.

 C. The Supreme Court ruled that the government had the right to break it up.

 D. It refers to the passage of the Eighteenth Amendment.

23. The Viceroyalty of New Spain can most accurately be described as which of the following?

 A. Lands conquered by Cortés from the Aztecs in 1521

 B. Alta California

 C. Outposts established by the Franciscan order

 D. Territories of the Spanish Empire in North America and Asia

24. On gaining a charter from the czar, the Russian-American Company established Fort Ross in 1812 for which of the following reasons?

 A. To expand its sea otter trade

 B. To search for gold in California

 C. To grow food for its other settlements

 D. To challenge the sovereignty of Spain

25. The Raker Act, passed by the U.S. Congress in 1913, allowed what project to proceed in Yosemite National Park?

 A. Yosemite Valley Railroad

 B. O'Shaughnessy Dam

 C. Griffith Observatory

 D. Hoover Dam

26. What famous obscenity trial took place in San Francisco in 1957?

 A. O. J. Simpson trial

 B. Patty Hearst trial

 C. *Howl* trial

 D. Rodney King beating trial

SUBTEST II

SCIENCE, MATHEMATICS

Multiple-Choice Answer Sheet

Science

QUESTION NUMBER	YOUR RESPONSE
1	
2	
3	
4	
5	
6	
7	
8	
9	
10	
11	
12	
13	

Mathematics

QUESTION NUMBER	YOUR RESPONSE
14	
15	
16	
17	
18	
19	
20	
21	
22	
23	
24	
25	
26	

Multiple-Choice Questions

1. A person on earth who weighs 135 pounds will weigh approximately 23 pounds on the moon. Which of the following is the best explanation for this phenomenon?

   A. The gravitational pull of the earth is stronger than that of the moon.

   B. The earth's core is made of a denser material than that of the moon.

   C. The diameter of the earth is 12,756.2 km, and the diameter of the moon is 3,474.8 km.

   D. The moon affects the motion and the orbit of the earth around the sun.

Use the figure shown here to answer the question that follows it.

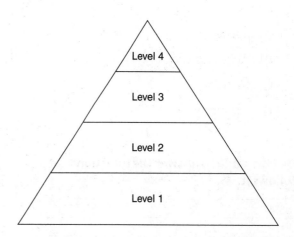

2. In an energy pyramid, the amount of available energy _____.

   A. increases from level 1 (producers) to level 4 (tertiary consumers)

   B. decreases from level 1 (producers) to level 4 (tertiary consumers)

   C. increases from level 1 (primary consumers) to level 4 (producers)

   D. decreases from level 1 (primary consumers) to level 4 (producers)

Use the following statement to answer the question that comes after it.

An object is traveling north at 56.1 km/hr.

3. This statement best represents which of the following concepts?

   A. Speed

   B. Acceleration

   C. Velocity

   D. Inertia

Use the table to answer the question that follows it.

85.47	87.62	88.71
Rb	Sr	Y
37	38	39

4. What is the atomic mass of Strontium (Sr)?

   A. 38

   B. 49.62

   C. 87.62

   D. 125.62

5. Two different isotopes of the same element will always have _____.

   A. the same number of protons and neutrons in their nuclei

   B. the same number of protons but a different number of neutrons in their nuclei

   C. the same number of neutrons but a different number of protons in their nuclei

   D. different numbers of protons and neutrons in their nuclei

6. In general, herbivores play which of the following roles in an ecosystem?

   A. Tertiary consumers

   B. Secondary consumers

   C. Primary consumers

   D. Producers

7. In humans, damaged or old skin cells are regularly replaced by new cells. The process through which these new cells are created is known as _____.

   A. hybridization

   B. meiosis

   C. diakinesis

   D. mitosis

8. Which of the following organelles is present in plant cells but not present in animal cells?

   A. Ribosomes

   B. Mitochondria

   C. Chloroplast

   D. Vacuole

9. Thunderstorms are most often associated with which of the following types of clouds?

   A. Cirrus

   B. Cumulonimbus

   C. Lenticular

   D. Stratus

10. In general, an acid will have _____.

    A. a higher pH than a base

    B. a lower pH than a base

    C. the same pH as a base

    D. the same or different pH as a base depending on the substance involved

11. With some exceptions due to weather conditions, temperature generally decreases with elevation. Which of the following statements provides the best explanation for this?

A. Higher elevations are physically closer to the sun during the day. Therefore, more light is reflected by the ground at these elevations.

B. The chemical makeup of the atmosphere is different at higher elevations, leading to different levels of heat retention.

C. The majority of the heating of the surface of the earth comes from the earth's core, and higher elevations are farther from this heat source.

D. The sun heats the surface of the earth, which in turn heats the atmosphere. Since the air is "thinner" at higher elevations, it has more difficulty retaining this heat.

12. A neuron is the primary cell of organs in which of the following systems?

A. Nervous system

B. Endocrine system

C. Digestive system

D. Skeletal system

13. According to Darwin's theory of evolution, traits that make an organism more suited for its environment can become more common over time through the process of _____.

A. adaptive selection

B. artificial selection

C. natural selection

D. prior selection

14. Which of the following numbers is larger than $\dfrac{152}{27}$?

A. $\dfrac{101}{85}$

B. $\dfrac{16}{17}$

C. $\dfrac{8}{1,003}$

D. $\dfrac{91}{15}$

15. Jake has saved $15 more than Sara, while Sara has saved $20 more than Harvey. If Harvey has saved $8, how much has Jake saved?

A. $23

B. $28

C. $35

D. $43

16. A student wishes to estimate the average GPA of students who are also varsity athletes. She takes a sample of 35 such athletes and asks them to write down their most recent GPA. Which of the following aspects of her study could produce a biased result?

A. She did not consider the size of the population when picking the sample size.

B. Her sample does not include students who are not athletes.

C. The students may lie about their GPA.

D. She did not ask the students their current age.

17. The probability of event A is 0.05, while the probability of event B is 0.08. Which of the following is the probability of the complement of event A?

    A. 0.03

    B. 0.13

    C. 0.92

    D. 0.95

Use the graph shown here to answer the question that follows it.

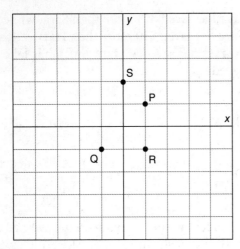

18. Which pair of points are on a line with negative slope?

    A. *S* and *P*

    B. *P* and *Q*

    C. *Q* and *R*

    D. *R* and *P*

19. Which of the following expressions is equivalent to $2\frac{1}{8} \div \frac{4}{3}$?

    A. $\frac{17}{8} \times \frac{4}{3}$

    B. $\frac{17}{8} \times \frac{3}{4}$

    C. $\frac{11}{8} \times \frac{4}{3}$

    D. $\frac{11}{8} \times \frac{3}{4}$

20. What is the first step in performing the following multiplication problem?

    1,459
    × 27

    A. Multiply 2 and 9.

    B. Multiply 2 and 1.

    C. Multiply 7 and 9.

    D. Multiply 7 and 1.

Use the equation provided to answer the question that follows it.

$8x + 4 = 9$

21. Which of the following equations is equivalent to the equation provided?

    A. $8x + 6 = 9$

    B. $16x + 4 = 18$

    C. $24x + 12 = 27$

    D. $8x + 4 = 8$

22. In the triangle shown here, angles *A* and *C* have the same measure. What is the measure of angle *C*?

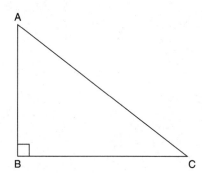

  A. 30 degrees

  B. 45 degrees

  C. 80 degrees

  D. 90 degrees

23. In a figure with 50 squares, if 20 squares are shaded, what percentage of the squares is shaded?

  A. 20%

  B. 30%

  C. 40%

  D. 70%

24. What is the slope of a line that is perpendicular to the line $y=\dfrac{1}{3}x+4$?

  A. −3

  B. $-\dfrac{1}{3}$

  C. $-\dfrac{1}{4}$

  D. 4

25. A company rents trucks for short-term rentals. The company charges a flat fee of $50 for any truck rental in addition to a rate of $8 per hour. If a truck is rented for *h* hours, which of the following expressions represents the total charge for the rental?

  A. $50 + 8h$

  B. $50h + 8$

  C. $58h$

  D. $8(50 + h)$

26. The Pythagorean theorem applies to triangles that _____.

  A. have at least two sides with the same length

  B. have one angle that is larger than 60 degrees

  C. have three sides of the same length

  D. have one angle that is exactly 90 degrees

SUBTEST III

PHYSICAL EDUCATION, HUMAN DEVELOPMENT, AND VISUAL AND PERFORMING ARTS

Multiple-Choice Answer Sheet

Physical Education

QUESTION NUMBER	YOUR RESPONSE
1	
2	
3	
4	
5	

Human Development

QUESTION NUMBER	YOUR RESPONSE
6	
7	
8	
9	
10	

Visual and Performing Arts

QUESTION NUMBER	YOUR RESPONSE
11	
12	
13	
14	
15	

Multiple-Choice Questions

1. Which of the following effects is NOT a benefit of fitness education?

   A. Reduced stress

   B. Increased body mass index

   C. Increased ability to perform motor skills

   D. Reduced likelihood of injury and disease

2. In which order are nonlocomotor skills developed?

   A. Stretch, bend, turn, twist

   B. Twist, turn, bend, stretch

   C. Bend, stretch, turn, twist

   D. Turn, stretch, bend, twist

3. The *Physical Education Framework for California Public Schools* establishes that physical education instruction should do all of the following EXCEPT _____.

   A. transfer learning

   B. encourage practice

   C. establish a safe environment

   D. promote participation in organized sports

4. In younger students, self-responsibility is one influence on social development. Self-responsibility includes _____.

   A. responding appropriately and respectfully to winning or losing

   B. motivating teammates and opponents to be successful

   C. working cooperatively with other members of a team

   D. accepting the physical abilities of others

5. Which of the following statements is true?

   A. Boys are generally more physically fit than girls.

   B. Muscle strength is the best way to assess the impact of exercise.

   C. The fitness level of young girls increases through elementary school.

   D. Low-intensity exercise provides greater cardiovascular benefits than high-intensity exercise.

6. Which of the following statements is accurate?

   A. A child's perception of his or her athletic ability often affects status in school.

   B. Children from lower-SES families are often more fit than those from higher-SES families.

   C. A child from an affluent family is less likely to participate in sports than less-affluent children.

   D. Children who participate in fitness activities are more likely to experience lower-back problems.

7. According to behaviorist B. F. Skinner's theory of operant conditioning, which is the best strategy for modifying students' behavior?

   A. Delayed rewards for desired behaviors

   B. Intermittent punishment for undesired behaviors

   C. Instant negative reinforcement for undesired behaviors

   D. Immediate positive reinforcement for desired behaviors

8. The greatest influence on children during the early years of life is _____.

   A. their family

   B. peer groups

   C. their own morals and beliefs

   D. authority figures such as teachers

9. Which of the following statements is true regarding successful learning?

   A. Students learn best when given small amounts of material that vary in difficulty.

   B. Students learn best when engaged in learning and expected to master the material.

   C. Students learn best when working independently at the appropriate difficulty level.

   D. Students learn best when in an environment where they are not corrected or criticized.

10. A child has mastered the concept that when the appearance of an object is altered, the basic properties of the object remain the same. This concept is known as _____.

    A. accommodation

    B. assimilation

    C. conservation

    D. seriation

11. A dance instructor commented that her students showed a flowing degree of energy. Which element of dance was the instructor evaluating?

    A. Force

    B. Level

    C. Space

    D. Time

12. A combination of musical tones creates a quality of tension. Which term describes this sound?

    A. Chord

    B. Consonance

    C. Dissonance

    D. Harmony

13. Early theater stages were semicircular, open-air amphitheaters. These were later replaced with a raised stage. Which other event also occurred during the period in which the raised stage was introduced?

    A. Official theater companies were licensed by the state.

    B. Women were allowed to have minor roles in theater performances.

    C. Women were permitted to be spectators but not actors in the theater.

    D. Bible stories were performed to educate the audience about religious events.

14. Which statement is true of art during the Baroque period, from 1600 to 1750?

    A. Frescoes, sculptures, and works that celebrated great events were popular during this time.

    B. Art during this period had a complex style, appealed to the senses, and involved strong emotion.

    C. Multiple images of a single subject appeared on a single surface, at times with overlapping geometric forms.

    D. Primary colors were placed beside each other in paintings in order to mix them, and little black or white was used.

15. Emphasis is one of the principles of art. Which description best explains emphasis?

    A. An object in the work is painted in such a way that it stands out, causing the viewer's eye to be drawn to a particular point.

    B. The elements of the piece are arranged in a harmonious manner, which may be symmetrical or asymmetrical.

    C. A piece gives the viewer a sense of how the work might actually feel, producing a tactile quality.

    D. The artist uses positive and negative space to create a feeling of depth within a piece.

CHAPTER 4

Diagnostic Test Results

Domain Answer Sheets

On the following pages, you'll find Domain Answer Sheets that will help you in evaluating your answers. The first two columns show the correct answer for each question. Use the other two columns to indicate whether you answered a specific question correctly or not. At the end of each answer sheet, there's a space where you can enter the total number of questions you answered correctly for that particular domain.

Interpreting Your Results

While the diagnostic subtests can't predict how you'll perform on the actual CSET, your results here will give you a reasonable idea as to which domains you may need to review more. You may consider the following guide helpful in determining how much time you should spend reviewing a particular domain:

All questions answered correctly → Review this domain relatively briefly

Most questions answered correctly → Spend less time reviewing this domain than others

Most questions answered incorrectly → Spend more time reviewing this domain than others

Learning from Your Mistakes

After the Domain Answer Sheets, you'll have the chance to look over explanations for each question. If you answered a question incorrectly, reading the explanation will enable you to determine whether you made a simple mistake and otherwise understand the material or whether you need to go back and review the subject matter.

SUBTEST I: DOMAIN ANSWER SHEET

READING, LANGUAGE, AND LITERATURE

QUESTION NUMBER	CORRECT ANSWER	YOUR ANSWER	
		Correct?	**Incorrect?**
1	A		
2	B		
3	D		
4	B		
5	A		
6	A		
7	A		
8	B		
9	A		
10	D		
11	A		
12	A		
13	D		

You answered _____ out of 13 questions correctly.

SUBTEST I: DOMAIN ANSWER SHEET

HISTORY AND SOCIAL SCIENCE

QUESTION NUMBER	CORRECT ANSWER	YOUR ANSWER	
		Correct?	**Incorrect?**
14	C		
15	D		
16	B		
17	B		
18	C		
19	A		
20	A		
21	B		
22	D		
23	C		
24	B		
25	B		
26	C		

You answered _____ out of 13 questions correctly.

SUBTEST II:
DOMAIN ANSWER SHEET
SCIENCE

QUESTION NUMBER	CORRECT ANSWER	YOUR ANSWER	
		Correct?	Incorrect?
1	A		
2	B		
3	C		
4	C		
5	B		
6	C		
7	D		
8	C		
9	B		
10	B		
11	C		
12	A		
13	C		

You answered _____ out of 13 questions correctly.

SUBTEST II:
DOMAIN ANSWER SHEET
MATHEMATICS

QUESTION NUMBER	CORRECT ANSWER	YOUR ANSWER	
		Correct?	Incorrect?
14	D		
15	D		
16	C		
17	D		
18	A		
19	B		
20	C		
21	C		
22	B		
23	C		
24	A		
25	A		
26	D		

You answered _____ out of 13 questions correctly.

SUBTEST III:
DOMAIN ANSWER SHEET

PHYSICAL EDUCATION

QUESTION NUMBER	CORRECT ANSWER	YOUR ANSWER	
		Correct?	Incorrect?
1	B		
2	A		
3	D		
4	A		
5	A		

You answered _____ out of 5 questions correctly.

SUBTEST III:
DOMAIN ANSWER SHEET

VISUAL AND PERFORMING ARTS

QUESTION NUMBER	CORRECT ANSWER	YOUR ANSWER	
		Correct?	Incorrect?
11	A		
12	C		
13	B		
14	B		
15	A		

You answered _____ out of 5 questions correctly.

SUBTEST III:
DOMAIN ANSWER SHEET

HUMAN DEVELOPMENT

QUESTION NUMBER	CORRECT ANSWER	YOUR ANSWER	
		Correct?	Incorrect?
6	A		
7	D		
8	A		
9	B		
10	C		

You answered _____ out of 5 questions correctly.

Subtest I Explanations

READING, LANGUAGE, AND LITERATURE; HISTORY AND SOCIAL SCIENCE

1. **A** The *ai* vowel pattern is associated with the long-*a* sound in words such as *rain, paid, raise.* Studies of sound-symbol correspondence in English have found very few exceptions to this rule. Choices B, C, and D are associated with multiple pronunciations.

2. **B** Phonology is the study of the way sounds function in a particular language. Choice A, syntax, is sentence structure. Choice C, morphology, is the study of word structure, of how sounds and syllables combine to produce meaning. Choice D, semantics, is the study of how sounds, words, phrases, and sentences combine to convey meaning and content.

3. **D** Universal grammar is the theory of linguistics that says there exists an underlying principle of grammar in all languages that children everywhere innately learn. The theory recognizes that the grammar may be different in the various languages, but children come to recognize the rules. In this case, choice D is correct. The child says "goed" instead of "went" because she has already understood that, in English, past tenses are formed by adding *-ed* to a present-tense verb. The child has not yet learned that the past tense of the irregular verb *go* is *went.* Choice A is not correct; the child has chosen an incorrect objective pronoun, *me,* instead of the correct pronoun, *I.* In choice B, the speaker uses a double negative. In choice C, the speaker uses a slang word, *ain't.*

4. **B** Holophrastic speech, which is one-word utterances, is typical of children from one to two years. Children from 18 months to 30 months typically use telegraphic speech, using mostly content words without affixes or function words, so choice A is incorrect. Choice C is incorrect because this time period typically displays emergent speech. Choice D is incorrect. From five to seven years, children display intermediate language fluency.

5. **A** Here *waiting* is a participle and part of the verb *was waiting.* Choice B is incorrect because an infinitive always has *to* with it, as in *to wait.* Choice C is not correct because *waiting* cannot be an adverbial. Choice D is not correct because a gerund, while it does end in *-ing,* is the form of a verb that is used as a noun.

6. **A** The word *discrete* means separate, distinct, or different. The word *discreet* means having good judgment. Choice A is the only sentence that is correct; it uses the word *discrete* correctly. Choice B incorrectly confuses the word *discreet* with *discrete.* Choices C and D also confuse the two words.

7. **A** Choice A is the only sentence to contain an adverb clause. The clause *as long as he was in charge* modifies the adjective *confident.* Choice B contains a relative clause. Choice C has a main clause and a subordinate clause. Choice D is a simple sentence with a compound subject.

8. **B** Choice B creates a logical flow of ideas in the passage. Choice A would not make sense, nor would choice C or D.

9. **A** This sentence properly places the entire adjective clause immediately after the noun that it modifies (Fight-Deer), rather than breaking up the clause so the meaning of the sentence is not clear. Choices B, C, and D do not have the clause adjacent to the noun, and the meaning of the sentence is confused.

10. **D** While relaxation is a good concept, it is not a presentation component, making choice A incorrect. The same holds true of organization, so choice B can be eliminated. Choice C is a possibility, since pacing and volume might be good components for a dramatic reading. But clearly, choice D, enunciation and gesture, is the best choice.

11. **A** A legend is usually based on a person and then enlarged to make the person bigger. Facts may be mixed with fiction about the person. Choice B has the trait of many

science fiction books. Choice C is what is usually found in myths, and choice D is a description of a tall tale.

12. **A** The images created by the poet talk about the many terrible things that occur in life. While there may be complexities of feelings, that is not what the images are reinforcing, so choice B is incorrect. Choices C and D are incorrect also. This is not what the images conjure up.

13. **D** In the last stanza, the viewpoint of the narrator of the poem is clear. He is the master of his fate, which translates to him being able to surmount his challenges. The other choices do not describe the narrator's viewpoint.

14. **C** Hammurabi's Code, a code of laws written around 1772 BCE, was the first written document to set down standards and laws for a society. The Rosetta stone, discovered in 1799, was written in both Greek and Egyptian hieroglyphics, which allowed scholars to learn how to translate ancient Egyptian writing. Abraham Lincoln delivered the Gettysburg Address in 1863, invoking the concept of human equality. The Mayflower Compact was a document signed by the settlers at Plymouth Colony in 1620.

15. **D** Krishna is a Hindu deity, depicted in the Sanskrit epic *Mahabharata*, written sometime between 6,000 and 4,000 BCE. Siddhartha Gautama lived around 600–400 BCE and handed down the principles of Buddhism to his followers. Taoism is an ancient Chinese way of living in harmony with Tao, or the way or path. Islam was founded by the prophet Muhammad, who lived around 570 to 630 CE and was believed to be a messenger of God. He recorded his beliefs in the Islamic holy book, the Qur'an.

16. **B** On August 24, 410 CE, the Visigoths, under the leadership of King Alaric, attacked and plundered the city. Julius Caesar was assassinated in 44 BCE, on the Ides of March (March 15). According to legend, 753 BCE is the date on which Rome was founded by the brothers Romulus and Remus. In 70 CE, the Roman army—under the command of Titus, who would later become emperor—laid siege to Jerusalem and destroyed the temple.

17. **B** Genghis Khan (c. 1162–1227 CE) united the many nomadic tribes that roamed the Asian steppes, creating the Mongol Empire. Vasco da Gama was an explorer; in 1498, he was the first European to reach India. Alexander the Great was Greek. He tried to extend his empire by invading India in 326 BCE, but he was turned back. He died a few years later. Hadrian was a Roman emperor from 117 to 138 CE. He is best known for building Hadrian's Wall, which marked the northern boundary of Roman Britain.

18. **C** The Roman Catholic Church was the most powerful institution during the Middle Ages, from 590, when Gregory proclaimed himself its supreme leader, until 1517, when Martin Luther began the Protestant Reformation. The Latin word *catholicus* means "universal." The Bulgarian Empire, which began in 690, is noted mainly for its many conflicts with the Byzantine Empire and was never as powerful as the Catholic Church. The Knights Templar was a military order started with the First Crusade in 1096. The Magna Carta was a document signed by King John of England in 1215; it forced the king to accept limits on his powers.

19. **A** The Spaniard Juan Ponce de León (1460–1521) discovered Florida in 1513, naming it Pascua de Florida (Feast of Flowers) because he and his crew landed on Palm Sunday. Although America is named after Vespucci, his voyages were to South America—Brazil and Guiana. De Champlain founded Quebec in 1603, and Gilbert founded St. Johns, Newfoundland, in 1583.

20. **A** The map shows that the New England colonies were the most northern of the 13 colonies and would have a harsher climate for farming. Choices B and D are based on the map but have nothing to do with farming. Choice C cannot be determined from the map.

21. **B** George Washington's Farewell Address was printed in a Philadelphia newspaper on September 19, 1796. In it, he warned of the political dangers to be avoided if the country were to remain true to its values. The Articles of Confederation, written in 1777, were the first constitution for the United States during

the Revolutionary War. *Marbury v. Madison* was a case in which the Supreme Court ruled in 1803 that the court had the power of judicial review of acts of Congress. The Monroe Doctrine, in 1823, warned European powers that any attempt to colonize or interfere with the nations of Latin America would be viewed as an act of aggression.

22. **C** The Northern Securities Company was a railroad trust that was broken up by the Supreme Court, which ruled, "The supremacy of the law is the foundation rock upon which our institutions rest." The Underground Railroad was the term used to define the network of secret routes and safe houses. The first transatlantic radio signal was received by Marconi in 1901. The Eighteenth Amendment authorized Prohibition, outlawing alcohol consumption, which began in 1920.

23. **D** The Viceroyalty of New Spain included the territory in North America and Asia claimed by the Spanish king. The capital was Mexico City. The land Cortés conquered was only a part of the viceroyalty. Alta (Upper) California was a province of the viceroyalty. The Franciscans established missions, or outposts, throughout Alta California to convert the Native Americans to Christianity.

24. **C** The company's other settlements were in Alaska, where raising crops was much harder. Because of overhunting, the sea otter population was actually declining. Gold was not discovered in California until 1848. Although the czar did defy the king of Spain by granting the charter, there was never any conflict between the two countries.

25. **B** The O'Shaughnessy Dam flooded the Tuolumne River in Hetch Hetchy Valley. Because the valley was located in a national park, an act of Congress was needed to allow the dam to be built. Conservationist John Muir opposed the project. The Sierra Club is now actively campaigning to tear down the dam and return the valley to its original pristine beauty. The Yosemite Valley Railroad opened in 1907, greatly increasing the number of visitors to the park. The Griffith Observatory is in Los Angeles, and the Hoover Dam is in Arizona.

26. **C** Poet and publisher Lawrence Ferlinghetti and the bookstore City Lights were accused of distributing obscenity when customs agents seized copies of Allen Ginsberg's poem *Howl*, which had been printed in England. The judge ruled that the work was not obscene. The trial put the Beat Generation into the national spotlight, and many young people flocked to San Francisco. The O. J. Simpson trial ended in 1992 with Simpson being acquitted of two counts of murder. Patty Hearst, a newspaper heiress, was convicted of bank robbery in 1976 and sentenced to 35 years in prison. She was released after 22 months. President Clinton pardoned her in 2001. The Los Angeles police officers who beat Rodney King were acquitted in 1992, setting off days of race riots in which 53 people were killed.

Subtest II Explanations

SCIENCE, MATHEMATICS

1. **A** Weight is a measurement of how much the force of gravity acts on an object. Since the person weighs more on earth, the force of gravity must be stronger on earth.

2. **B** The most available energy can be found at the producer level, where producers derive energy from sunlight through photosynthesis.

3. **C** Velocity is the speed of an object along with the direction in which the object is moving.

4. **C** The atomic number of an element will always be a whole number, since it is a count of the number of protons found in the nucleus of a single atom of that element. Therefore, the atomic mass must be 87.62.

5. **B** The number of protons "defines" an element and will always stay the same. What changes for different isotopes is the number of neutrons.

6. **C** Herbivores derive their energy from producers (plants, etc.). Since they are one level above producers, they are known as primary consumers.

7. **D** Mitosis is a process of cell division that yields two identical cells. This is commonly confused with meiosis, which yields genetically different cells.

8. **C** Photosynthesis takes place in chloroplasts, which are not found in animal cells.

9. **B** Thunderstorms are formed when warm, humid air rises. This air cools, resulting in condensation and the formation of a large thunderhead cloud (cumulonimbus).

10. **B** Low pH values are associated with acids, while high pH values are associated with bases.

11. **D** In a sense, the atmosphere is heated from the "ground up." The sun heats the ground, which in turn heats the dense air near the surface. At higher levels of elevation, the air is less dense, and less heat is retained.

12. **A** Neurons are the main cells found in the brain and the nerves throughout the body.

13. **C** If a trait is more likely to lead to survival, then that trait is more likely to be passed on to the next generation. This process is called natural selection.

14. **D** 152/27 is 152 ÷ 27, which is approximately 5.63. Only answer choices A and D are larger than 1, since their numerators are larger than their denominators. Answer choice D is approximately equal to 6.1.

15. **D** Harvey has saved $8, and Sara has saved $20 more. Therefore, Sara has saved $8 + $20 = $28. Since Jake has saved $15 more than that, Jake has saved $28 + $15 = $43.

16. **C** As long as the sample size is larger than approximately 30, the population size will not have much of an influence on the estimate. Additionally, she did not need to include any other students, since she wishes to estimate only the GPA of athletes. Her biggest risk is her data collection method, which asks students to self-report their GPA.

17. **D** The probability of an event and its complement always add to 1. Therefore, the probability of event A complement is 1 − 0.05 = 0.95.

18. **A** A line with negative slope will fall from left to right, as would a line through the points S and P.

19. **B** The mixed fraction $2\frac{1}{8}$ is equivalent to $\frac{2 \times 8 + 1}{8} = \frac{17}{8}$. Finally, division by a fraction is equivalent to multiplication by its reciprocal.

20. **C** When multiplying two multidigit numbers, you will always multiply the ones or units digits first.

21. **C** If the same number is added to both sides or multilpied by both sides of an equation, you will get an equivalent equation. Only in answer choice C was the same number used on both sides. In this case, both sides were multiplied by 3.

22. **B** The pictured triangle is a right triangle. You know this by the square marking at angle B (which is 90 degrees). Since the total of the measures of the angles in any triangle is 180 degrees, there are 90 degrees remaining for angles A and C. If these two angles have the same measure, then they must have measure 90 ÷ 2 = 45 degrees.

23. **C** $\frac{20}{50} = \frac{40}{100} = 40\%$

24. **A** Perpendicular lines have negative reciprocal slopes.

25. **A** Since $50 is a flat fee, it should not be multiplied by any variable. For each hour, $8 is charged. This means the total hourly charge will be $8h$. Adding the flat fee yields answer choice A.

26. **D** The Pythagorean theorem applies only to right triangles.

Subtest III Explanations

PHYSICAL EDUCATION , HUMAN DEVELOPMENT, AND VISUAL AND PERFORMING ARTS

1. **B** Body mass index (BMI), which is calculated from the weight and height of a person, indicates the amount of body fat. Generally, fitness education would cause a decrease, rather than an increase, in BMI.

2. **A** The order in which nonlocomotor skills are developed is stretch, bend, turn, twist.

3. **D** The *Physical Education Framework for California Public Schools* establishes that physical education instruction should achieve the goals named in answer choices A, B, and C, as well as including class management and employing effective teaching behaviors.

4. **A** Social development is influenced not only by self-responsibility, but also by team activities and social interaction. Self-responsibility includes taking responsibility for one's own fitness as well as taking responsibility for one's own reaction to the outcome of competition.

5. **A** Typically, the fitness level of young girls decreases throughout elementary school. Boys are usually more physically fit, and their fitness level remains constant throughout these years. The most effective way to assess the impact of exercise is to monitor the heart rate of the students. While low-intensity exercise does offer a range of significant health benefits, high-intensity exercise, performed on a regular basis, provides the greatest benefit.

6. **A** One of the benefits of being involved in fitness activities and athletics is the fact that a student's ideas about his or her own athletic ability can influence his or her status in school and society. Another positive impact is the reduced likelihood of lower-back problems (contradicting choice D). Choices B and C are incorrect because students from higher-SES families are more likely to participate in sports and physical activities, so those from lower-SES families are often less physically fit than their higher-SES peers.

7. **D** Skinner's operant conditioning relies on positive reinforcement, or reward, for desired behavior; negative reinforcement, which is the escape of punishment by demonstrating desired behavior; extinction, or not reinforcing undesired behaviors; and punishment of undesired behaviors. He believed that immediately offering positive reinforcement for desired behaviors, paired with extinction or punishment for undesired behaviors, was the best strategy to use with students.

8. **A** The family provides the greatest influence on young children. However, changes in families over the years have given more influence over children's values to schools, peers, and social or religious groups, while the role of parents has diminished in many cases.

9. **B** Successful learning should include the expectation of mastery of materials at the appropriate difficulty level. Students should receive positive corrections and constructive criticism, and they learn best when engaged in learning activities supervised or instructed by the teacher.

10. **C** Conservation of numbers, volumes, and weights is generally mastered during Piaget's concrete operational stage, which occurs between the ages of 7 and 11. Assimilation is the way children blend new information with prior knowledge. Accommodation is the adjustment of existing knowledge to fit a new experience. Seriation is the ability to arrange objects in a logical progression, such as from shortest to longest.

11. **A** The quality and degree of energy refer to the element of force. Examples of other ways to describe the degree of energy of a dance include *dynamic*, *static*, *tense*, and *light*.

12. **C** Several notes played together are a chord; however, a feeling of tension produced by these notes is dissonance. Consonance, in contrast, is a combination of tones that has a relaxing quality.

13. **B** Amphitheaters were used in ancient Greek theater from approximately 600 to 400 BCE. During this time, women were not permitted to perform onstage. The raised stage was introduced in Roman theater between 300 BCE and 500 CE. By this time, women were allowed to play minor roles. Medieval theater, from 500 to 1300, focused on teaching religion, rather than entertaining. Later, during the Renaissance and Reformation, from 1400 to 1600, theater companies were hired by the state.

14. **B** In addition to having a complex style, appealing to the senses, and involving strong emotion, Baroque art also emphasized depth and space. Landscapes were popular; these works usually did not include people.

15. **A** Emphasis is also the center of interest in visual art. The viewer's eye is drawn to a specific point, causing that point to attract attention.

PART 3

Review

CHAPTER 5

Subtest I

Reading, Language, and Literature
History and Social Science

Reading, Language, and Literature

Domain 1: Language and Linguistics

Language is a system of communication, and linguistics is the scientific study of language. All languages are governed by structural rules that tell us how to organize words, phrases, and sentences. The term *grammar* refers to both the rules and the study of those rules.

Parts of Speech

The parts of speech tell us how a word is used within a sentence. Learning grammar begins with understanding the eight parts of speech:

▶ A **verb** is an action word. Examples: *run, walk, be.*
▶ A **noun** is the subject or object of a sentence. Examples: *Mary, house, table.*
▶ A **pronoun** stands in for a noun. Examples: *he, she, it.*
▶ An **adjective** modifies a noun. Examples: *beautiful, tall, strong.*
▶ An **adverb** modifies a verb, an adjective, or another adverb. Examples: *quickly, greatly.*
▶ A **preposition** stands before a noun or pronoun and connects it to another word in a sentence. Examples: *on, in, of, to, by, through, for.*
▶ A **conjunction** connects two words, sentences, or phrases. Examples: *and, but, or, yet.*
▶ **Interjections** express an emotion or pause. Examples: *hooray, ah, uh, er.*

Syntax and Sentences

Syntax is the study of how sentences are constructed. A sentence is a group of words organized in a meaningful way according to the rules of grammar. Languages differ in many aspects, but they are most similar in the way they construct a sentence, with most using the subject-predicate structure. A sentence fulfills one of four major functions:

▶ A **declarative** sentence makes a statement of fact or opinion. Example: *I'm going to the store.*
▶ An **imperative** sentence gives an order to someone. Example: *Don't park there.*
▶ An **interrogative** sentence asks a question. Example: *May I have a piece of cake?*
▶ An **exclamatory** sentence expresses an emotion or states a fact or opinion strongly.

Example: *I can't listen to this music anymore!*

Several major concepts structure a sentence:

▶ A **clause** is a group of words containing a subject and verb. Clauses may be independent/main or dependent/subordinate (i.e., noun, relative, and adverbial clauses). Independent clauses can stand alone and make sense as a sentence; dependent clauses can support an independent clause but cannot stand alone. Examples:

I know why you did that.

Why you did that is a dependent clause supporting *I know.*

I work at the office, and my husband works at home.

I work at the office and *my husband works at home* are two independent clauses that make sense on their own.

▶ A **phrase** is a group of words that work together in a sentence but cannot stand alone. Example:

The bicycle leaning against the fence is blue.

The bicycle leaning against the fence is a phrase that cannot stand alone in this sentence.

▶ The **subject** is a single word or phrase in a sentence that is doing or being something. It can be a person, place, thing, or idea. Examples:

She goes to the store every day.

She is the subject.

Living in the country was a challenge for them.

Living in the country is the subject.

▶ The **predicate** is a verb, an action word or phrase. Examples:

The dog ran after the car.

Ran is a verb.

John is the tallest boy in the class.

Is is a verb.

Semantics

While syntax guides us in constructing logical sentences, semantics focuses on what words, sentences, and texts mean. Syntax and semantics are related. The way we structure our speech and writing through word choice, clauses, phrases, and sentence complexity can affect the interpretation of what our communication means. Several concepts in semantics are important:

▶ **Etymology** helps us understand the meaning of words by tracing their history and origins and by studying how their use has changed over time. Words that originate from the same parent language can have similar spellings and meanings in English. Many English words have Latin or Greek origins, but a significant number can be traced to Sanskrit and Arabic. The word *cotton*, for example, has its origins in the similar-sounding Arabic word for the Egyptian cotton plant, *qutn*.

▶ **Denotation** is the literal, or dictionary, meaning of a word.

▶ **Connotation** refers to the subjective meaning of a word or phrase. Connotation can be influenced by emotion and culture, and it may carry an implicit value judgment.

▶ Readers and listeners must locate words in **context** in order to understand their meaning. Context can refer to a word's place in a sentence or to the larger culture that helps determine the meaning of words and phrases.

Pragmatics

Pragmatics studies how context helps us decipher the meaning of words. While syntax is important for organizing written and spoken communication, semantics and pragmatics govern meaning. Context can be something as encompassing as culture or as particular as one's facial expression and body language. You can tell someone to "close the door" with either a smile or a frown on your face, and that context will signal a particular meaning to the other person. Pragmatics is especially important in cross-cultural and cross-class situations. Contexts of cultural differences and power relations can create ambiguity in communication. Pragmatics looks at the interconnection between language, meaning, and the social and cultural context of the communicators.

Phonology

Phonology is the study of a language's sound system and how sounds convey meaning. Do not confuse phonology with phonetics, which is concerned with how sounds are transmitted and perceived through the senses. Phonology delves beneath the level of the word to find meaning in the smallest units of sound, called phonemes. A phoneme is a sound or group of sounds. Phonemes help us distinguish differences in the meaning of words. For example, the words *ball* and *hall* mean different things because the phonemes /b/ and /h/ signal that these are two different words, even though they both end in *all*.

Phonological Awareness. As children develop language skills, phonological awareness is crucial for their ability to read and write. Reading problems are likely to stem from poor phonological processing.

Phonological awareness (or phonemic awareness) refers to the understanding that words are built upon sounds and that sounds can be combined to form words. Phonological development begins with the easiest skill, identifying the first sound in a word. Teachers can promote phonological development and awareness through exercises using rhyming, segmenting, and blending:

▶ **Rhyming.** Listening to rhymes helps children identify sounds and common word patterns. Children learn to hear the similarities and differences in word sounds.
▶ **Segmenting.** Breaking down a word into separate sounds helps children divide words into phonemes.
▶ **Blending.** Once children learn to segment words, they can then recombine the individual phonemes into smooth-flowing words.

Morphology
Morphology is the study of morphemes, which are the smallest units of meaning in a language. Morphemes may or may not stand alone, and all words are composed of one or more morphemes. For example, in the word *payment*, *pay* is a morpheme—a meaningful unit—that can stand alone as a word, but *-ment*, a suffix meaning an action or product, is a morpheme that cannot stand alone. Together, these two morphemes build a word whose meaning refers to a product that results from an action. Like phonemes, morphemes help build language and convey meaning.

Alphabetic Principle
The alphabetic principle refers to the relationship between symbols and sounds. According to this principle, letters in an alphabet are symbols that represent the sounds in a language. Teachers should be aware of cultural differences that come into play regarding symbols and sounds. Some cultures have one alphabet letter for every speech sound, while other cultures recognize several letters or letter combinations with the same sound. The term *grapheme* refers to the alphabetic unit that represents a single phoneme. English has an especially complex relationship between symbols and sounds, since the English alphabet has 26 letters but the English language has 40 sounds. This means that some sounds must be represented by more than one letter. An example is the graphemes *ph* and *gh*, which both represent the phoneme /f/, as in *graph* and *laugh*. Mastering the alphabetic principle, the relationship between letters and sounds, is a major step to reading competency.

First Language Development
Children develop language competency in stages, beginning with hearing sounds and recognizing speech patterns. Biology and social environment may influence, but not determine, language skills and development. Many theories try to explain language development.

Psychologist B. F. Skinner argued that children learn language, or verbal behavior, just as they learn other types of behavior, through conditioning and reinforcement. Children will learn to use correct grammar by being positively reinforced, and will be discouraged from using incorrect grammar through negative reinforcement.

Linguist Noam Chomsky's views differ from Skinner's and revolutionized thinking about linguistic development. Chomsky argued that, unlike other animals, humans have an innate ability to learn language. He called this ability the language acquisition device (LAD). Chomsky theorized that universal rules of grammar underlie all languages, and only surface aspects of language, such as vocabulary, differ.

Primary language development occurs in six major stages:

▶ **Birth to one year.** Children make cooing and babbling sounds in imitation of the vowel and consonant-vowel combination phonemes they hear.
▶ **One to two years.** Phonological awareness increases as children begin to recognize when

speakers use correct pronunciation. Their vocabulary, especially nouns and verbs, grows between 18 and 24 months. They begin to join words into two-word combinations.

▶ **Three to five years.** Children's pronunciation improves, and they begin to construct three-word sentences. Words and sentences become increasingly complex as children learn to add morphemes. They also begin to grasp metaphors.

▶ **Six to ten years.** Children know all vowels and most consonants, and they can break down words into syllables. They learn denotation, the literal or dictionary meaning of a word. Their understanding of metaphor increases. They begin to use more complex grammatical structures.

▶ **Seven years.** Children are capable of simple reading and writing.

▶ **Eight years.** Children can use complex and compound sentences, know all speech sounds, and can regulate the rate and volume of their speech.

Second-Language Acquisition (SLA)

Students learning a second language also learn in stages. According to Stephen Krashen and Tracy Terrell, there are five stages of second-language acquisition, or SLA:

▶ **Preproduction.** Students at this stage have little or no comprehension of the second language and usually are not verbal.

▶ **Early production.** The student is beginning to comprehend. The student responds to the teacher with one- or two-word answers and uses verbs in the present tense.

▶ **Speech emergence.** The student's comprehension improves, and the student can use simple sentences with some grammar and punctuation errors.

▶ **Intermediate language fluency.** Students have vastly improved comprehension but make occasional grammatical errors.

▶ **Advanced fluency.** The student can speak almost at the level of a native speaker.

Theories of Second Language Acquisition

Several theories attempt to explain how students learn a second language:

▶ **Comprehensible input hypothesis.** One SLA theorist is the linguist Stephen Krashen, who developed five hypotheses for SLA, based on the notion of comprehensible inputs, or linguistic knowledge and information that students can understand and acquire:

▶ **Acquisition-learning hypothesis.** Acquiring and learning a second language are independent processes. Acquisition takes place at the subconscious level, while learning is the conscious study of grammatical rules.

▶ **Input hypothesis.** Each step in learning a second language should build on the inputs from the previous step.

▶ **Natural-order hypothesis.** Students must acquire the rules of a second language in a natural, comprehensible order in order to learn that language.

▶ **Monitor hypothesis.** Students of a second language use their internal self-monitors to correct errors before speaking.

▶ **Affective filter hypothesis.** Emotional and environmental contexts may act as filters to inhibit understanding and learning a second language.

▶ **Comprehensible output hypothesis.** Not all theorists agree with Krashen's comprehensible input hypotheses. Merrill Swain developed a theory based on comprehensible outputs. According to Swain, students acquire a second language by perceiving the gap between what they already know and what they should know. When students notice the gap in their language skills, they modify their output and become open to learning new skills.

▶ **Skill acquisition theory.** Developed within cognitive psychology, the skill acquisition theory states that learning a second language is a skill that depends on practice and perseverance. This skill, like any other, progresses from declarative knowledge (consciously learning the rules) to procedural knowledge (unconsciously learning how to apply the rules).

▶ **Processability theory.** Another cognitive approach to SLA, developed by Manfred Pienemann, attempts to understand how students deal with "interlanguage" systems—the idiosyncratic system a student creates, blending features of the native and second language, before being completely proficient in the second language.

▶ **Sociocultural theory.** Cultural anthropologists, cultural psychologists, and sociologists emphasize the social and cultural context of language development, and this is especially important in second-language acquisition. Sociocultural approaches emphasize cultural sensitivity, cultural themes and traditions, and the culturally specific use of words and body language in communication.

Literacy Development and Assessment

Literacy refers to the skills a child needs to properly communicate with others. This broad and developing category includes vocabulary acquisition, listening skills, critical thinking, spelling, writing ability, reading comprehension, understanding body language, and reading symbols and pictorial clues.

Many of the processes we've covered will help children learn to decode words and become fluent readers. Phonemic awareness, phonetics, the alphabetic principle, and building an extensive vocabulary are crucial first steps to literacy. As children learn to recognize sounds and identify them with alphabetic letters and letter patterns, their word recognition and reading abilities grow. Advanced readers will learn to understand the meaning of words from their context in a sentence, even if they are not familiar with the dictionary definition of the word. Spelling development also depends on phonemic awareness. Children may initially sound out words and eventually memorize their correct spelling.

Difficulty with reading usually stems from poor phonemic awareness. If children cannot break down words into phonemes and recombine those sounds into whole words, they cannot learn to read.

There is a range of formal and informal literacy assessment techniques. Observation, standardized tests, checklists, student self-evaluations, performance evaluations, and literature critiques are all conventional techniques intended to assess listening, speaking, and reading abilities. No particular technique is right for everyone, and teachers should tailor their assessment procedures to the individual student or group of students. Teachers should also be aware of unintended cultural bias in assessment techniques, which may skew results. The important thing is to use these techniques consistently.

Domain 2: Nonwritten and Written Communication

Written communication requires knowledge of the conventions used in Standard English, such as sentence structure, spelling, capitalization, and punctuation.

Principles of Composition

Standard English employs certain conventions for writing. A well-written composition will follow this general outline:

▶ **Introductory paragraph.** This opening paragraph should get your reader's attention and state your thesis, or argument, in a concise way.
▶ **Body paragraphs.** These paragraphs will expand, analyze, and support the main argument.
▶ **Concluding paragraph.** The final paragraph should restate the thesis, summarize the main points, and offer a conclusion, solution, or call to action.
▶ **Transitional phrases.** Words and phrases signal transitions that hold all these paragraphs together. These transitional phrases can be introduced by simple conjunctions such as *and, but, nor, or, for,* and *yet* or by more complex conjunctive adverbs such as *furthermore, consequently, however, moreover, nevertheless,* and *meanwhile.*

Sentence Structure

Students should learn to vary sentence structure to add interest to their writing. There are four main types of sentence structure:

▶ **Simple.** Simple sentences contain a single independent clause and no dependent clauses. Example: *The movie was delightful.*
▶ **Compound.** Compound sentences contain two or more independent clauses but no dependent clauses. The clauses are joined

by a correlative conjunction, a semicolon, a conjunctive adverb, or a coordinating conjunction, such as *for, and, nor, but, or, yet,* and *so* (to memorize the conjunctions, remember that their first letters spell FANBOYS). Example: *Mary wanted to go to the cinema, but John insisted on staying home.*

▶ **Complex.** Complex sentences contain one independent clause, expressing the more important idea, and one dependent clause, stating the subordinate idea. Example:

> *Susan wore the necklace that John had given her.*

Susan wore the necklace is the independent clause, and *that John had given her* is the dependent clause.

▶ **Compound-complex.** Compound-complex sentences contain several independent clauses and at least one dependent clause. Example:

> *Doris drove to work, but Don, who did not have a car, took the bus.*

Doris drove to work and *Don took the bus* are independent clauses; *who did not have a car* is a dependent clause.

Spelling

Spelling is a characteristic of alphabetic languages, but not all languages are consistent in the spelling of words. Like language, spelling competency develops in stages. According to *Words Their Way*, these are the five stages of spelling:

▶ **Emergent.** Children ages 1 to 7 acquire phonemic awareness and learn the alphabet.
▶ **Letter name/alphabetic.** Between ages 4 and 10, children learn the connection between letters and sounds, begin to include vowels in their words, and learn to blend basic sounds.
▶ **Within-word patterns.** Between ages 6 and 12, children learn long vowels, consonant patterns, diphthongs, homographs, and homophones.
▶ **Syllables and affixes.** Children between ages 8 and 18 understand polysyllabic words, double consonants, word roots, prefixes, and suffixes.

▶ **Derivational relations.** After age 10, children grasp the connection between spelling and meaning, and they understand word origins, consonant and vowel changes, and absorbed prefixes.

Capitalization

Basic rules of capitalization include capitalizing proper nouns, the first word in a sentence, and official titles that precede a name.

Punctuation

Punctuation marks structure and clarify our writing and give clues to the reader about its rhythm and tone. Rules for punctuation cover a range of uses for commas, semicolons, colons, en and em dashes, apostrophes, hyphens, and many other marks. There are stylistic differences in punctuation use across cultures. For example, in British English, quotation marks go inside the period at the end of a sentence, whereas in American English, the period goes inside the closing quotation mark. Teachers should be aware of these differences when teaching second languages.

Writing Strategies

The writing process can be broken down into five steps, and teachers can evaluate students' progress after each step.

▶ **Step 1: Prewriting.** Prewriting is the thinking and brainstorming stage of writing. There are many techniques teachers can use to help children access their creativity: visual cues, discussion, freewriting, mapping, webbing, and story charts.
▶ **Step 2: First draft.** Next, it's time to put those ideas on paper. Students may feel more confident about the first draft if they have a structure to follow. Review basic sentence structure (subject, predicate, clauses, and phrases). Outline the structure of a paragraph (introductory sentence, supporting body sentences, and concluding sentence).
▶ **Step 3: Revising.** When the first draft is complete, revise it to ensure the argument makes sense and is supported with examples. Check sentence structure, and vary the length of

sentences. See that sentences and paragraphs are linked by transitional phrases or words.

▶ **Step 4: Editing.** The editing stage is the time to look for mistakes in grammar, spelling, capitalization, and punctuation.

▶ **Step 5: Sharing.** Sharing can take various forms, from publishing to oral presentation to posting on the Internet.

Writing Applications

Writing can be divided into two main categories: fiction and nonfiction. Within these categories, there are four rhetorical modes—expository, persuasive, descriptive, and narrative—which identify the conventions and purposes of various genres. There is also a fifth type of writing distinct from these four: interpretive writing.

▶ **Expository writing** is most often used for nonfiction, such as letters, reports, news stories, and textbooks. It explains, analyzes, discusses, or simply presents factual information.

▶ **Persuasive writing** attempts to convince the reader of something or to prove an idea or point of view. We see this type of writing in advertising, newspaper editorials, political speeches, and letters to the editor. Persuasive writing should be based on solid evidence, but some genres use emotional appeals and exaggeration, which do not always rely on facts.

▶ **Descriptive writing** attempts to describe a situation, place, or person so readers may visualize and experience it in their imagination. Journaling is an example of descriptive writing.

▶ **Narrative writing** tells a story, usually in a descriptive mode. Fictive narrative writing, such as novels and short stories, involves characters, setting, plot, and point of view. Narrative writing can also be used for nonfiction, as in biographies and autobiographies.

▶ **Interpretive writing** goes beyond description and attempts to help the reader decode and understand the meaning of events. Interpretive writing accepts that there may be several interpretations of a piece of literature, and it does not try to prove that one is correct. But an interpretive piece must at least present a logical explanation of why a particular interpretation was chosen over others, and it must base that choice on quotations from the text being interpreted.

Nonwritten Communication

Learning to speak in small or large groups enhances a student's confidence. Teachers should be aware of cultural differences that may inhibit a child's ability or desire to speak in public. You should also note the effect that a speaker's dialect or idiolect may have on an audience, and avoid situations of stereotyping and bias. The importance of nonverbal language—posture, facial expression, and gestures—cannot be stressed enough.

PRESENTATION COMPONENTS OF SPEECH

▶ **Volume.** Tailor your volume for the setting. Do not speak excessively loud in a small room or at a somber occasion. Conversely, do not speak too softly at a political rally.

▶ **Pace/rate.** A slow pace will give your audience time to absorb your words and argument. Increasing the rate, or pace, of your speech can also build a sense of excitement.

▶ **Tone/pitch.** Vary your tone to keep listeners alert, interested, and emotionally involved.

▶ **Rhythm.** Establish rhythm by alternating the stress on your words. Rhythm can also enhance the emotional effect of your speech.

▶ **Body language, eye contact, posture, and facial expression.** These nonverbal forms of communication will send messages to your audience.

GENRES OF NONWRITTEN COMMUNICATION

▶ **Narrative speech.** A narrative speech, similar to narrative writing, tells a story about a person, place, or thing in order to make a point. Much like a written short story, it unfolds in a sequence of events and uses conventions like plot and characterization.

▶ **Persuasive speech.** A persuasive speech tries to convince the audience to do something. The "something" should be clearly stated at the beginning, and the speaker should use most of the allotted time presenting evidence for the argument. Speakers may also use language that rouses emotions. Rate, pitch, and rhythm are especially important in persuasive speeches.

- ▶ **Research presentation.** A research presentation provides a summation of the process and results of a research project. Students should incorporate the conventions of expository writing and build a strong introduction explaining why the particular research topic is relevant. They should explain their methodology and resources, present important data, and tell the audience whether or not the data support their thesis.

- ▶ **Poetry recitations.** Volume, rate, pitch, and rhythm are very important when reading poetry aloud. The speaker's body language will also help the audience visualize the words and feel the emotional impact of the poem. Electronic media, such as background music and videos, may accompany a poetry recitation and enhance its impact.

- ▶ **Responses to literature.** Students can use an analytical or interpretive perspective to give their response to a piece of literature.

Research Strategies

Research is only as good as the sources on which it is based. Students must learn to be selective in choosing sources and must learn the difference between primary and secondary sources. There is a flood of information on the Internet, but much of it is untested and possibly incorrect. Starting with an Internet search may be a good way to brainstorm and develop the main points that the student can investigate further, but eventually students must learn to explore their library.

Gathering data is just the first step. At a certain point, students must learn to stop gathering and begin analyzing and interpreting. Once they have a thesis, they can construct their report following the writing strategies and the conventions of composition previously outlined.

Students must learn to cite sources properly and never to claim words as their own if they are taken from another source. There are several formats that professionals use to cite sources. Students should learn when it is proper and necessary to cite a source, whether quoted or paraphrased, and should be taught what constitutes plagiarism. They should be familiar with the different ways to cite various types of texts,

such as books, short stories, poetry, newspaper articles, encyclopedia entries, web pages, journals, and magazines.

Domain 3: Texts

Reading fiction and nonfiction is one way children learn vocabulary. Narrative and expository writing are common rhetorical modes found in children's literature, whether it is prose or poetry.

Concepts and Conventions

Students should be familiar with literary elements including plot, characterization, setting, and point of view.

Plot

Plots are built around conflict, struggle, and obstacles. They follow a rhythm of action, starting with the introduction of the main character's dilemma, through his or her struggle against all odds, and ending with the resolution of the conflict.

Characterization

Characters and their dialogue move the plot along. The main character, called the protagonist, should be a sympathetic figure with whom the readers can identify. The protagonist is the character who must overcome all the obstacles in the plot. These obstacles will come from the antagonist, the character who attempts to prevent the main character from reaching his or her goals.

Setting

Stories take place in specific geographical, climatic, and historical contexts. Good writing does not simply explain or state the character of the setting, but makes the reader feel and visualize it. If it is raining, muggy, or cold, the reader should sense the chill or heat. Historical and geographical settings must be accurate and believable in their details.

Point of View

The storyteller may be the author of the story or a character in the novel. Whoever is narrating the story is doing so from a certain point of view. Point of view can be consistent throughout the story, or it can shift from chapter to chapter, depending on the author's purpose and goal. Several points of view are possible:

- **First person.** The narrator as protagonist tells the story from his or her perspective. This can be limiting, since we can only know about action witnessed by the narrator. Examples: *My Ántonia; Treasure Island.*
- **Omniscient.** The narrator is all-seeing, and the reader is privy to every thought, motive, and action of each character. Examples: *A Tale of Two Cities; Silas Marner.*
- **Third-person subjective.** This perspective is most common in fiction. We know the protagonist's thoughts, intentions, ideas, and motives, but from the narrator's third-person perspective, without having them spoken from the first-person point of view. Examples: *The Age of Innocence; Wise Blood.*
- **Third-person objective.** The narrator describes the actions performed by the characters but does not gain access to the thoughts and intentions of the characters. Examples: *The Maltese Falcon; To Have and Have Not.*
- **Mixed perspectives.** The point of view alternates among different characters, with each character giving his or her limited perspective in each chapter. The reader eventually gets a comprehensive view by reading each partial view. Examples: *Dr. Jekyll and Mr. Hyde; The Silence of the Lambs.*

Literary Themes and Devices

Humans are more alike than different, and literature throughout the world attests to this fact in the common themes that run through folktales, novels, and mythologies. Literary themes often teach us a lesson, and similar themes can be found in literature from diverse cultures: themes of love, revenge, jealousy, and greed are common throughout the world. A typical character in many traditional folktales, from the ancient Greeks to the Native Americans, is the trickster, a cunning figure and culture hero who doesn't follow society's conventional rules. Students should learn to identify common cross-cultural themes in religions and myths.

Students should also understand the structural devices, or stylistic elements, used in prose and poetry. Here are some common literary devices:

- **Rhyme** is the repetition of similar word endings in a meaningful pattern. It is usually used in poetry but can also be a device in persuasive speeches and other types of written and oral communication. Example: *The rain in Spain falls mainly on the plain.*
- **Alliteration** is the repetition of sounds at the beginning of words or phrases. Example: *The gleeful girls' glee club met yesterday.*
- **Simile** uses *as* or *like* to suggest a comparison between two different things or ideas. Example: *My neighbor, who is a plumber, thinks like a lawyer.*
- **Metaphor** is a figure of speech suggesting a comparison between two things or ideas without using *as* or *like*. Example: *When John brought up that subject, he opened a can of worms.*
- **Personification** gives human characteristics to animals or inanimate objects. Example: *Mary was able to penetrate to the heart of the matter.*
- **Hyperbole** uses exaggeration to affect an audience. Hyperbolic phrases are so extreme that the audience knows not to take them literally, but they can have an emotional impact. Example: *I'm so happy I could die.*
- **Onomatopoeia** is a word that is supposed to imitate a real sound. Examples: *moo; ruff.*

Genres

A range of literary genres appeal to children. Here are some of the most popular genres:

- **Novels** tell a story, generally about overcoming interior or exterior obstacles, through structural devises like plot, character, and setting.
- **Short stories** can also use plot, character, and setting and revolve around a conflict, but the time frame for their unfolding is usually more condensed than in novels.
- **Poetry** includes long and short poems, from heroic epic poems of thousands of stanzas to short sonnets, which are usually about 14 lines. Poems can use literary devices like rhyming and alliteration. Poetic language is meant to be aesthetic, rather than literal.

▶ **Myth and legends** tell stories that are popular in particular cultures, although they may have cross-cultural themes. The origin of humans and the earth is a popular universal theme.

▶ **Fables** are short fictional stories that use anthropomorphized animals and mythical creatures to teach a lesson. One of the most popular collections of fables from Greek literature is *Aesop's Fables*, where cunning foxes, ingenious crows, and steady tortoises have moral lessons to teach.

▶ **Fairy tales** use a simple narrative structure and make a point with a plot about good versus evil.

Interpretation of Texts

Themes running throughout various genres are both implicit and explicit, and they may contain both literal and figurative meanings. Students should learn to recognize the difference between literal and figurative meanings and base their interpretations on the actual content in the text. Students may also place texts in historical, cultural, and social contexts to enrich their understanding of an author's work. Teachers must be aware of ethnic, class, and gender stereotyping in any literary genre and use it to help students recognize stereotypes as forms of bias, rather than natural truths.

History and Social Science

Domain 1: World History

Ancient Civilizations

"Civilization" has various meanings, and teachers should be aware of the hidden moral bias in the term. The word generally refers to societies with a dominant urban core, writing, hierarchical political system, and agricultural economic base. History and the social sciences are interested in understanding how societies originated, developed, and declined; how they organize themselves economically and politically; how people relate to one another in kinship groups; what kind of art they produced; and how they structure their belief systems. Whether or not civilizations are "superior" to other forms of society, like hunter-gatherer or nomadic societies, is not a question for history or science.

We have two sources of information about ancient societies: archeology and ancient texts. Students should understand the benefits and deficiencies of both. Texts must be read critically, since most were written by biased observers and conquerors. Archeological findings may not be accurate 100 percent of the time, but the science of archeology is continually developing.

> **Visual Aids**
> Maps, charts, graphs, and tables are all useful tools for teaching history. The expansion of empires and the annexation of territories can best be demonstrated by maps. Tables and graphs require interpretation and analysis of the data presented. Charts are used to compare two or more items, usually with numerical data.

Geography and Ancient Civilizations. People need water and food sources to survive. From the Paleolithic era to the Neolithic agricultural revolution, humans lived in small kinship groups and survived by hunting animals and gathering wild food. These hunter-gatherers spread throughout the world and adapted their skills, culture, and social organization to the environments they lived in. Today, only a few societies still use hunting and gathering as a major survival strategy, and they have been pushed into marginal areas in Africa, Indonesia, and North and South America.

As humans domesticated plants and animals, they began living in larger and more settled communities. Agriculture became more important, and large agricultural societies developed along major water systems in Egypt (Nile), Cush (Nile), Mesopotamia (Tigris and Euphrates), India (Indus), China (Yellow and Yangtze), Greece (Achelous, Europas), and Rome (Tiber). Persia did not have any major rivers, but the Persians developed an ingenious water management system known as *qanāts*, which carried water throughout the land for irrigation and human use.

Waterways were necessary not only for agriculture, but also for trade, and the major ancient civilizations were great agricultural producers and traders. Agriculture and trade were also the source of political power, warfare, and slavery. People living in ancient civilizations no longer lived in small kinship groups, as hunter-gatherers did; rather, their societies were hierarchical and divided into classes. Hinduism in ancient India, for example, was based on four classes, or castes: the Brahman priesthood; the Kshatriya warriors, kings, and governing groups; the Vaishya farmers, cattle herders, and traders; and the Shudra servants and workers.

In ancient civilizations, politics and religion were closely connected, and kings were associated with deities and divine rule. In some societies, the king was believed to be descended from the god—to be the son of the god. This association was the source of the king's legitimacy, which could not be contested by ordinary people.

Not all ancient civilizations were great empires. In Greece, which is made up of thousands of small islands, separate city-states developed and rivaled one another in trade and warfare. Two of the most important city-states were Sparta, known for its military training, and Athens, which introduced a form of democracy around 508 BCE.

Intellectual Contributions. Societies of all types have made artistic and intellectual contributions to human history. Hunter-gatherers developed fire, tools, and musical instruments and created magnificent cave art, rock art, and figurative art, like the Upper Paleolithic Venus figurines found in France and Germany.

The ancient civilizations of Egypt, Mesopotamia, Persia, Greece, and Rome produced pottery, glass, wall murals, jewelry, architecture, and sculpture. They also developed writing, alphabets and hieroglyphics, metalworking, standardized weights and measures, coinage, sciences, laws, political systems, and architectural principles.

From Mesopotamia, the Code of Hammurabi, dating to the Old Babylonian period about 1772 BCE, is one example of an ancient code of law. It establishes the idea that one is innocent until proven guilty and that both sides in a dispute have a right to present evidence for their defense.

Hatshepsut, a female Egyptian pharaoh from 1473 to 1458 BCE, enriched Egypt financially and culturally by establishing extensive trade networks, and building great temples and monuments throughout the kingdom. Ramses the Great, an Egyptian pharaoh who reigned from 1279 to 1213 BCE, also built magnificent cities, temples, and monuments, and established Egyptian control over much of Nubia and the Middle East.

Egyptian art included painting, sculpture, and architecture, rich with symbolic significance. Egyptians used hieroglyphics and images in their art forms and depicted important figures, like pharaohs, larger than women and servants.

Chinese civilization developed in the valleys of the Yellow and Yangtze Rivers. It has given the world the two great philosophies of Confucianism and Taoism. The Chinese also introduced paper and gunpowder.

Greek artists, playwrights, and philosophers set the standards for Western art and rational argument for centuries. Homer, Socrates, Plato, Aristotle, Euclid, Thucydides, Euphronios, Praxiteles, Sophocles, and Euripides are some of the names students should be familiar with. Greece also gave us two classic epic poems, Homer's *Odyssey* and *Iliad*, and a wealth of mythological figures, such as Hercules, that have filtered down into contemporary popular literature.

The legacy of the Roman Republic and Empire touches on almost every aspect of contemporary culture, from language to law to art. Many English words have Latin roots and retain their original meaning. Rome also gave us a code of laws, a written constitution, a tripartite government, a system of checks and balances, and the concept of civic duty. The Romans were also master military strategists, architects, and road builders.

Trade and Commerce. Ancient civilizations were not self-contained regions. Their rulers and merchants established overland and sea routes, and they traded extensively with one another. Merchants also carried and transmitted culture, and ancient trade routes are one reason we often see common cultural traits on different continents. Buddhist and Hindu rituals and deities, for example, traveled to Southeast Asia along with Indian monks and merchants; early Greeks brought their deities and alphabet to Italy before the rise of Roman Republic; trade was extensive between Egypt, the Mediterranean, and Mesopotamia; and the famous "silk roads" connected China by sea and land with Southeast Asia, India, Persia, Arabia, Egypt, and Rome, carrying trade goods, religions, and philosophies throughout the ancient world.

Medieval and Early Modern Times

Decline of the Roman Empire. No empire lasts forever, and Rome finally lost its power around 476 CE. Internal problems, such as corruption and competition between military commanders, weakened Rome's political structure until the Germanic tribes, long enemies of Rome, finally overthrew Romulus Augustus, the last emperor of the west. Rome's fall marks the end of classical antiquity and the beginning of the Middle Ages in western Europe.

During the Middle Ages, which lasted from the fifth to the fifteenth centuries, Europe became decentralized into many smaller kingdoms, or fiefdoms. Lords controlled the land and protected their vassals—knights and nobles—who were allowed to collect rents and services from peasants, or serfs, in return for their military service to the lord.

Pre-Columbian America. After Columbus's voyage to the Americas in 1492, the Spanish expanded their empire into the Americas by sending conquistadores to conquer indigenous peoples, administrators to rule them, and Catholic missionaries to convert them. Spanish expansion and rule lasted for over four hundred years, from 1492 to 1898. The period prior to Columbus (the pre-Columbian era) saw a number of flourishing civilizations, among which the Maya, Aztec, and Inca were the most powerful:

▶ The **Mayas** were an agricultural people who lived in an area that today encompasses Honduras, Guatemala, northern El Salvador, and central Mexico. They had a hieroglyphic writing system; sophisticated knowledge of mathematics and astronomy; urban centers; temples, palaces, and stepped pyramids;

carvings and reliefs, ceramics, and murals; ritual ball courts; and a calendar system.

▶ The **Aztecs** also were agriculturalists and lived in central Mexico. They spoke a language called Nahuatl, which is still spoken by more than a million people in Mexico. Their social structure was hierarchical, based on nobles and commoners, and they worshipped a pantheon of deities. They were highly cultured and produced written books called codices, poetry, drama, music, ceramics, body ornaments, pyramids, temples, and palaces.

▶ The **Incas** constituted the largest of the pre-Columbian empires. Originating in Peru, the Inca empire eventually grew to incorporate parts of Ecuador, Bolivia, Argentina, Chile, and Colombia. Quechua, still spoken today, was the official language. Their main deity was a sun god, and their king was considered a child of the sun god. The Inca people produced ceramics, gold and silver items, and metallurgy, and their healers performed successful skull surgery. Their agricultural system was based on terrace agriculture on steep mountain slopes and used sophisticated engineering technologies, including retaining walls and river diversion.

Christianity and Europe. By the fourth century, Emperor Constantine had legitimized Christianity, and after the fall of Rome in the fifth century, Christianity became the dominant religion in Europe. The rise to power of the Roman Catholic Church depended on a combination of its political alliances with powerful emperors and its consistent persecution of "heretics"—any individual or group with whom the church disagreed on issues of doctrine. By eliminating all rivals, aligning with kings and emperors, and building its land and tax base, the Catholic Church grew in numbers and wealth during the Middle Ages. Between 1095 and 1291, the church organized a series of military campaigns, called the Crusades, against Muslims in the Middle East.

The church's attempt to conquer Muslim lands failed, but the Crusades had an important political, economic, and social impact on western Europe. They opened up trade routes between Europe and the East that had been closed for centuries, and they brought Eastern knowledge of mathematics, optics, architecture, and medicine to western Europe.

Islam and the Middle Ages. Islam developed in Arabia in the seventh century but reached its golden age in the mid-eighth century. While western Europe was in a "dark age," Islam preserved and increased our scientific knowledge. Rather than building wealth based on agriculture, Islamic cities and states developed their merchant class and built extensive trade networks throughout Africa and Asia. Islamic artists were masters in ceramics, glass, metallurgy, textiles, calligraphy, illuminated manuscripts, and woodworking. Scientists advanced knowledge in trigonometry, algebra, astronomy, and optics, and physicians translated the works of Galen and Hippocrates, the preeminent Greek physicians, from the Greek into Arabic. They added their own medical knowledge to this body of work, and preserved this medical tradition for centuries.

Renaissance and the Scientific Revolution. The Renaissance, meaning "rebirth," began in Italy in the fourteenth century. It was an attempt to revive the culture of classical antiquity after the dark period of the Middle Ages. Renaissance scholars were humanists, meaning they recognized the importance of the human mind in understanding the world, and they based their analysis of literature and science on reason and empirical evidence.

The arts flourished during this period, in part because the Catholic Church and the nobility became great patrons. Artists like Leonardo da Vinci and Michelangelo, political theorists like Niccolò Machiavelli and Thomas More, and poets and writers like Dante Alighieri, Giovanni Boccaccio, and Francesco Petrarch left their mark during the Renaissance.

One of the most important inventions during this period was the printing press, introduced into Europe by Johannes Gutenberg around 1440. This invention helped bring literacy to the masses and spread scientific knowledge among intellectuals, and it laid the groundwork for the scientific revolution and the Enlightenment. The scientific revolution, beginning in the sixteenth century, grew out of the Renaissance and brought changes to research and experimentation in the sciences, especially physics, mathematics, astronomy, biology, medicine, and chemistry. Some of the major findings during this time included the following:

- The earth is not the center of the universe but instead revolves around the sun.
- Matter is composed of atoms, not elements (earth, air, water, fire).
- Bodies move according to the same laws of physics.
- Blood circulates from arteries to veins in one closed system.
- An object will resist any change in its motion from an outside force.

The Enlightenment. The seventeenth- and eighteenth-century Enlightenment, or age of reason, was a cultural movement that laid the groundwork for the overthrow of monarchies and the introduction of a market system. Intellectuals emphasized reason and empirical observation, and opposed religious superstition and dogma. Although there was a range of Enlightenment ideas circulating throughout North America, Europe, and Russia, there were a few central concepts: freedom, democracy, rationality, and the notion that rights are based on a social contract rather than divine right.

Early Modern Capitalism. Merchant capitalism began to replace feudalism by the sixteenth century. European merchants made their wealth by trading spices and other commodities with Asia and Africa and through the slave trade. Merchants accumulated enormous amounts of capital through trade and slavery, and they were in a position to invest it in industry by the time of the Industrial Revolution, around 1750. By the eighteenth century, mercantilism declined, and industrial capitalism became the dominant economic system in Europe.

European Colonialism. The Industrial Revolution created a demand in Europe for raw materials that did not grow in European soil. European colonialism from the eighteenth century focused on bringing to Europe raw materials from Africa and Asia, to be manufactured in European factories and then sold back to colonial nations at high prices. The introduction into colonial countries of European-made goods devastated local craft businesses and created poverty in what are today called Third World countries. India is a good example of this process. Cotton from India was shipped to England to be made into clothing that was shipped back to India to be sold. This ruined the indigenous Indian textile industry, since machine-made British goods could undersell local, handmade Indian goods. When Gandhi protested British rule, one of his tactics was to demand that Indians wear only Indian cloth goods—an early version of "buy local."

Democracy. Ancient Athens, Native Americans, and small aboriginal groups throughout the world have long had forms of political organization based on the concept of democracy, from the Greek meaning "rule of the people," or "people power." Some large state societies practice variants of democracy, such as representative democracy, rather than direct democracy. The Magna Carta, introduced in England in 1215, challenged the undemocratic authority of the monarch and established the right of individuals to due process, meaning the government cannot harm any individual unless it strictly follows the law. Enlightenment thinkers in the eighteenth century also challenged the notion that the aristocracy had an inherent right to rule. Using reason, and believing in liberty and equality, they argued that all people are created equal. The Magna Carta and the values of the Enlightenment became a model for the U.S. Constitution.

Domain 2: United States History

European Exploration and Settlement

By the fifteenth century, most western European countries were engaged in economic competition (which often led to warfare) under the mercantile system. Governments chartered mercantile companies to carry out expeditions in search of gold, silver, and commodities like spices and sugar. These expeditions found that the new lands were already inhabited by people whom the Europeans called "heathens and infidels." Europeans dealt with these indigenous people in a variety of ways, including establishing trade relations, enslaving the population, warfare, and, in some cases, extinction. Merchants weren't the only group vying for power, since the Roman Catholic Church and, after the Protestant Reformation in 1517, Protestant sects also competed for the souls of the indigenous people.

Christopher Columbus's explorations in the Caribbean opened the way for European explorers and the mercantile interests looking for new lands to exploit for resources. The first European to set foot in North America since the eleventh-century Viking voyages was an Italian navigator named Giovanni Caboto, known by his English name, John Cabot. In 1496, England's King Henry VII granted Cabot the right to sail west under the English flag. Cabot landed on the island of Newfoundland in 1497.

The first permanent English settlement in North America was founded in Jamestown, Virginia, in 1607. This colony was originally welcomed by the Virginia Algonquians, the indigenous inhabitants of the area. The settlers, however, established their settlement in a malarial swampy area, were not familiar with agricultural work, and had to depend on the Indians for survival. Eventually their demands on the Algonquians led to conflict and three Anglo-Powhatan Wars, in 1609, 1622, and 1644.

The second successful English settlement in North America was the Plymouth Colony. In 1620, a group of English Dissenters—Christians who had separated from the Church of England—landed in Provincetown Harbor in Massachusetts. They established a social contract, known as the Mayflower Compact, and pledged themselves to work for the good of the colony. Their initial contact with the indigenous people was hostile, since earlier the Indians had been killed and enslaved by the English captain and slave trader Thomas Hunt.

Slavery

Although slavery as a social institution has existed since ancient times and still exists, under the mercantile system slave trading was a major means of accumulating wealth. Slavery began early in the settlements (the Jamestown settlement bought 20 captive Africans in 1619), and by 1750 slavery was legal in all 13 colonies. Massachusetts was the first colony to legalize slavery in 1641, and in 1662 Virginia passed a law declaring slavery to be hereditary.

The slave trade was an organized system that involved shuttling slaves, crops, and manufactured goods between America, West Africa, and Europe. Europeans manufactured the goods that were bartered for the African slaves brought to America, and slaves in America grew the crops that were exported to Europe.

Farming with slave labor was especially profitable in agricultural areas that grew export crops, such as tobacco, cotton, sugar, and coffee, and most of those plantations growing these crops were located in the southern part of the United States.

War for Independence

The original 13 colonies established between 1607 and 1733 were initially part of the British Empire, but over time, grievances developed. In 1765, the British imposed the Stamp Act, which levied a tax on the American colonies. The colonies rebelled, demanding "no taxation without representation." The British Parliament ignored the protests and continued to impose taxes, including a tea tax, which led to the 1773 Boston Tea Party, in which colonists dumped the tea into the Boston Harbor. In 1774, the British Parliament passed what the colonists called the Intolerable Acts, limiting self-government in Massachusetts.

In response, the Committees of Correspondence, formed in 1772 as a shadow government, set up the First Continental Congress to petition against the Intolerable Acts. The British reacted by declaring the members of the congress to be traitors, and in 1775 the colonists held the Second Continental Congress. The Second Continental Congress organized an army, naming George Washington as commander, and in 1776 adopted the Declaration of Independence, which declared the colonies' independence from Britain.

Thomas Jefferson wrote the original draft of the declaration, and it was signed by 56 delegates to the Continental Congress, including Benjamin Franklin, John Adams, and John Hancock. The declaration listed the grievances against King George III and asserted the natural and legal rights of the colonists. Today the declaration is considered to be an important statement on human rights.

The American Revolutionary War was fought between 1775 and 1783. The Battles of Lexington and Concord opened the war, and France, Spain, and the Netherlands supplied the revolutionaries with weapons. France entered the war as an American ally in 1778, after the American victories in the 1777 Battles of Saratoga. French involvement is considered a turning point in the war. The French were victorious in the Battle of the Chesapeake and Battle of Yorktown in 1781, forcing the British into treaty talks. The Treaty of Paris in 1783 officially ended the war and declared the United States to be a sovereign nation.

Women of the Revolution. Women played an important role during the American Revolutionary War:

- Abigail Adams was the wife of John Adams and the mother of John Quincy Adams, both presidents of the United States. She favored women's rights and opposed slavery. She requested that the Continental Congress not put unlimited power into the hands of men, or the women also would rebel.
- Molly Pitcher may be the nickname for Mary Ludwig Hays, who brought water to soldiers during the American Revolutionary War. At the Battle of Monmouth in June 1778, her husband was killed, and Molly took his place loading the cannon. George Washington honored her with the status of noncommissioned officer, and she was afterward known as Sergeant Molly.
- Phillis Wheatley was a Gambian woman sold into slavery and brought to Boston. She became a well-known poet in the 13 colonies, supported the revolution, and wrote a poem in praise of George Washington that was later published by Thomas Paine in the *Pennsylvania Gazette*.

▶ Mercy Otis Warren was a poet, playwright, political writer, and historian of the Revolutionary War who criticized British royalty and urged colonists to rebel. Warren's home was the birthplace of the Committees of Correspondence, formed in 1772.

The U.S. Political System

The United States is a republic of representatives elected by the people. It is based on a system of checks and balances between three branches: executive, legislative, and judicial. The "separation of powers" among these branches allocates specific duties to each branch: the executive upholds the laws and the Constitution, the legislature makes laws, and the judicial branch interprets the law as the final court of appeals. Citizens participate in government through the democratic process of voting for their representatives in the executive and legislative branches.

U.S. Constitution and Bill of Rights. The Articles of Confederation was the first constitution of the 13 colonies, drafted by the Continental Congress between 1776 and 1777 and ratified by all 13 states in 1781. The articles were meant to protect the sovereignty of the colonies. They legitimized the authority of the colonies during the Revolutionary War and authorized the colonies to sign treaties with Indian groups. The articles did not provide a way to finance the government, however, so in 1787 the Articles of Confederation were replaced by the U.S. Constitution. In 1791, the 10 amendments of the Bill of Rights were added to the Constitution.

The Constitution lays out the reasons for its existence: to establish justice, ensure domestic tranquility, provide for the common defense, and promote the general welfare. It describes the three branches of government and their powers, and it defines how power is to be shared between the federal and state governments. It also identifies the limits to government power.

The Constitution and Bill of Rights enshrine the major principles of government that the three branches have a duty to uphold, including the separation of powers; federalism; the right to trial by jury; separation of church and state; freedom of speech, the press, and assembly; the right to bear arms; and protection against unreasonable search and seizure.

Evolution of Political Parties. Early debates over the form the new government would take centered around the role of the federal government versus the role of the states. The "federalists" included Alexander Hamilton, James Madison, and John Jay. Hamilton formed the Federalist Party, the first political party in the United States. Party members were upper-class bankers, businessmen, industrialists, and investors. They did not believe in equality, and they wanted a national bank and a strong central government. Their major base of support was New England and the urban centers. Opposing the federalists was the Democratic-Republican Party, led by Thomas Jefferson and James Madison. They were strong in the rural south among free farmers and plantation owners. Jefferson was in favor of states' rights and rejected the idea of a national bank.

Jefferson's Democratic-Republican Party dominated state and federal governments through three presidential administrations: Thomas Jefferson (1801–1809), James Madison (1809–1817), and James Monroe (1817–1825). After Monroe's presidency, the Democratic-Republican Party split between supporters of Andrew Jackson and supporters of John Quincy Adams. Adams won the presidency and served from 1925 to 1929. Jackson became president in 1829, and his supporters formed the new Democratic Party.

The era of Jacksonian democracy saw greater democracy for white males. Land ownership was no longer a voting requirement for white men, and white farmers were encouraged to move west and claim land, supported by an ideology known as "manifest destiny," a belief that the United States was destined to stretch from the Atlantic Ocean to the Pacific Ocean.

In the 1830s, the Whig Party was formed to oppose Jackson's policies. The Whigs favored congressional power over executive power, as well as government support for urban modernization, railroad construction, and the banks. Henry Clay, Daniel Webster, William Henry Harrison, Zachary Taylor, and Abraham Lincoln were members of the Whig Party.

Westward Movement

From its original 13 colonies, the United States grew to incorporate 50 states. The following list describes some of the major treaties and acquisitions:

▶ **Louisiana Purchase.** In 1803, the United States acquired from France most of what is today the Midwest, including Arkansas, Missouri, Iowa, Oklahoma, Kansas, and Nebraska plus parts of Minnesota, North Dakota, South Dakota, New Mexico, Texas, Montana, Wyoming, Colorado, and Louisiana.

▶ **West Florida.** James Madison declared western Florida a U.S. possession in 1810.

▶ **East Florida.** East Florida was ceded from Spain in 1819.

▶ **Texas.** The United States annexed Texas in 1845. After the Mexican-American War, the Mexican Cession, and the Compromise of 1850, the United States also acquired all or part of Kansas, Colorado, Wyoming, Oklahoma, and New Mexico.

▶ **Oregon.** The United States acquired Oregon from Great Britain in the 1846 Oregon Treaty.

▶ **Treaty of Guadalupe Hidalgo (1848).** The Treaty of Guadalupe Hidalgo ended the Mexican-American War and brought the United States vast new territories that had previously belonged to Mexico, Gradually, these territories were granted statehood. Between 1850 and 1912, California, Nevada, Utah, and Arizona all became states.

▶ **Gadsden Purchase.** In 1853, the United States purchased parts of New Mexico and Arizona from Mexico.

▶ **Alaska.** In 1867, the United States purchased Alaska from Russia. In 1959, Alaska became the forty-ninth state.

▶ **Hawaii.** Hawaii became a U.S. Territory in 1900 and the fiftieth state in 1959.

As settlers moved west, they displaced Indian groups already living in those areas. Settlers and the federal government often joined forces to remove Indians, sometimes by purchasing their land through treaties, but more often by waging wars, decimating forests and buffalo herds, and breaking treaties with native peoples.

In colonial America, the predominant ethnic groups were English, Irish, Welsh, Scottish, German, and Dutch. Farming, trading, and crafts were the main occupations. Slavery of Africans and Native Americans was an important aspect of the American economy. Plantations were the economic base of many colonies, and they depended on slave labor, so American agriculture and slavery were interconnected. In colonies where the land was not suitable for farming, including Massachusetts, merchants were involved in the slave trade, transporting slaves and supplies between Africa, New England, and the West Indies.

Time Lines of the Civil War and Reconstruction

Although there were many slave uprisings between 1776 and 1860, by 1860 there were about four million slaves in the United States, most living in the South. The northern states were the first to oppose slavery after the American Revolutionary War. Antislavery sentiments and protests have a long history in America. Following are some major landmarks in the antislavery movement:

1688	German and Dutch Quakers in Pennsylvania protested slavery and signed a document called the "Germantown Quaker Petition Against Slavery."
1775	Thomas Paine publishes "African Slavery in America" in the *Pennsylvania Magazine.* This was the first published article calling for emancipation and abolition.
1775	The Society for the Relief of Free Negroes Unlawfully Held in Bondage, organized in Philadelphia, was the first American abolition society.
1780	Pennsylvania passes a law titled An Act for the Gradual Abolition of Slavery, which prohibited the importing of slaves but did not free current slaves. It also required slaveholders to register their slaves, and it declared that children born to slave mothers would be considered indentured servants. This act gradually abolished slavery.

1787 The Northwest Ordinance established the Northwest Territory and prohibited slavery in that area.

1833 The American Anti-Slavery Society, founded in Philadelphia, called for the immediate and unconditional abolition of slavery. Important leaders were William Lloyd Garrison, Arthur Tappan, and Frederick Douglass.

1839 The Liberty Party was founded in New York as an abolitionist party.

1847 Pennsylvania freed all remaining slaves who were enslaved before the 1780 law.

1854 The Republican Party was created by antislavery activists.

1856 In what became known as the Pottawatomie Massacre, John Brown and a group of abolitionists killed five proslavery activists in response to the 1854 attack on Lawrence, Kansas, an antislavery settlement.

1859 John Brown led a raid on the Harpers Ferry armory in Virginia to obtain weapons for a slave uprising throughout the south. He was caught and hanged.

1863 The Emancipation Proclamation, an executive order issued by President Lincoln, freed the slaves in 10 secessionist states.

1865 The Thirteenth Amendment to the U.S. Constitution abolished slavery.

The Civil War (1861–1865). In the 1800s, North and South became polarized. States in the North passed antislavery laws and gradually eliminated slavery beginning in 1804. Northern states became more urbanized and industrialized, with water-powered factories in New England and the Northeast. In 1828, the U.S. Congress passed a tariff law to protect Northern industries. This angered the South and led to a debate over "nullification" in 1832, when South Carolina declared the federal tariff null and void within its state borders. President Andrew Jackson ignored this states' rights argument and threatened South Carolina with military force. The state backed down, but the Southern states feared that the federal government might use the same tactics with regard to slavery—that an antislavery president would ignore states' rights and convince Congress to abolish slavery.

In contrast to the industrial development of the North, the South maintained its plantation agriculture based on slave labor. The invention of the cotton gin in 1793 increased cotton production and the demand for slaves, and Southern states wanted to expand slavery into the new territories annexed through wars with Mexico.

By the 1850s, the fight over slavery came to a head. The Supreme Court issued its 1857 *Dred Scott* decision stating that slaves had no rights, and in 1858 Abraham Lincoln made his famous "House Divided" speech condemning slavery. Lincoln's Republican Party wanted to eliminate slavery, and when he took office as president in 1861, seven slave states seceded from the union and formed the Confederate States of America, with their capital at Montgomery, Alabama. In his inaugural address, Lincoln refused to accept the secession or to sign any treaties with the secessionists, as this would legitimize their secession.

The Civil War began when the new Confederate army attacked Fort Sumter near Charleston, South Carolina. The fort's commander surrendered, but President Lincoln called for volunteers to put down the Confederate rebellion. As both sides raised armies, Lincoln blockaded Southern ports, leading to the end of the cotton trade and the devastation of the Southern economy.

Some military actions of the Civil War were the Peninsula Campaign, Battle of Antietam, Battle of Gettysburg, Battle of Shiloh, Siege of Vicksburg, and Siege of Petersburg.

Reconstruction. After the Civil War, the federal government began the task of restoring national unity and ending slavery. Under Republican control, the Congress placed the Southern civilian governments under military control and held elections, allowing freed slaves to vote but prohibiting white Confederacy leaders from voting. Southern governments formed through alliances of freedmen, carpetbaggers, and scalawags. Some of the reforms included establishing schools, raising taxes, and government aid for railroads to help rebuild the economic infrastructure of the South.

Opposition to these efforts included the creation of the Ku Klux Klan, a violent, racist organization that opposed abolition. Extremists within the Southern Democratic Party also helped destroy the Republicans and their reconstruction efforts through paramilitary groups like the White League. The 1876 presidential election put Republican Rutherford B. Hayes in office, but only after the two parties made a deal to exchange Hayes's victory for the Republican agreement to withdraw federal troops from the South. This deal ended Republican reconstruction efforts. By 1877, white Democrats had regained power in the South and enacted Jim Crow laws to segregate whites and blacks. The laws restricted voter registration; imposed a poll tax and literacy tests for voting; segregated schools, public spaces, and public transportation; and succeeded in disenfranchising blacks and poor whites.

Urban Growth, Immigration, and Nativism. After the Civil War, the North prospered through increased industrialization and urbanization. The United States, especially its major cities including New York, Chicago, and Philadelphia, became a magnet for immigrants from southern and eastern Europe. Many lived in ethnic enclaves, such as Little Italy, Little Bohemia, and Chinatown, for mutual protection and aid. Immigrants were hardworking people and helped develop America's entrepreneurial and industrial base.

Racist attitudes that had been directed toward Native Americans and African slaves for centuries were turned, after the 1880s, toward the new immigrants. Nativism—the ethnocentric or racist belief that only native-born members of one's own group are true citizens—was rampant during the turn of the century and contributed to many stereotypes of immigrants. Congress responded to nativist fears by passing immigrant restriction laws, such as the Chinese Exclusion Act of 1882, which was renewed every 10 years until its repeal in 1943.

Industrial Revolution

The Industrial Revolution began in Britain in 1750 and spread to the United States in the late eighteenth century. The greatest innovations were in the textile industry. Inventions such as the spinning jenny, spinning mule, and water-powered spinning frame allowed workers or machines to produce more yarn in less time, and the cotton gin increased the production and processing of cotton. The steam engine increased transportation in the shipping and railroad industries and allowed raw materials to be shipped faster. The expansion of the railroad and telegraph networks in the late nineteenth century was the primary reason for the development of a market economy in the United States.

While the Industrial Revolution introduced inventions that improved the lives of many, these same inventions also harmed some groups. The cotton gin increased the demand for slaves, the spinning mule increased cancer among male spinners, and women and children were often forced to work long hours in unsafe factories.

Domain 3: California History

Geography

California's geography is a mix of mountains, deserts, plateaus, basins, valleys, rivers, lakes, glaciers, and coastline. The Pacific Ocean borders California on the west, and the mountains along the coast are part of the Pacific Coast Ranges that run from Canada to Mexico. The Sierra Nevada runs along the eastern border and includes Mount Whitney, Yosemite Valley, and Lake Tahoe. The Central Valley contains the Sacramento and San Joaquin Valleys and is a major agricultural region fed by the Sacramento and San Joaquin Rivers. To the north lie the Cascade Range, the Modoc Plateau, and the Klamath Mountains, rich in coniferous forests. The Mojave Desert and Death Valley lie to the southeast.

California's American Indian Peoples

California is home to diverse Native American groups, many of which have ancient roots in the region. In pre-Columbian times, indigenous groups ranged from small hunter-gatherer bands to large tribal villages. Hunting, trapping, gathering, fishing, and trading were major economic activities.

Native groups adapted their economies to the geography and climate of the regions they inhabited. In forest and basin areas, people collected wild foods like acorns, berries, roots, mushrooms, and seeds, and they fished and hunted small animals. In coastal and river areas, people fished for salmon, ocean fish, and shellfish; they also hunted game and gathered wild plants. Indigenous people made their clothing, baskets, homes, tools, medicines, and weapons from the natural resources at their disposal.

Kinship was central to their social organization, and kin networks included clans and lineages that intermarried and assisted one another in disputes, farming, hunting, trading, rituals, and food collecting. Because social relations were based on kin, hierarchy and gender inequality were minimal and, in some groups, nonexistent. Religious rituals focused on the community and its needs. Rituals revolved around rain, food, health, birth, death, marriage, and other life events. Religious beliefs varied, and cosmologies and traditions were highly sophisticated, often incorporating several deities and supernatural worlds. Myths, folklore, and legends were elaborate and shared some common themes, such as origins, and common characters, such as the trickster, culture-hero, and creator.

Spanish Exploration and Colonization

Explorers from Catholic and Protestant European countries thought of native people in America as "uncivilized heathens," and as military expeditions conquered new lands, missionary groups followed to "convert and civilize" the native population. Spanish colonization of the Americas, between 1492 and 1898, followed this pattern. As the conquistadores colonized new territory, they set up forts, towns, and missions.

The Jesuits initially established missions in Baja California, beginning in 1683, but were expelled from New Spain by King Carlos III in 1768. The Spanish government then sent in the Franciscans to replace the Jesuits. In 1769, the Franciscan friars Junípero Serra and Juan Crespí joined the expedition of the Spanish soldier Gaspar de Portolà to San Diego. At San Diego, Serra founded the Mission San Diego de Alcalá, the first of 21 California missions established by the Spanish.

Not only were Native Americans mission converts, but they also became the major workforce in each mission. It was the responsibility of the missions to provide the Spanish forts with food and manufactured goods, and for this, the missionaries needed Indian labor. Eventually, agriculture became the dominant industry of the missions. The missionaries brought seeds for oranges, grapes, apples, peaches, pears, and figs, and developed the cultivation of fruit trees throughout California. They made wine, raised cattle and sheep, cultivated olive trees, and developed the citrus industry.

After native peoples came under the influence of the missions, their traditional lives changed. Missionaries promoted male authority, the worship of one deity, corporal punishment of men and women, housing of children separately from their parents, restriction of interaction with kin groups, prohibitions on traditional ceremonies, and strict sexual norms.

The conditions at the missions often provoked rebellion. In 1771 Indians attacked the San Gabriel Mission, charging that the Spanish soldiers guarding the mission had raped an Indian woman. In 1775 Indians burned the mission of San Diego, charging the Spanish with forced labor and rape. In 1776 Indians attacked the mission at San Luis Obispo, and in 1785 six Indian villages revolted against the San Gabriel Mission. In 1824 the Chumash at La Purísima Mission revolted and resisted the Spanish military for more than a month. There are also accounts of Indians running away from the missions only to be hunted down by soldiers, returned to the mission, and subjected to severe punishment.

Mission lands were supposed to pass to Native Americans after they became Spanish subjects, but the Franciscans never turned over the missions.

Mexican Rule

Mexico won independence from Spain by 1821, after an 11-year war of independence. This victory ended European rule in California and reduced the power of the missions. There had been growing criticism of the abuses of the mission system, and in 1827 the Mexican government passed a law expelling all Spanish-born people, many of whom were missionaries. In 1834 the government provided the final death knell to the missions when it passed a law secularizing California's missions. This law allowed the Mexican government to take much of the mission land, leaving the friars only their churches and the priests' homes and gardens.

The Mexican government also established large land grants, called ranchos, for raising cattle and sheep. Previously, the Spanish crown had granted use rights for these lands, but the Mexican government actually allowed individuals to own title to the land if they built a house on it within one year. This encouraged settlement and farming in California.

The Mexican-American War (1846–1848). On May 13, 1846, the United States declared war on Mexico. The war came after the United States annexed the Republic of Texas, which Mexico claimed. The Bear Flag Revolt of 1846 initiated hostilities in California. In June 1846, American settlers revolted against the Mexican fort in Sonoma and raised the Bear Flag, signifying the California Republic. In July, Commodore Robert F. Stockton arrived in Monterey, and by January 1847, the Mexicans conceded defeat and signed the Treaty of Cahuenga, ending the Mexican-American War in California.

In 1848 the war ended for the rest of America with the Treaty of Guadalupe Hidalgo. Mexico ceded much territory, including California and New Mexico, and established the Rio Grande as the official border between the United States and Mexico. California was admitted to the union as the thirty-first state on September 9, 1850.

The Gold Rush (1848–1855)

In January 1848, gold was discovered at Sutter's Mill in California, and after its announcement in the press and President James Polk's address to Congress, migrants from as far away as China, Europe, and Australia flooded into the area. They were called the "forty-niners," since many arrived in 1849. As increased financing and more sophisticated technology were needed to extract the metal, gold companies began to outnumber individual prospectors.

The gold rush had a significant effect on California's cities and economy. By 1852 San Francisco had grown from 200 residents just five years earlier to 36,000. Cities sprung up throughout the state, and their rapid population growth led to a boom in building homes, schools, roads, temples, churches, hotels, and saloons.

The beginning of the gold rush was a chaotic time, since California was only an American possession, under U.S. military control, and didn't become a state until 1850. There was no local U.S. government, and the Mexican government no longer had authority in the region. There were no laws controlling the land or mines.

Miners squatted in camps and staked their claims on any open land. Native American villages were attacked, and their lands were confiscated. Indians, having lost their hunting and gathering areas, were pushed into marginal zones. Many thousands died from disease and starvation in the 20 years after the rush began. As gold became more difficult to extract, American miners competed with and attacked foreign miners, especially Chinese and Mexicans.

The gold rush caused significant environmental damage. Miners would descend on an area, work it until it no longer yielded gold, and then abandon it. In some cases, miners would divert rivers in order to expose the riverbed to dig for gold. By 1853 miners began to use hydraulic mining, similar to fracking, which destroyed all flora along the hillsides and washed pollutants, such as gravel, silt, and heavy metals, into streams and rivers.

The California Constitution

The growth of population and towns during the gold rush stimulated the demand for California to become a state, which occurred on September 9, 1850. The California Constitution, ratified in 1879, defines the duties, structure, and powers of the state government.

Reforms during the Progressive Era (1890–1920) were meant to break the monopoly over government by powerful interests and give more power to the people. Popular sovereignty, a major principle of the California Constitution, is guaranteed by reforms such as these:

▶ **Initiative.** Voters can bypass the state legislature and force a vote on laws and constitutional amendments by collecting enough signatures on a petition.
▶ **Referendum.** Voters can directly vote on a specific issue on the ballot.
▶ **Recall.** Voters can vote to end the term of an elected official before the term has officially ended.

The California Constitution differs from the U.S. Constitution in several ways:

▶ It affords more substantial rights to California citizens: it prohibits capital punishment and allows free speech even in privately owned spaces (for example, shopping centers).
▶ It allows the California governor to veto parts of a bill; the U.S. Constitution allows the president to veto only an entire bill.

The California Constitution is similar to the U.S. Constitution in its Declaration of Rights, found in Article 1 of the constitution, which is similar to the U.S. Bill of Rights in asserting individual freedoms, including the freedom of speech, freedom to assemble and petition grievances, the right to due process, and freedom of religion. The California Constitution also contains a separation-of-powers clause and a system of checks and balances.

California's Government

At the state level are the governor; the bicameral legislature, consisting of senators and assembly members; and the California Supreme Court.

Locally, California is divided into 58 counties, 460 cities, 22 towns, and more than 1,000 school districts (either unified, elementary, or high school). The county is the most important unit of the local government. Counties can hold elections, collect property taxes, and record and maintain public records. Cities can be either charter cities (governed by the city charter) or general law cities (governed by state law). School districts are governed by school board members and school superintendents. California's constitution provides a minimum amount of funding annually for K–12 education and community colleges,

depending on economic growth and student enrollment.

Indian Rancherias and Reservations

Rancherias are small Native American villages, settlements, or land reservations. In 1958 the California Rancheria Act attempted to redistribute rancheria lands and assets to individual tribal members, on condition that they forfeit any future federal assistance, including federal protection of their traditional lands. In the 1970s, the Inter-Tribal Council of California formed local task forces to protest the termination of rancherias. In 1975, as a result of these local actions and the actions of the American Indian Movement and the civil rights movement, a federal law called the Indian Self Determination and Education Assistance Act restored federal grants to federally recognized Indian tribes.

Rancherias in California include the following examples:

▶ Redwood Valley Rancheria is located northeast of Redwood Valley in Northern California. It is home to the Redwood Valley Band of Pomo Indians.
▶ Graton Rancheria is also in northern California. It is a rancheria for the Coast Miwok and Southern Pomo Indians.
▶ Buena Vista Rancheria, located in the foothills of the Sierra Nevada, is a rancheria of the Me-Wuk Indians of California.
▶ Redding Rancheria, in Redding, California, is home to diverse tribes, including descendants of the Pit-River, Wintu, and Yana.

Immigration to California

After gold was discovered in California in 1848, immigrants from all over the United States and from several foreign countries flooded into the state. There already was a community of Chinese in California and elsewhere in the country, working in various service industries, but many more came from China, and by 1852 Chinese immigration was booming. In 1863 construction began on the Central Pacific Railroad and required the labor of thousands of Chinese immigrants. But anti-Chinese racism was high in California and the United States, and in 1882 the federal Chinese Exclusion Act restricted the immigration of Chinese people. Businesses turned to Japanese migrants for labor.

Japanese immigrants began arriving in America after the Japanese emperor was restored to power under the 1868 Meiji Restoration and the Japanese loosened emigration laws. Japanese workers first stopped in Hawaii, around 1885, before arriving in California. Most Japanese immigrated as families, not individuals, and they attempted to assimilate into American society. But racism turned toward the Japanese, especially with the formation of the Japanese and Korean Exclusion League in 1905.

After the San Francisco fire in 1906, the school board placed the Japanese students into Chinese and Korean schools, which angered Japanese parents. They appealed to the Japanese media, and to prevent an embarrassing international situation, President Theodore Roosevelt signed the 1907 Gentlemen's Agreement, offering to have the Japanese children admitted to public schools in return for Japan restricting further Japanese emigration to the United States. Although the Gentlemen's Agreement never became law, it was superseded in 1924 by the Immigration Act, which banned the immigration of all Asians. With the passage of the Immigration and Nationality Act of 1965, early quota systems based on country of origin were abolished and Asians and Pacific Islanders once again migrated to California in large numbers.

Throughout much of the 1930s, severe dust storms caused by drought and poor farming techniques prompted migration from Oklahoma, Arkansas, Missouri, Iowa, Nebraska, Kansas, Texas, Colorado, and New Mexico. Over 200,000 of these migrants, called "Okies," went to California's Central Valley hoping to find work. They performed low-wage work, such as harvesting hay, picking fruit and vegetables, and picking cotton. The Okies also brought their music to California and introduced the state to hillbilly bands.

Mexicans have always lived and created communities in the states that once belonged to Spain and Mexico, including California, Texas, Arizona, Nevada, Utah, and New Mexico. After the Mexican-American War in 1848 and the Gadsden Purchase in 1853, a majority of the Latino population living in those territories became American citizens. In California, about 25,000 Mexicans migrated to the state during the gold rush. They were driven out of the mining camps by Anglo immigrants, and prevented from fighting for their rights in the courts by discriminatory laws. Research shows that about 163 Mexicans were lynched in California between the start of the gold rush and 1860.

Mexicans have also emigrated from California to Oregon and Washington to find work in orchards. Another wave of Mexican immigrants came after 1890. They were mostly agricultural laborers and found work in the farming valleys like the Imperial Valley. The 1920s saw another wave, as Mexico was exempt from the restrictions imposed on other countries in the 1924 Immigration Act. Between 1926 and 1930, internal wars in Mexico caused the emigration of over 400,000 people, many of whom fled to California.

Mexicans and other immigrants are responsible for California being a major agricultural state. They have not always been treated fairly, but they have organized in unions to protect their rights. Under the leadership of organizers like César Chávez and Dolores Huerta, Mexican grape growers and lettuce workers in California have gained some ground with the Democratic Party and have helped elect Mexican-Americans to office. By the 1990s, the increasing proportion of Latinos in California also increased their political power, and there were significant Mexican-American politicians in high elected offices. Cruz Bustamante was the lieutenant governor from 1999 to 2007, and in 2005, Antonio Villaraigosa was elected mayor of Los Angeles.

Mexican-Americans in California have also fought legal battles to educate their children in nonsegregated schools. The 1947 case of *Mendez v. Westminster* declared racial segregation in Orange County schools to be unconstitutional. The Chicano movement also was active in California and helped get Chicano studies into university curricula.

Immigration in California, as in the rest of the United States, is still a volatile issue. California has more immigrants than any other state, and most of them are from Latin America and Asia. They still face strong discrimination and are often the subject of anti-immigrant crimes and police harassment. But California also offers hope to immigrants: effective January 2012, the California Dream Act will allow even undocumented workers to pay cheaper in-state college tuition.

California's Major Economic Activities

California's major economic activities include mining, large-scale agriculture, entertainment, aerospace, electronics, and international trade.

California ranks third in the United States in mineral production. According to the National Mining Association, California had 629 active mines in 2007 that provided, directly and indirectly, 97,480 jobs statewide. Coal and metal mining are two major industries.

California's climate and immigrant population have made it the major large-scale agricultural state in the nation. California produces more than 350 crops and grows more than half of the fruits and vegetables produced in America. There are about 81,000 farms, with an average size of 313 acres.

Debates over sustainability are becoming stronger, and California's water crisis threatens the future of large-scale farming. Analysts fear that Central California is heading for a second dust bowl as global climate change brings shifting weather patterns, loss of much of the Sierra Nevada snowpack, and severe drought.

The Sacramento–San Joaquin River Delta in the Central Valley, the heart of California's agriculture industry, is the meeting place where the northern Sacramento River meets the southern San Joaquin River. The delta contains 1,100 miles of levees to protect farmland in the Central Valley from flooding and contamination. But some of these levees are more than 100 years old and may not be able to withstand earthquakes and heavy flooding. California's water reserves are already low, and if the levees fail, as they have in other states, there will be a severe shortage of water for both agriculture and public use.

California was once a center of the aerospace industry, but that may be changing due to mergers since the 1960s. Following the mergers, Douglas Aircraft and Lockheed and other companies moved to other states.

Trade is one of California's largest job sectors. International trade is one-quarter of California's economy. The major export products, accounting for almost half of all exports, are computers and electronics.

When most people think of entertainment, they think of Hollywood, the home of American cinema. The entertainment industry also benefits local services, including hotels, restaurants, tourism, transportation, retail businesses, bars and clubs, and housing.

CHAPTER 6

Subtest II

Science, Mathematics

Science

Domain 1: Physical Science

Structure and Properties of Matter

Anything that has mass and volume is classified as matter. Matter occurs in four different states: solid, liquid, gas, and plasma, each with its own properties. Regardless of the state, however, all matter will share the following physical properties:

▶ **Color.** Matter can be described in terms of the general color observed.
▶ **Mass.** The matter's mass describes the amount of matter present.
▶ **Density.** The density is the matter's mass per unit of volume.
▶ **Hardness.** Hardness is the ease or difficulty of penetrating the material.
▶ **Electrical conductivity.** Electrical conductivity is a measure of how well electricity "moves" through the matter.
▶ **Thermal conductivity.** Thermal conductivity measures how well heat "moves" though the matter.

Physical and Chemical Changes. Changes in matter can be classified into two types: physical and chemical changes. In a physical change, only the state of the matter or the shape of the matter changes; there is no change at the molecular level. For example, if we were to put an ice cube into a hot pan, the ice cube would melt. This change in state is brought on by the introduction of heat energy but doesn't change the basic makeup of the water. Only the physical properties are affected.

However, if we instead were to take a piece of wood and place it on the hot pan, allowing it to burn, this would result in a chemical change. This change is irreversible and affected the chemical properties and makeup of the piece of wood.

Atoms and Molecules. Atoms are the most basic building block of matter, but they themselves are made up of smaller particles. Those particles are called protons, neutrons, and electrons. Together, protons (which carry a positive charge) and neutrons (which carry no charge) make up the nucleus of an atom. Atoms also carry negatively charged electrons, which are located outside of the nucleus.

When two or more atoms are combined chemically, they form a molecule and will behave as a single particle.

Elements and Compounds. An element is a substance that contains only one type of atom. Some of the common elements are oxygen (represented with the chemical abbreviation O), helium (He), mercury (Hg), and sulfur (S).

When we chemically combine two or more elements in such a way that we can break them down again through chemical reactions, we have a compound.

The Periodic Table. The periodic law states that when you arrange atoms by increasing atomic number (the number of protons in the nucleus), similar properties will occur at regular and predictable intervals. The periodic table is a way of arranging elements to express this.

The periodic table provides a great deal of information if we know how to read it. For example, let's look at the entry for the element xenon (Xe):

```
131.3
Xe
54
```

Xenon's atomic number is 54, which means its nucleus contains 54 protons. The atomic mass of xenon is 131.3, which represents the total mass of protons, electrons, and neutrons in each xenon atom.

On a larger scale, the periodic table is divided into groups or columns. Elements in the same column share similar chemical properties. Moving across rows from left to right in the periodic table, elements have increasing electronegativity, which is the tendency of the element to attract electrons.

Acids and Bases. The pH scale, which ranges in value from 0 to 14, is used to measure how acidic or basic a substance is. Substances with a low pH (less than 7) are said to be acidic, while substances with a high pH (more than 7) are said to be basic. Substances are considered neutral if they have a pH of 7. Following are the pH measurements for some common substances:

```
Pure water . . . . . . .  pH 7
Tomato juice . . . . .  pH 4.5
Vinegar . . . . . . . .  pH 3
Baking soda . . . . . .  pH 9
Ammonia . . . . . . .  pH 11
```

Principles of Motion

The motion of an object can be described in several ways:

- **Displacement.** Displacement is the change in position due to some type of motion. It can be thought of as the distance the object moved.

- **Speed.** Speed is the rate at which the displacement is changing with respect to time.
- **Velocity.** Velocity indicates the speed and the direction of the motion.
- **Acceleration.** Acceleration is the rate of change in speed with respect to time.

To understand this concept further, let's use the example of a car speeding up to enter a freeway. At a specific moment in time, the displacement is the distance the car has driven, while the speed is simply the number on the speedometer, such as 55 mph. To know the velocity, however, we also need to know the direction in which the car is traveling. If it were traveling north, we could say that the velocity is 55 mph north. Now suppose we look at the same car moments later, and it is now traveling at a speed of 60 mph. The acceleration would measure the change in speed we saw over that period of time.

NEWTON'S LAWS OF MOTION
- **First law.** An object in motion will stay in motion, and an object at rest will stay at rest unless an outside source acts on it. For example, a ball rolling on the floor will continue to roll on the floor until the forces of friction and gravity slow it to a stop.
- **Second law.** The force acting on an object is proportional to the mass of the object and its acceleration (expressed mathematically, $F = ma$). We can see this law in action when we consider the difference in an airplane engine and a car engine. The airplane's engines require much more power to move the airplane forward, due to the plane's heavier weight.
- **Third law.** If an object exerts a force on another, the other object will exert an equal and opposite force. When a rubber ball hits the ground, it bounces back up because of the opposite force from the ground as it hits.

Conservation of Energy

Energy can come in many forms, including solar, chemical, electrical, magnetic, nuclear, and electromagnetic (light). According to a principle known as conservation of energy, energy cannot be created nor can it be destroyed.

To interpret examples of this, we need to distinguish between two general types of energy: potential and kinetic. When an object has energy based on its position alone, we say it has potential energy. An easy way to picture this is to imagine a ball being held above the ground. The ball has potential energy, since work will be done if it is let go. In this sense, work is done if there is force being applied to an object to move it.

Kinetic energy is the energy an object has due to its motion. For example, a bicycle that is traveling at 30 mph has kinetic energy. If the ball in our previous example is dropped, its potential energy is converted to kinetic energy. This is an example of the conservation of energy.

Heat and Temperature

In everyday experience, heat and temperature seem to be the same thing, but they are not. The temperature of an object is a measure of the average kinetic energy of the molecules that make up that object. Heat, in contrast, is the transfer of this "internal" energy.

Heat spontaneously flows from hot objects to cold objects. This heat transfer is typically classified in one of three ways:

- **Conduction.** When two objects are in contact with each other, the molecules collide, and the heat in the warmer object is transferred to the cooler object. For example, if you were to hold an ice cube, the heat from your hand would be transferred into the ice cube, warming it and eventually melting it.
- **Convection.** When the heat transfer is caused by a fluid (gas or liquid) in motion, we say it is a result of convection. An example of this can be seen when boiling a pot of water on the stove. As the water heats up, it rises to the top and is replaced by cooler water. The water that was heated cools and then falls back. In this process, heat is transferred by the movement of the water.
- **Radiation.** Heat transferred by electromagnetic waves is said to be transferred by radiation. When the sun heats your face on a warm day, you are experiencing heat transfer by radiation.

Light

Light can come from many sources, including natural and human-made light. Most sources of light involve the production of heat also. Human-made sources of light include the following:

- **Candles, oil lamps, and torches.** These and similar sources of light rely on some source of combustible fuel and a flame to produce light.
- **Incandescent light bulbs.** In the classic style of light bulb, electricity heats a filament until it glows.
- **Neon light bulbs.** When electricity is applied to a gas such as neon held at a low pressure, the atoms become excited and emit light. Fluorescent lights work similarly, except that the gas contained in them emits light that is not visible to the human eye. Instead, the inside of the tube is coated in phosphorous, which absorbs the light and emits visible light.
- **Chemiluminescence.** This is a form of light caused by a chemical reaction that produces light *without* heat. A common example is the "glow sticks" sold at fairs and carnivals.

Natural sources of light include both terrestrial and astronomical sources, including the following:

- **The sun, stars, moon, and other astronomical phenomena.** Clearly, the sun, the closest star to the earth, is our main source of light. Other stars also produce light visible on earth, as do comets. Comets and asteroids (hunks of space rock) that enter the earth's atmosphere are called meteors. The friction caused by the object's entry into the atmosphere causes meteors to heat temporarily to high temperatures and also creates visible light. Dust from comets can also enter the atmosphere in a phenomenon known as a meteor shower.
- **Lightning and auroras.** On earth, common forms of natural, if short-lived, light are formed by electrical activity in the atmosphere. Lightning is caused by a discharge of electrical energy. Auroras, colored light displays visible at extreme northern and southern latitudes, are caused by the collision

of electrically charged particles high in the earth's atmosphere.

▶ **Bioluminescence.** Some life forms on earth, such as fireflies, emit a natural source of light caused by a chemical reaction within them. This is a natural form of chemiluminescence.

▶ **Volcanic eruptions.** Deep beneath the earth's surface is a layer of molten rock called magma. Through cracks in the earth's surface, magma can erupt, at which point it is called lava. Hot lava, like other highly heated objects, emits light.

Refraction and Reflection. When light is traveling through the air and hits a substance such as a glass of water, which will slow it down, it bends. This process, called refraction, can be seen any time light changes media through which it is traveling.

When light hits a smooth surface, it changes direction. This is known as reflection. The angle at which the light is reflected is exactly the same as the angle at which it hit the surface.

Domain 2: Life Science

Life can be divided into two main groups: plants and animals. These groups have evolved separately, and while they have some similarities, there are also important differences.

Cellular Structure

The cells of plants and animals are eukaryotic, meaning they contain a nucleus that stores DNA. Both types of cells also share several other structures, called organelles, including the following:

▶ **Cell membrane.** The cell membrane is the outer layer of the cell, separating the interior from the exterior environment.

▶ **Mitochondria.** The mitochondria are responsible for the energy of the cell through the generation of adenine triphosphate (ATP). Cells, depending on their particular function, may have many mitochondria.

▶ **Ribosomes.** The ribosomes are organelles responsible for protein synthesis within the cell.

While sharing some other structures, plant and animal cells also differ in some important ways. Specifically, most plant cells contain the following structures that are not found in animal cells:

▶ **Cell wall.** Many plant and animal cells have a cell membrane, which separates the interior and exterior of the cell. Additionally, most plants have a strong cell wall made of cellulose, which allows them to take in a larger amount of water than animal cells can.

▶ **Plastids.** Plastids such as chloroplasts play a central role in photosynthesis, the process by which plants obtain energy from sunlight. These structures are not found in animal cells.

▶ **Vacuoles.** In animal cells, there may be a handful of small vacuoles, but in plant cells, there is a single large vacuole. The vacuoles in plant cells collect water and waste products, becoming rigid and giving the plant cell an even stronger structure.

Human Organ Systems

The human body has 11 primary organ systems, which are responsible for different overall processes. These systems work together to ensure that natural processes work correctly. The following list describes each organ system, its makeup, and its underlying processes:

▶ **Skeletal system.** Made up of all the bones, ligaments, cartilage, and tendons, the skeletal system is the primary support system in humans. It also provides protection to vital organs and anchor points for the muscles.

▶ **Muscular system.** The muscular system is responsible for all movement, including movement of materials through some organs.

▶ **Integumentary system.** Consisting of the skin, hair, and fingernails, the integumentary system is primarily responsible for protecting the body against the outside world. It also helps provide sensory information along with the nervous system.

▶ **Circulatory system.** The circulatory system, which consists of the heart and blood vessels, transports oxygen, nutrients, hormones, and some waste products throughout the body.

▶ **Respiratory system.** Primarily consisting of the lungs and trachea (along with other organs such as the pharynx), the respiratory system is responsible for intake of oxygen and expulsion of carbon dioxide.

▶ **Digestive system.** The digestive system breaks down food and absorbs nutrients. The main organs for this process are the esophagus, stomach, and the large and small intestines.

▶ **Nervous system.** The nervous system is the control center for the body, processing information and controlling movements through electrical signaling. The brain, spinal cord, and nerves make up this system.

▶ **Endocrine system.** Through the various glands in the body such as the pituitary gland and the thyroid, the endocrine system regulates the body through hormones secreted directly into the bloodstream.

▶ **Excretory system.** The kidneys, bladder, urethra, and ureters are all part of the excretory system, which filters waste and excess water from the body.

▶ **Reproductive system.** Consisting of the sex organs, the reproductive system is responsible for all aspects of the reproduction process.

▶ **Immune system.** The spleen, thymus, lymph nodes, and other organs of the immune system help the body fight off infection by keeping bacteria and other organisms out of the body and destroying those that do enter the body.

Ecology. Ecology is the study of how environments and organisms interact. Ecologists study these interactions such as how energy flows, how changes in the environment affect the organisms living within it, and how the environment regulates itself.

An ecosystem is a group of interacting organisms that function as a unit within a specific habitat such as a small pond or a large forest. In any ecosystem, the flow of energy can be described using a food chain or food web, with various groups of species being assigned roles in this flow:

▶ **Primary producers.** These are organisms such as plants that produce their own energy through methods such as photosynthesis. Primary producers do not feed on other organisms.

▶ **Primary consumers.** These are organisms such as herbivores that feed on primary producers but do not feed on other consumers.

▶ **Secondary consumers.** These organisms feed only on primary consumers.

▶ **Tertiary consumers.** Consumers at this level feed only on secondary consumers.

From the tertiary level, the chain may continue on to additional levels.

This flow of energy can be thought of as a pyramid with the primary producers on the bottom and the tertiary consumers on the top. The most energy is available to the primary producers, so their biomass will be the greatest in the ecosystem. Much less energy is available to the tertiary consumers, and they will represent the smallest portion of the ecosystem's biomass.

In an ecosystem, organisms may interact in a symbiotic way, meaning a long-term interaction between two different species. This type of interaction can often be classified in one of the following three ways:

▶ **Commensalism.** One of the organisms benefits, while the other is unaffected (neither harmed nor helped).

▶ **Mutualism.** Both organisms involved in the relationship benefit.

▶ **Parasitism.** One of the organisms benefits, while the other is harmed.

Evolution. Evolution is the gradual change of entire species over many generations through a process of natural selection. In natural selection, inherited traits and mutations that are favorable to the survival of the organisms become more prevalent as these traits are passed to offspring. These changes are actual changes in the DNA over time and are the result of the modification of previous forms.

While some consider evolution a controversial idea, it is a well-established fact with a great deal of evidence supporting its existence, such as the similarities in the basic structure (DNA, skeletal) of many organisms and the fossil record showing species that are transitional in nature.

Mendel, Punnett, and Genetic Inheritance. Gregor Mendel was a nineteenth-century monk who conducted some very illuminating experiments cross-breeding garden peas. He observed various characteristics of different types of pea plants and was able to theorize and correctly predict how often certain characteristics were likely to be expressed in offspring pea plants. Mendel's theories became the foundation of modern genetic theories.

A hundred years after Mendel's experiments, Reginald Punnett, a British professor and great admirer of Mendel's work, picked up where Mendel left off. He is perhaps best known for developing a simple model called the Punnett Square, which can be used for predicting how often dominant or recessive traits from a male and female will be expressed in their offspring. For example, let's say there are two squirrels, a male and female, and each carries a dominant and recessive trait for fur color. The dominant color is brown and the recessive color is gray. We will let "A" represent the dominant trait and "a" represent the recessive trait. Our Punnett Square would look something like this, with the male's traits on the top and the female's traits on the side (although it doesn't really matter whether the male or female traits are aligned on top or side):

Cross: Aa x Aa

	A	a
A	AA	Aa
a	Aa	aa

Offspring receive pairs of genes from their parents. Whenever the offspring receives two dominant genes, the characteristics expressed by those genes will be apparent in the offspring. Whenever the offspring receives one dominant and one recessive gene, the dominant gene will still be expressed. If, however, the offspring receives two recessive genes, the recessive trait will be expressed. We can see by this chart of possible combinations that if our male and female squirrels had four offspring, the odds are that three of them would have brown fur and one would have gray fur.

Domain 3: Earth and Space Studies
Basic Astronomy

The solar system consists of the sun at the center and the planets and asteroids that orbit it in an elliptical fashion. In order from the closest to the sun to the furthest, the planets are Mercury, Venus, Earth, Mars, Jupiter, Saturn, Uranus, and Neptune. There are also several small "dwarf" planets, including Pluto, which was once classified as a planet.

Between the orbits of Mars and Jupiter, the majority of asteroids in the solar system can be found in the asteroid belt. Comets, in contrast, have very large and eccentric elliptical orbits around the sun. While asteroids are almost completely rocky or metallic, comets are made up of frozen water, methane, ammonia, and some rocky materials. This water and the gases are responsible for the unique appearance of comets from Earth as they vaporize near the sun.

Our solar system is one of many elements of the Milky Way Galaxy, a spiral-shaped grouping of billions of stars all revolving around the center.

The Moon. The moon revolves around the earth every 27 days with the same side always facing the earth, since the moon rotates on its axis with the same period. The phase of the moon is dependent on where the moon is in relation to the earth and the sun. When the moon is completely opposite the sun, we will have a full moon, where the entire surface of the side facing the earth is visible. As the moon continues to revolve around the earth, the phases change until it is between the earth and sun. At this time, the phase is the new moon, and the moon appears dark.

The moon is also responsible for the tidal variations in ocean level on the coastlines. As the earth rotates, the side that is closest to the moon and the side directly opposite will experience high tide. The rest of the earth's coastlines will experience low tide. The sun's gravity has some influence over this, but it is minor compared with the gravitational effect of the moon.

The Seasons. The earth is slightly tilted on its axis of rotation, and because of this, different parts of the earth receive greater sunlight during different parts of the earth's orbit around the sun. For example, in December, the Northern Hemisphere of the earth is tilted away from the sun, and the Southern Hemisphere receives more sunlight (where it is summer) than the Northern Hemisphere (in winter). However, in July, the Northern Hemisphere of the earth is tilted toward the sun, resulting in summer in the Northern Hemisphere.

Time Zones. The earth rotates on its axis once every 24 hours, with noon being recognized as the time at which the sun is directly overhead at a particular spot on the earth. To define time in this way, it is necessary to have different time zones across the earth.

The length of a day is equivalent to the earth turning by 15 degrees of longitude every hour. Therefore, the boundaries for the time zones are set 15 degrees apart. For instance, if it is noon in your time zone, then 15 degrees to the east, it is 1 p.m., and 15 degrees to the west, it is 11 a.m.

Basic Geology

Geologists study the physical makeup of the earth, such as the formation of mountains, the creation of rocks and minerals, and phenomena such as volcanoes and earthquakes.

Rocks consist of homogenous materials referred to as minerals. Many types of minerals, including quartz, calcite, and mica, are common in the earth's crust. However, rocks can be classified into three main types:

- **Igneous.** Igneous rocks are formed when molten rock cools. A common example is granite.
- **Sedimentary.** These rocks are formed as the fragments of other rocks and sediment are compressed over a long period of time.
- **Metamorphic.** Metamorphic rocks were originally igneous or sedimentary but were transformed by heat and pressure under the earth's surface in a way that gave them new characteristics.

The Layers of the Earth. The earth consists of three main parts. In the center of the earth is the earth's core, consisting of a solid inner core and a liquid outer core made up of molten iron and possibly other materials. Beyond this layer is the mantle, which is a largely solid layer consisting of ferromagnesian minerals, meaning minerals containing iron and magnesium.

The surface of the earth, such as the continents and the ocean basin, makes up the outermost layer of the earth. This layer, along with the outermost portion of the mantle, makes up the lithosphere.

Plate Tectonics. The lithosphere consists of several large plates that float upon a more fluid part of the mantle called the asthenosphere. These plates grow as they drift apart, allowing molten rock to form new ocean floor and get destroyed as a plate slides under another. As these plates have shifted and moved around the earth, the continents have shifted as well.

It is widely believed that 200 million years ago, there was a single large continent (Pangaea) and a single large ocean. Over millions of years, the continents have drifted apart as the plates beneath them have shifted.

Evidence for these processes comes from several different sources. For example, the sea floor near ridges is much younger than the sea floor away from the ridges, suggesting that the plates are pulling apart. Further, evidence of glacial erosion is found in regions near the equator such as India and in paths that would suggest the glaciers moved across the oceans and back onto land. Fossil evidence would also suggest movement of animals and plant life across oceans in ways that are not possible today.

Meteorology

Meteorology is the study of the earth's atmosphere. All weather as we experience it on the surface of the earth can be traced back to the sun warming the earth unevenly. As the air warms, it rises, and cooler air replaces it. When the warm air rises, it leaves behind an area of lower pressure. Any moisture that has evaporated is carried upward and condenses as it cools, forming clouds. If these clouds are substantial enough, precipitation will result. Regions of low pressure are generally associated with wet and windy weather conditions, while regions of high pressure are generally associated with clear and calm weather.

Winds are created by pressure differences between regions where the air is falling (high pressure) and where the air is rising (low pressure). The greater the pressure difference, the stronger the winds.

Mathematics

Domain 1: Number Sense

The Number Systems

Many of the numbers we encounter in algebra come from a set of numbers called the real numbers. The number line shown here is a graph of this set. Notice that it contains all of the negative and positive numbers, as well as fractions and decimals.

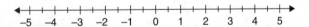

Mathematicians have divided the real numbers up into many smaller groups based on their properties or form. The most common of these follow.

The Whole Numbers {0, 1, 2, 3, 4, 5, . . .}. You can think of the whole numbers as the numbers we use to say how many of something we have. This set contains zero as well as all of the positive whole numbers.

The Natural Numbers {1, 2, 3, 4, 5, . . .}. If we leave zero out of the set of whole numbers, we have the natural numbers. These are sometimes thought of as the "counting" numbers and also include all of the positive whole numbers.

The Integers {. . . , –3, –2, –1, 0, 1, 2, 3, . . .}. The integers contains zero, all of the positive whole numbers, and all of the negative whole numbers.

The Rational Numbers. Any number that can be written as a fraction of whole numbers is considered a rational number. This includes the integers, since, for example, $-\dfrac{3}{1} = -3$; therefore, the set of rational numbers also contains the whole numbers and the natural numbers. Even decimals that never end but follow a recurring pattern, such as $0.\overline{6}$, are included, since $0.\overline{6} = \dfrac{2}{3}$. As long as a number can be written as a fraction of whole numbers, it will be included in the set of rational numbers.

The Irrational Numbers. Of course, if there are rational numbers, there must be irrational numbers. If a number cannot be written as a fraction of whole numbers, then it is called an irrational number. This includes all never-ending decimals that have no pattern, such as π and $\sqrt{2}$.

Properties of the Real Numbers

The real numbers have many important properties. Three of these come up even with simple operations like addition and multiplication.

The Associative Property: (a + b) + c = a + (b + c). The associative property says we can associate any two values and add them first. Example:

$$(1+2)+5 = 3+5 = 8$$
$$1+(2+5) = 1+7 = 8$$

It also holds true for multiplication:

$$5 \times (2 \times 3) = 5 \times 6 = 30$$
$$(5 \times 2) \times 3 = 10 \times 3 = 30$$

Place Value

Place value is used to describe the size of numbers in words. Let's look at an example to see how it works. The number below is 1,257,120.74.

1	2	5	7	1	2	0	7	4
millions	hundred thousands	ten thousands	thousands	hundreds	tens	ones	tenths	hundredths

Moving from one place value to the next, as we move to the left, place value increases, and each place value is 10 times bigger than the previous. As we move to the right, place value decreases, and each place value is one-tenth as big as the previous.

The Commutative Property: a + b = b + a. The commutative property says that the order in which we add does not matter. In other words, 1 + 2 will give us the same answer as 2 + 1. This property is also true for multiplication.

The Distributive Property: a(b + c) = ab + ac. The distributive property comes up a great deal in algebra as well as arithmetic. Using this property, we can simplify large expressions. Example:

$$-5(4+9) = -5 \times 4 + -5 \times 9 = -20 - 45 = -65$$

Ordering

When you look at a number line, the numbers get larger as you move left to right, and they get smaller if you move right to left. We can use this to understand the ordering of real numbers.

On the number line, 7 is to the right of 3, so 7 is larger than 3. This can be denoted as 7 > 3. Similarly, 0 is to the left of 1, meaning 0 is smaller than 1, and this can be denoted as 0 < 1.

To compare fractions or find where a fraction should be placed on a number line, one method is to convert the fraction to a decimal. Example:

Which is larger, $\dfrac{3}{17}$ or $\dfrac{8}{21}$?

To compare the two fractions, divide 3 by 17, and divide 8 by 21:

$$\frac{3}{17} \cong 0.17647$$

$$\frac{8}{21} \cong 0.38095$$

Now we can see that $\dfrac{8}{21} > \dfrac{3}{17}$. We can also use these decimal representations to place each of these fractions on a number line.

Exponents

Suppose we had the multiplication problem $4 \times 4 \times 4$. This problem can be rewritten using exponents. When exponents are positive whole numbers, they are used to tell us how many times to multiply a number by itself. In the example, $4 \times 4 \times 4 = 4^3$.

By definition, any number with a 0 exponent is considered to be 1 (except 0^0, which is an indeterminate form), and any number with an exponent of 1 is simply the number itself. But what about negative exponents or even fractional exponents? For a negative exponent n, take the reciprocal of the number to the nth power:

$$a^{-n} = \frac{1}{a^n}$$

For fractional exponents where the exponent has the denominator n, you take the nth root (assuming the exponent uses whole numbers m and n):

$$a^{\frac{m}{n}} = \sqrt[n]{a^m}$$

Examples:

$$\left(\frac{1}{2}\right)^3 = \frac{1}{2} \times \frac{1}{2} \times \frac{1}{2} = \frac{1}{8}$$

$$3^{-2} = \frac{1}{3^2} = \frac{1}{9}$$

$$81^{\frac{1}{2}} = \sqrt{81} = 9$$

Scientific Notation

The concept of exponents can be used to write numbers in an almost shorthand way called scientific notation. As was mentioned before, place value is based on tens. In this sense, we can think of moving a decimal place as either multiplying or dividing by 10.

Consider the number 80,000. The 8, which is in the ten thousands place, is four zeros to the left of the decimal place. That means we could get 80,000 by multiplying 8 by 10 four times. In symbols, $80,000 = 8 \times 10 \times 10 \times 10 \times 10$. Using exponential notation simplifies this expression with an exponent:

$$80,000 = 8 \times 10 \times 10 \times 10 \times 10 = 8 \times 10^4$$

Now we have written 80,000 in scientific notation.

When rewriting a number from scientific notation, we can think of the exponent on the 10 as telling us which direction to move the decimal. The sign on the 10 (positive or negative) tells us whether to move the decimal left or right. For example, to rewrite 1.2×10^{-7}, we move the decimal place seven spaces to the left (since the exponent is negative):

$$1.2 \times 10^{-7} = 0.00000012$$

Finding Prime Factorizations

When considering the integers, there are two major groups of numbers:

▶ **Prime numbers.** Prime numbers are numbers that can be evenly divided only by 1 and themselves. By convention, 1 is not considered prime, but 2, 3, and 11 are examples of prime numbers.

▶ **Composite numbers.** If a number is not a prime number, it is called a composite number. These numbers have factors other than 1 and themselves. Factors are simply numbers you can multiply to get the original number. For example, 6 is a composite number and has 2 and 3 as factors. You would also be correct if you said that 6 and 1 are factors of 6.

Every composite number can be written as a product of prime numbers. Finding these prime numbers is called finding the "prime factorization" of the number. Finding the prime factorization of a number always starts off with finding two factors of that number.

For example, let's find the prime factorization of 192. First, we need to find just two factors of 192. Instead of randomly checking numbers on a calculator, it can be helpful to use one of the following divisibility rules (if 10 is divisible by 2, it means 2 is a factor of 10):

▶ All even numbers are divisible by 2. This includes numbers ending in 0, 2, 4, 6, and 8, such as 1,240 and 158,972.
▶ If the sum of the digits is divisible by 3, then the number is divisible by 3. For example, the sum of the digits of 336 is 3 + 3 + 6 = 12, which is divisible by 3. Therefore, 336 is divisible by 3.
▶ If the last two digits in the number are divisible by 4, then the number is divisible by 4. Since 48 is divisible by 4, so is 30,548.
▶ If the number ends in 0 or 5, then it is divisible by 5. The numbers 1,000 and 250 are both divisible by 5.

While these aren't all of the divisibility rules, they are the most useful ones.

With our example of 192, it is even, so it is divisible by 2. Divide: $192 \div 2 = 96$, so $192 = 96 \times 2$. Since 2 is a prime number and we are trying to write 192 as a product of all prime numbers, we now focus on the 96.

The sum of the digits of 96 is 9 + 6 = 15, which is divisible by 3. This means that 3 is a factor of 96. By dividing, we find that $96 = 3 \times 32$. Now we can state the factors as $192 = 96 \times 2 = 32 \times 3 \times 2$. As before, since 3 and 2 are prime, we now need to focus on breaking down the 32. Since this number is smaller, we can use our knowledge of the multiplication tables to write 32 as 4×8. Neither the 4 nor the 8 is prime, so we still must break them down further.

The following steps review and complete the work:

$$
\begin{aligned}
192 &= 96 \times 2 \\
&= 32 \times 3 \times 2 \\
&= 4 \times 8 \times 3 \times 2 \\
&= 2 \times 2 \times 4 \times 2 \times 3 \times 2 \\
&= 2 \times 2 \times 2 \times 2 \times 2 \times 3 \times 2
\end{aligned}
$$

Notice that in each step, if the number wasn't prime, we broke it down into smaller factors until all of the numbers were prime. In addition, we can simplify the prime factorization of 192 by using exponential notation: $2^6 \times 3$.

Greatest Common Factors

When we have two numbers, the greatest common factor (GCF) is the largest number that divides both of the numbers. We will review one common technique for finding this useful value by working through two examples.

Find the greatest common factor of 120 and 84. To solve, first we find the prime factorization of each number:

$$120 = 2^3 \times 3 \times 5$$

$$84 = 2^2 \times 3 \times 7$$

Next, to make our GCF, we use the prime factors that the two numbers share. The factors 2^2 and 3 are shared by 120 and 84. Multiply them to obtain the GCF:

$$2^2 \times 3 = 4 \times 3 = 12$$

Let's try another example: Find the greatest common factor of 180 and 150. First, find the prime factorization of each:

$$180 = 2^2 \times 3^2 \times 5$$

$$150 = 2 \times 3 \times 5^2$$

The GCF is $2 \times 3 \times 5 = 30$.

Rounding and Estimation

Rounding numbers can be helpful for estimating large quantities like $38,001 \times 5$ or even smaller quantities such as $1.023 + 2.511$. Before you can estimate values such as these, you must be able to round numbers.

To round a number to a certain place value, we look at the digit to the right of that place value. If the digit to the right is 5 or greater, we round up, and if it is less than 5, we round down. Examples:

Round 11.2577 to the tenths place.

Since the digit to the right of the 2 (which is in the tenths place) is 5, we round the 2 up to 3, giving us 11.3.

Round 1,317.11 to the nearest hundreds place.

The number in the hundreds place is 3. The number to the right of the 3 is less than 5, so we do not change the value of the 3. Therefore, the answer is 1,300.

Estimate the value of 1.27 + 5.33.

We can round 1.27 to 1 and 5.33 to 5 to estimate this sum as about 6.

Domain 2: Algebra and Functions

Simplifying Linear Expressions

Linear expressions involve variables of degree 1 and no equals sign. The "degree" is the highest power to which a variable is raised, so a linear expression of the first degree, or "degree 1," has no variables raised beyond the first power. When it comes to linear expressions, the two big skills you will need are the ability to determine when two linear expressions are equivalent and the ability to write a linear expression that will represent a real-life situation. In both of these cases, there are a couple of key points to remember:

▶ **Order of operations.** If you are simplifying an expression with several operations and parentheses, you must work in this order to get an equivalent expression: parentheses, exponents, multiplication, division, addition, and subtraction. To remember the order, use the mnemonics based on the first letters of the operations: P.E.M.D.A.S. or "Please excuse my dear Aunt Sally."

▶ **The Distributive Property, a(b + c) = ab + ac.** If the operation inside parentheses is addition or subtraction, you must remember to multiply each of the terms inside of the parentheses by the term on the outside of the parentheses; otherwise, you will not get an equivalent expression. A simple example shows that this is true: You can see that $2 \times 3 + 2 \times 4 = 6 + 8 = 14$ by the order of operations. It is also true that $2(3 + 4) = 2(7) = 14$ by the same properties. We also get the same answer if we use the distributive property: $2(3+4)=2\times3+2\times4=14$. If we had instead multiplied 2 by only the first term in parentheses, we would have $2\times3+4=6+4=10$, which is, of course, completely different.

▶ **Like terms.** Two terms are "like" if they have the same variable with the same exponent. For example, x and $-5x$ are like terms, while x^2 and $2x^7$ are not (since they have different exponents). You can only add and subtract like terms when simplifying. Thus, to simplify the linear expression $5x-6(2+x)-1$, we would first distribute the -6 and get $5x-12-6x-1$. The $5x$ and $-6x$ are like terms, so they can be combined further to $-x$. The -12 and -1 also are like terms, which can be combined to get -13. As a result, we simplify the expression to $-x-13$.

Writing Linear Expressions

When trying to represent a relationship where one or more of the values could change, we can write a linear expression. A useful approach is to read the question very carefully and decide what values are fixed and what values are dependent on a variable value. Example:

Suppose a car rental company charges a base fee of $15 a day to rent a compact car and 2 cents for every mile the car is driven during the rental period. Which of the following expressions would represent the final bill if the car is rented for a single day and driven n miles during that period?

  A. $(\$15+\$0.02)n$

  B. $\$15+\$0.02n$

  C. $\$15n+\$0.02$

  D. $\$15.02n+\$15$

Since we had the car for only one day, the company would charge us $15 whether we drove it or not. This value is fixed, meaning it won't depend on our variable n, which represents the number of miles.

But if we drove the car exactly 1 mile that day, then we would have an extra charge of 2 cents (or $0.02). If we instead drove it 10 miles, we would have an extra charge of 2 cents for each of those miles. This would be a total extra charge of

$(10\times\$0.02)=\$0.2$, or 20 cents. Therefore, the extra charge depends on the number of miles, n. In both of these cases, we were multiplying the number of miles by the 2 cents to find the extra charge. Applying this to the variable n, the extra charge would be $\$0.02n$ for our rental. Since this is in addition to the $15 fee we would pay no matter what, the final charge would be $15 + $0.02n (answer choice B).

Notice how all the other answer choices treated the wrong value as dependent on the number of miles. If we didn't reason it out with numbers first, we might have been tempted to pick a different answer. Thinking about the problem with real examples (1 mile or 10 miles) helped us figure out how the process works in general.

Solving Linear Equations

Many of the same skills we need for simplifying or writing algebraic expressions also apply to linear equations. While expressions do not have an equal sign and hold true for any value of the variable, equations have an equal sign and hold true only for some values of the variable (and possibly none). To solve a linear equation means to find those values that make the equation true.

There are two big ideas to keep in mind when solving linear equations:

▶ Whatever you do to one side of the equation, you must do to the other. To help this make sense, let's look at an example with numbers. It is certainly true that $5 + 6 = 11$. If we add 1 to both sides of this equation, we end up with $5 + 6 + 1 = 11 + 1$, which is a true statement, since both sides now add up to 12. But if we had added 1 only to the left side of the equation, we would have ended up with $5 + 6 + 1 = 11$, which is not true. The same would hold true if we were subtracting, multiplying, or even dividing.

▶ If you want to move a term, do the "opposite" operation. Why might we want to move a term to the other side of the equation? If we want to solve a linear equation, we will want to end up with an equation that states what one variable equals—say, $x = 5$ or $n = 15$. To simplify to such a statement, we need to have the variables on one side of the equation and the constants (or numbers) on the other side. This usually means we will have to move terms. But simply moving a term from one side to the other will change the equation so that the sides are no longer equal. For example, let's look back at 6 + 5 = 11. Simply moving the 5 to the other side would change the equation to 6 = 5 + 11, which is clearly wrong. For the equation to remain true, you need to do the same operation on both sides. We want to remove the 5 from the left. The 5 was added to 6, so we do the opposite operation; we subtract the 5. Then we must do the same thing on the right side: subtract the 5 from 11. Now the equation remains equal: 6 + 5 – 5 = 11 – 5. The same holds true when there are variables involved.

Using these ideas, we will now solve a couple of example equations.

Solve: $4x + 1 = 2x - 3$

Since both sides of this equation are simplified completely, the next step is to get every x term on one side of the equation and all of the constants (numbers) on the other side of the equation. We will remove the $2x$ from the right side of the equation by subtracting it from both sides:

$$\begin{aligned} 4x + 1 &= 2x - 3 \\ -2x &\quad - 2x \\ 2x + 1 &= -3 \end{aligned}$$

Similarly, to remove the 1 on the left, subtract 1 from both sides:

$$\begin{aligned} 2x + 1 &= -3 \\ -1 &\quad -1 \\ 2x &= -4 \end{aligned}$$

Finally, since x is multiplied by 2, we will solve for x by dividing both sides by 2:

$$x = -2$$

Solve: $8 + 2(x - 5) = 6$

The left side of this equation is not simplified, so before doing any other step, we need to distribute the 2 in front of the parentheses and collect like terms:

$$\begin{aligned} 8 + 2x - 10 &= 6 \\ 2x - 2 &= 6 \end{aligned}$$

As before, we need to remove the –2 from the left side. Since the 2 is subtracted on the left, we will add 2 to both sides:

$$\begin{aligned} 2x - 2 &= 6 \\ +2 &\quad +2 \\ 2x &= 8 \end{aligned}$$

To solve for x, we divide by 2 on both sides. That gives us our final answer: $x = 4$.

Applied Problems

Solving applied problems—also known as story or word problems—really involves two steps: (1) writing an equation to represent the situation and (2) solving the resulting equation.

When writing the equation, we will use the same ideas that we used when writing algebraic expressions, but when reading the problem, we will be looking for one more thing: what the question is asking for.

An example will help clarify this idea: Suppose that Bobby is three years older than Lisa and that their ages sum to 75. How old is Bobby?

Notice that Bobby's age is written in terms of Lisa's age. This is a clue that we can let Lisa's age be represented by a variable and write Bobby's age in terms of it. If we let Lisa's age be represented by x, then, since Bobby is three years older, Bobby's age will be $x + 3$. The next piece of information we have is that their ages sum to 75. This means that if we add Bobby's age ($x + 3$) and Lisa's age (x), we will get 75. Using our current variables, we get the following equation, which we can solve for x:

$$\begin{aligned} x + (x + 3) &= 75 \\ 2x + 3 &= 75 \\ 2x &= 72 \\ x &= 36 \end{aligned}$$

We have an answer, but to what question? The question asked, "How old is Bobby?" We let x represent Lisa's age, which we just found to be 36. Therefore, Bobby is $x + 3 = 36 + 3 = 39$ years old.

Applications with Ratios and Proportions. Some applied problems involve proportions and can be approached a little differently. A ratio or proportion is a way of quantifying the relationship between two values. This is common in recipes, where you may see a statement such as "Flour and sugar are in a 2:1 ratio," meaning for every two units of flour, you will use one unit of sugar. Example:

> A recipe calls for 2 cups of flour for every $\frac{1}{2}$ pound of butter. If Joe is making this recipe for a large group and uses 5 cups of flour, how much butter should he use?

The ratio 2 cups of flour for every $\frac{1}{2}$ pound of butter can be expressed this way:

$$\frac{2 \text{ cups flour}}{\frac{1}{2} \text{ pound butter}}$$

To follow the recipe, we must keep this ratio. If we let the unknown amount of butter Joe should use be represented by x, we have the following equation to solve:

$$\frac{2 \text{ cups flour}}{\frac{1}{2} \text{ pound butter}} = \frac{5 \text{ cups flour}}{x \text{ pounds butter}}$$

To solve, we can cross multiply:

$$\frac{2}{\frac{1}{2}} = \frac{5}{x}$$

$$5 \times \frac{1}{2} = 2x$$

$$\frac{5}{2} = 2x$$

$$\frac{5}{4} = x = 1\frac{1}{4}$$

Joe should use $1\frac{1}{4}$ cups of butter.

Graphs of Linear Equations

Linear equations can be graphed on the Cartesian coordinate plane by using points or by using the slope and y-intercept of the equation. A point in the Cartesian coordinate plane is expressed in the form (x, y). Plotting just two points will allow us to graph linear equations, since they are always straight lines.

Any linear equation can be simplified to the form $y = mx + b$, where m is the slope, or steepness of the graph, and b is the y-intercept of the graph (the point at which it crosses the y-axis). Consider the linear equation $y = 5x + 4$. This line described by this equation has a slope of 5 and a y-intercept of 4.

The y-intercept is actually a point on the graph $(0, b)$. In our example, the point $(0, 4)$ is on the graph of $y = 5x + 4$. Recall that we only need two points to plot the entire graph, so the question becomes "How do we find another point?"

To find another point on this graph, plug in any convenient (easy to work with) value of x. For example, 1 is very easy to work with, and plugging 1 into our equation, we get $y = 5(1) + 4 = 9$. Therefore, the point $(1, 9)$ also is on the graph, and we can now sketch the graph, as shown here.

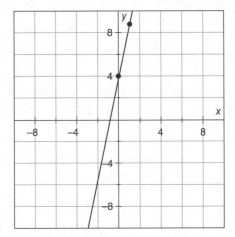

While the slope and the y-intercept can be found simply by looking at the equation when it is in this form, the x-intercept requires a bit more work. The x-intercept is the point where the graph crosses the x-axis, which means it is the point where $y = 0$. Using this knowledge, we can find any x-intercept by setting $y = 0$ and solving for x.

In our example where $y = 5x + 4$, the x-intercept is $\left(-\frac{4}{5}, 0\right)$. We can find that point by solving with the following steps:

$$5x + 4 = 0$$

$$5x = -4$$

$$x = -\frac{4}{5}$$

An important formula to remember for graphing linear equations is the point-slope formula, which is:

$$y - y_1 = m(x - x_1)$$

To make this formula work, you need the coordinates for a single point on a graph, and you need to know the slope. With that information you can graph the linear equation. So say you know you have point (1,–3) and a slope of 2. You would plug this information into the equation like so:

$$y - (-3) = 2(x - 1)$$

The remaining y and x are any other points that will appear on our graphed line:

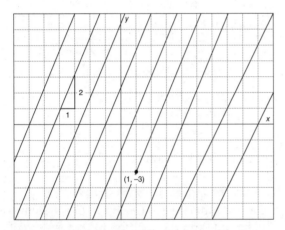

Parallel and Perpendicular Lines. Two lines are parallel if they have the same slope. For example, $y = 3x - 2$ and $y = 3x + 1$ are parallel lines, shown in the graph where the two lines do not cross one another.

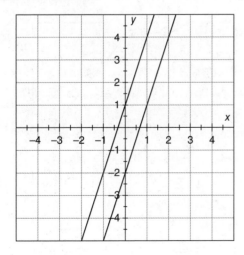

Two lines are perpendicular if they have negative reciprocal slopes. The reciprocal of a fraction is the fraction with the numerator and denominator switched, as in the following examples: $\frac{2}{3}$ and $\frac{3}{2}$; $\frac{1}{4}$ and 4. The lines $y = 2x - 4$ and $y = -\frac{1}{2}x + 2$ are perpendicular. Their slopes, $-\frac{1}{2}$ and 2, are reciprocals with opposite signs.

These functions are shown here in the graph of two lines that cross at right angles.

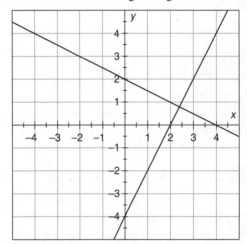

Systems of Two Linear Equations
In a system of two linear equations, we are trying to find values for two variables that make both of the equations true at the same time. There are two common methods for solving systems of linear equations: substitution and elimination.

Substitution. With the substitution method, we solve for one of the variables in one of the equations and then substitute this value in the other equation. This method is best when one of the coefficients (the number attached to a variable—for example, in $7y$, the coefficient is 7) is 1, as you can see in the following example:

$$x + 2y = 8$$
$$5x + 4y = 22$$

Since the x in the first equation has a coefficient of 1, it is easier to solve for it than for any of the other variables. We can do this by subtracting $2y$ from both sides of the equation:

$$x + 2y = 8$$
$$x = 8 - 2y$$

Now we have a formula for x and can plug this into the second equation, $5x + 4y = 22$:

$$5(8 - 2y) + 4y = 22$$

This is a linear equation in terms of y only. Now we can solve for y:

$$5(8 - 2y) + 4y = 22$$
$$40 - 10y + 4y = 22$$
$$40 - 6y = 22$$
$$-6y = -18$$
$$y = 3$$

Finally, we can substitute this value for y back into either one of the original equations. Using the first equation, $x + 2(3) = 8$, and $x = 2$. So the solution to this system is (2, 3).

Elimination. With the method of elimination, we multiply one or both equations by a value that is "convenient" in the sense that one of the variables will be eliminated when we add both of the equations. This way, we will end up with a simple linear equation to solve. Let's try it out on the same system as before:

$$x + 2y = 8$$
$$5x + 4y = 22$$

With this method, we can choose to eliminate either variable. In this example, since the coefficient of the x is 1, it would be easier to eliminate the x. Why? Well, this means we would only have to multiply one of the equations. If we multiply the first equation by –5, for example, we would have the following system:

$$-5x - 10y = -40$$
$$5x + 4y = 22$$

Now, when we add these two equations together, the x terms will cancel out:

$$-5x - 10y = -40$$
$$\underline{5x + 4y = 22}$$
$$-6y = -18$$

This allows us to divide by –6 and find that $y = 3$. As before, once we know one value, we can simply substitute into either equation to find the other value. In this case, $x = 2$.

As was mentioned, sometimes we will need to multiply both equations by some number to have the same effect. This is the case in the next example:

$$2x + 3y = 15$$
$$3x + 4y = 19$$

If we multiply the first equation by –3 and the second equation by 2, we will be able to eliminate the x and then solve for y:

$$-3(2x + 3y = 15) \rightarrow -6x - 9y = -45$$
$$2(3x + 4y = 19) \rightarrow \underline{6x + 8y = 38}$$
$$-y = -7$$

Since $y = 7$, we can plug into the first equation:

$$2x + 3(7) = 15$$
$$2x + 21 = 15$$
$$x = -3$$

Therefore, our solution is (–3, 7).

Systems of Equations and Graphs

A connection between the graph of a system of equations and the solution to that system of equations is worth noting. The following graph shows the first system of equations we worked with:

$$x + 2y = 8$$
$$5x + 4y = 22$$

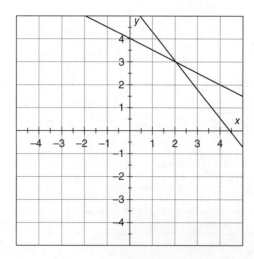

The solution to this system was (2, 3), which is also the intersection of the two lines. This will be the case with every system of two linear equations you come across. For example, the next graph shows that the solution to the system $y + x = 3$ and $2y - x = 0$ is (2, 1).

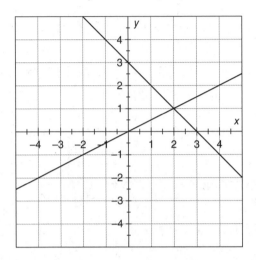

Solving Linear Inequalities

Instead of a statement about equality, linear inequalities have a statement such as $>$, $<$, $\leq$, or $\geq$. When we solve a linear inequality, we are finding all of the values of x that make the inequality true. We use the same techniques we did with linear equations, but we must watch for one important case: *If we divide or multiply by a negative number, the inequality will "flip."*

To see this in action, let's take a look at two different examples:

Solve for x: $3x - 1 \geq x + 1$

$$3x - 1 \geq x + 1$$
$$3x \geq x + 2 \quad \text{Add 1 to both sides.}$$
$$2x \geq 2 \quad \text{Subtract } x \text{ from both sides.}$$
$$x \geq 1 \quad \text{Divide by 2 on both sides.}$$

This means that all values of x from 1 and up will make this inequality true. We can graph this solution on a number line. Notice that the graph has a solid circle at 1, which indicates 1 is part of the solution set.

Solve: $-2x + 1 > -5$
$$-2x + 1 > -5$$
$$-2x > -6 \quad \text{Subtract 1 from both sides.}$$
$$x < 3 \quad \text{Divide by } -2 \text{ on both sides.}$$

Notice that since we divided by a negative number, the inequality flipped from greater than to less than.

The graph of this solution set will contain an open circle at 3, since our inequality is strictly less than 3. The values for which it is true do not include 3.

Addition and Subtraction of Polynomials

A polynomial is an expression that involves the addition and subtraction of variables with constants and exponents that are positive, whole numbers. Examples:

$$x^2 - 5x + 1$$

$$x^4$$

$$x^6 + 7x^4 - 2x^2 + x + 5$$

When adding two polynomials, you simply are collecting like terms. Recall that like terms are terms with the same variable and the same exponent. The following examples illustrate how to add polynomials:

$$(x^2 - 8x + 4) + (2x^4 - 2x^2 + 1)$$
$$= x^2 - 8x + 4 + 2x^4 - 2x^2 + 1$$
$$= -x^2 - 8x + 5 + 2x^4$$

$$(x^3 + 2x^2 - 8x + 4) + (x^3 + 5x^2 - x - 1)$$
$$= x^3 + 2x^2 - 8x + 4 + x^3 + 5x^2 - x - 1$$
$$= 2x^3 + 7x^2 - 9x + 3$$

When subtracting polynomials, we also must remember to distribute the negative before combining like terms. Distributing the negative changes all of the signs in the second polynomial. Examples:

$$(x^3 + x^2 - 8x) - (4x^3 - x^2 - 9)$$

Distribute the negative:
$$= x^3 + x^2 - 8x - 4x^3 + x^2 + 9$$

Combine like terms:
$$= -3x^3 + 2x^2 - 8x + 9$$

$$(x^5 - x + x^2 + 5) - (3x^5 + 9x^2 + x - 1)$$

Distribute the negative:
$$x^5 - x + x^2 + 5 - 3x^5 - 9x^2 - x + 1$$

Combine like terms:
$$-2x^5 - 2x - 8x^2 + 6$$

Multiplying Polynomials

When multiplying two polynomials, we must make sure to multiply every term in the first polynomial by every term in the second polynomial. You can think of this as an extension of the distributive property. In fact, if we are multiplying a single-term polynomial (called a monomial) and a larger polynomial, we will just distribute.

Consider this example of multiplying a monomial and a trinomial (a polynomial with three terms):

$$-4x^2(x^2 + 2x - 5)$$

$$= -4x^2(x^2) - 4x^2(2x) - 4x^2(-5)$$

The term distributes to every term in the trinomial.

Before we can finish this example, we must remember an important property of exponents. If you multiply two terms with the same base, you must add the exponents. Symbolically this rule is stated as follows:

$$a^m a^n = a^{m+n}$$

We will now apply this to the example:

$$= -4x^2(x^2) - 4x^2(2x) - 4x^2(-5)$$

Repeating our previous step:

$$= -4x^{2+2} - 8x^{2+1} + 20x^2$$

Multiply the coefficients and add exponents (x has an exponent of 1).

$$= -4x^4 - 8x^3 + 20x^2$$

In the case of the product of a binomial (a polynomial with two terms) and another binomial, we have a shortcut to keep track and make sure every term was multiplied. This shortcut is called FOIL, which stands for *first, outer, inner, last*, referring to the four pairs of terms we must multiply. Example:

Multiply $x + 5$ and $x - 2$.

$$(x + 5)(x - 2)$$

▶ **First.** We start by multiplying the first term in each binomial. In this case, the first two terms are both x, so this product is $x \cdot x = x^2$.
▶ **Outer.** Next, we multiply the outer terms, which in this case are x and -2. This product is $-2x$.
▶ **Inner.** For our third step, we multiply the inner terms, 5 and x, which results in $5x$.
▶ **Last.** As our last step, we multiply the last term of each polynomial: 5 and -2. This gives us -10.

Adding all of these terms together gives us our product, $x^2 - 2x + 5x - 10$. However, this product is not completely simplified, since it contains like terms. After we combine these like terms, we come to our final answer: $x^2 + 3x - 10$.

This process will work regardless of the form of the two binomials you are multiplying. Examples:

Find the product: $(x^2 - 3x)(x + 1)$

$$(x^2 - 3x)(x + 1)$$

$$x^3 + x^2 - 3x^2 - 3x \quad \text{Apply FOIL.}$$

$$x^3 - 2x^2 - 3x \qquad \text{Combine like terms.}$$

Find the product: $(x - 8)(4 + x)$

$(x - 8)(4 + x)$

$4x + x^2 - 32 - 8x$ Apply FOIL.

$-4x + x^2 - 32$ Combine like terms.

For larger polynomials, we have to be careful to make sure every term is multiplied by every other term. For instance, let's look at the product $(x + 5)(x^2 - 2x + 3)$. To find this product, we first multiply the x from the $x + 5$ term by every term in the trinomial:

$$x(x^2) - x(2x) + x(3) = x^3 - 2x^2 + 3x$$

Then multiply the 5 in the $x + 5$ term by each term in the trinomial:

$$5(x^2) - 5(2x) + 5(3) = 5x^2 - 10x + 15$$

When we combine these two expressions, we will have our product:

$$x^3 - 2x^2 + 3x + 5x^2 - 10x + 15$$
$$= x^3 + 3x^2 - 7x + 15$$

Find the product: $(x + 1)(x^3 - 2x^2 + x + 2)$

$(x + 1)(x^3 - 2x^2 + x + 2)$

$= x(x^3) + x(-2x^2) + x(x) + x(2) +$

$1(x^3) + 1(-2x^2) + 1(x) + 1(2)$

Multiply every term in the second polynomial by each term in the first.

$= x^4 - 2x^3 + x^2 + 2x + x^3 - 2x^2 + x + 2$

Simplify.

$= x^4 - x^3 - x^2 + 3x + 2$

Combine like terms.

Find the product: $(x^2 - 2x + 2)(x^2 + 5x + 3)$

$(x^2 - 2x + 2)(x^2 + 5x + 3)$

$= x^2(x^2) + x^2(5x) + x^2(3) +$

$-2x(x^2) - 2x(5x) - 2x(3) +$

$2(x^2) + 2(5x) + 3(2)$

Multiply every term in the second polynomial by each term in the first.

$= x^4 + 5x^3 + 3x^2 - 2x^3 - 10x^2 - 6x + 2x^2 + 10x + 6$

Simplify.

$= x^4 + 3x^3 - 5x^2 + 10x + 6$

Combine like terms.

Factoring Polynomials

Much like finding the prime factorization of a number, factoring a polynomial is a way of writing out what terms would be multiplied to get that polynomial. For example, we showed that $(x + 5)(x - 2) = x^2 + 3x - 10$. This means that the polynomial $x^2 + 3x - 10$ factors into $(x + 5)$ and $(x - 2)$, since these two terms can be multiplied to get the original polynomial.

We will start with factoring polynomials that are somewhat simple, that is, polynomials with terms that share a single factor such as $5x^3 - x^2$. Although we would likely never write this down, it is helpful to think of this polynomial as $5x \cdot x^2 - 1 \cdot x^2$. Looking at it this way, we can see that both terms of this polynomial share the factor x^2. By the distributive property, we can rewrite this as $x^2(5x - 1)$, which is the factored form of the polynomial. As you can see with the following examples, the goal is to bring out the shared factor.

You can always check your answer by multiplying and seeing if you get the original polynomial.

Factor: $2x^4 + 8x^3 - 4x$

Each term shares the factor $2x$, so this polynomial factored is $2x(x^3 + 4x^2 - 2)$.

Factor: $5x^5 - 3x^4$

Each term shares the factor x^4, giving us the factored form $x^4(5x - 3)$.

While polynomials can come in many different forms, a special group of polynomials come from the product of two binomials. Many but not all trinomials can be factored in this way:

$(ax + b)(cx + d)$, where a, b, c, d are all real numbers.

To factor a polynomial of the form $x^2 + bx + c$, we will find factors of c that add up to b. This will give us factors of the form $(x + ?)(x + ?)$. Additionally, if c is negative, we will use opposite signs on the factors, and if c is positive, we will use the same sign on both factors as we have on b. For example, with the polynomial $x^2 + x - 12$, we are looking for factors of 12 that add up to 1, using opposite signs, since the 12 is negative.

FACTORS OF 12
1, 12
2, 6
3, 4

Notice that only 3 and 4 are 1 apart, and if we put a negative sign on the 3, the sum will be +1. Therefore, the polynomial $x^2 + x - 12$ will factor into the terms $(x - 3)$ and $(x + 4)$. You can check this by multiplying.

Consider some more examples:

Factor: $x^2 - 9x + 14$

Since 14 is positive and the 9 is negative, we are looking for two negative factors of 14 that add to −9. Since $14 = 7(2)$, we can use −7 and −2. Therefore, this polynomials factors into $(x - 7)(x - 2)$.

Factor: $x^2 + 8x + 16$

The 16 is positive and so is the 8, so we are looking for two factors of 16 that add to +8. Since $16 = 4(4)$, the polynomial factors into $(x + 4)(x + 4)$.

Solving Quadratic Equations by Factoring

A quadratic equation is an equation of the form $ax^2 + bx + c = 0$ where a is not zero. If the polynomial in the equation can be factored, then we can use a simple idea called the zero-product rule to solve the equation.

The zero-product rule states that if $ab = 0$, then either $a = 0$ or $b = 0$. In other words, you can't multiply two nonzero numbers and still get zero, so one of them must be zero. By applying this to the two terms in a factored trinomial, we will have two simple linear equations to solve. Examples:

Solve: $x^2 - 3x + 4 = 0$

$$x^2 - 3x + 4 = 0$$

$(x - 4)(x + 1) = 0$ Factor.

$x - 4 = 0$, $x + 1 = 0$ Apply the zero-product rule.

$x = 4$, $x = -1$ Solve the resulting linear equations.

Solve: $x^2 + 2x - 15 = 0$

$$x^2 + 2x - 15 = 0$$

$(x + 5)(x - 3) = 0$ Factor.

$x + 5 = 0$, $x - 3 = 0$ Apply the zero-product rule.

$x = -5$, $x = 3$ Solve the resulting linear equations.

Solving Quadratic Equations with the Quadratic Formula

We can also solve a quadratic equation using the quadratic formula:

$$x = \frac{-b \pm \sqrt{b^2 - 4ac}}{2a}$$ where the quadratic

equation is $ax^2 + bx + c = 0$

Simply plug in the numbers from your formula and solve. The quadratic formula is derived from the process of completing the square, which is described next.

Solving Linear Equations by Completing the Square

If a polynomial is of the form $x^2 + 2ax + a^2$ for some nonzero number a, then the polynomial can be factored into $(x + a)(x + a) = (x + a)^2$. Such a polynomial is called a perfect-square trinomial. However, not all polynomials are perfect-square trinomials, and not only that, but not all trinomials can be factored in the first place.

Completing the square is a process that allows us to algebraically manipulate any trinomial so that we can somehow use the factoring we reviewed to solve a quadratic equation even if it is not factorable. There are several steps for completing the square on an equation of the form $ax^2 + bx + c = 0$. We will use the sample equation $3x^2 + 4x - 1 = 0$ to go through these steps.

1. Subtract the last term from both sides (subtracting –1 is the same as adding 1):

$$3x^2 + 4x - 1 = 0$$
$$3x^2 + 4x = 1$$

2. Divide by the coefficient of the x^2 term on both sides. We will divide by 3 on both sides:

$$3x^2 + 4x = 1$$
$$x^2 + \frac{4}{3}x = \frac{1}{3}$$

3. Take half the coefficient of the x term, square it, and add it to both sides.

Half of the coefficient: $\frac{1}{2}\left(\frac{4}{3}\right) = \frac{4}{6} = \frac{2}{3}$

Squared: $\left(\frac{2}{3}\right)^2 = \frac{4}{9}$

Add it to both sides:

$$x^2 + \frac{4}{3}x = \frac{1}{3}$$
$$x^2 + \frac{4}{3}x + \frac{4}{9} = \frac{1}{3} + \frac{4}{9}$$
$$x^2 + \frac{4}{3}x + \frac{4}{9} = \frac{7}{9}$$

4. Factor the left side, which is now a perfect-square trinomial. This will always factor into $\left(x + \frac{1}{2}(\text{coefficient of } x)\right)^2$. Note that we already found this to be $\frac{2}{3}$.

$$x^2 + \frac{4}{3}x + \frac{4}{9} = \frac{7}{9}$$
$$\left(x + \frac{2}{3}\right)^2 = \frac{7}{9}$$

5. Use the square root property. The square root property states that if $x^2 = c$, then $x = \pm\sqrt{c}$. In this case:

$$\left(x^2 + \frac{2}{3}\right)^2 = \frac{7}{9}$$
$$x + \frac{2}{3} = \pm\sqrt{\frac{7}{9}}$$

6. Solve for x in the resulting linear equation, and simplify:

$$x + \frac{2}{3} = \pm\sqrt{\frac{7}{9}}$$
$$x = -\frac{2}{3} \pm \sqrt{\frac{7}{9}}$$

Since the square root of 9 is 3, we can simplify this a bit more.

$$x = -\frac{2}{3} \pm \sqrt{\frac{7}{9}}$$
$$x = -\frac{2}{3} \pm \frac{\sqrt{7}}{3} = \frac{-2 \pm \sqrt{7}}{3}$$

This last step means that there are two answers: $x = \dfrac{-2 - \sqrt{7}}{3}$ and $x = \dfrac{-2 + \sqrt{7}}{3}$.

As you can see, completing the square involves a lot of steps and careful calculation. However, it will always result in a solution, even if the original trinomial could not be factored, as with the preceding example. If the trinomial can be factored, this method will result in the same answer as we would have found by factoring.

Consider two additional examples:

1. Solve $x^2 + x - 6 = 0$

$x^2 + x - 6 = 0$	No need to divide by the coefficient of the squared term, since it is 1.
$x^2 + x = 6$	Move the last term to the other side of the equation.
$x^2 + x + \dfrac{1}{4} = 6 + \dfrac{1}{4}$ $x^2 + x + \dfrac{1}{4} = \dfrac{25}{4}$	Square half the coefficient of x^2, and add it to both sides. $\left(\dfrac{1}{2}\right)(1) = \dfrac{1}{2}$ and $\left(\dfrac{1}{2}\right)^2 = \dfrac{1}{4}$
$\left(x + \dfrac{1}{2}\right)^2 = \dfrac{25}{4}$	Factor the trinomial.
$x + \dfrac{1}{2} = \pm\sqrt{\dfrac{25}{4}} = \pm\dfrac{5}{2}$	Apply the square root property.
$x + \dfrac{1}{2} = \pm\dfrac{5}{2}$ $x = -\dfrac{1}{2} \pm \dfrac{5}{2}$	Solve for x.
$x = -\dfrac{1}{2} + \dfrac{5}{2} = \dfrac{4}{2} = 2$ $x = -\dfrac{1}{2} - \dfrac{5}{2} = -\dfrac{6}{2} = -3$ x = 2, -3.	Simplify.

2. Solve: $2x^2 + 7x + 5 = 0$

$2x^2 + 7x = -5$	Move the 5 to the right side.

$x^2 + \dfrac{7}{2}x = -\dfrac{5}{2}$	Divide by 2 on both sides so we can begin to isolate x.
$x^2 + \dfrac{7}{2}x + \dfrac{49}{16} =$ $-\dfrac{5}{2} + \dfrac{49}{16} = \dfrac{9}{16}$	Add $\left(\dfrac{7}{2} \cdot \dfrac{1}{2}\right)^2 = \left(\dfrac{7}{4}\right)^2 = \dfrac{49}{16}$ to both sides.
$\left(x + \dfrac{7}{4}\right)^2 = \dfrac{9}{16}$	Factor.
$x + \dfrac{7}{4} = \pm\sqrt{\dfrac{9}{16}} = \pm\dfrac{3}{4}$	Apply the square root property.
$x = -\dfrac{7}{4} \pm \dfrac{3}{4}$	Solve for x.
$x = -\dfrac{7}{4} + \dfrac{3}{4} = -\dfrac{2}{4} = -\dfrac{1}{2}$ $x = -\dfrac{7}{4} - \dfrac{3}{4} = -\dfrac{8}{4} = -2$ $x = -2, -\dfrac{1}{2}$	Simplify.

Graphing Quadratic Equations

Many techniques can be used to sketch a graph of a quadratic equation of the form $y = ax^2 + bx + c$. One of the quickest methods is to find the vertex of the graph and use two points to sketch the remaining portion of the graph.

To be able to do this, we use the fact that the graph of every quadratic equation will be a parabola. The simplest parabola, $y = x^2$, is graphed here.

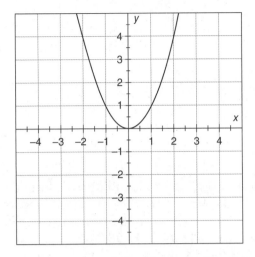

This parabola is said to "open up," and any parabola with a positive x^2 term will open up. Those with a negative x^2 term will open down, as in the graph of the second parabola.

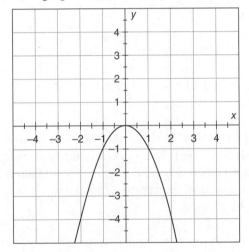

The vertex is the highest or lowest point in the graph. In both examples graphed, the vertex is (0,0). If we know just the x-coordinate of the vertex, then we can begin to sketch the graph of any quadratic equation. The general formula for the x-coordinate of the vertex is $x = -\dfrac{b}{2a}$. Our general strategy for graphing quadratic equations will be to begin by finding the x-coordinate of the vertex, then to find a single point on each side of the vertex. Once these points are plotted, we will sketch a parabola through them.

Let's use this method to graph the equation $y = x^2 - 4x + 7$. Here $a = 1$, $b = -4$, and $c = 7$. Therefore the x-coordinate of the vertex is $x = -\dfrac{-4}{2(1)} = 2$.

We will now make a table of values including this point, one to the left of it, and one to the right of it. The specific points do not matter, so we should pick points that will be easy to plug into the original equation. However, if we pick points that are the same distance from the vertex, the graph will be that much simpler to draw. This is why we choose 0 and 4, since both are 2 units away from $x = 2$.

X	Y
0	$(0)^2 - 4(0) + 7 = 7$
2	$(2)^2 - 4(2) + 7 = 3$
4	$(4)^2 - 4(4) + 7 = 7$

Since we now know that the points (0, 7), (2, 3), and (4, 7) are on the graph, we can go ahead and sketch it, as shown in the next illustration.

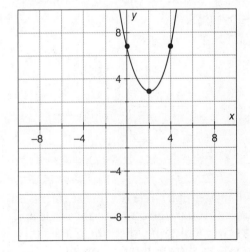

Domain 3: Measurement and Geometry

Squares and Rectangles

A rectangle is a quadrilateral (a shape with four sides) in which opposite sides are parallel and all of the interior angles measure 90 degrees. A square has these properties along with the additional property that all the sides have equal length.

To find the area of a square or a rectangle, we multiply the length by the width. For example, the rectangle shown here has an area of $5 \times 10 = 50$.

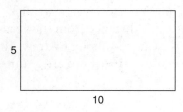

The perimeter of a square or rectangle is the sum of all the lengths. In the rectangle shown here, the perimeter would be $5 + 10 + 5 + 10 = 30$.

Circles

Circles have several important properties, many of which are expressed in terms of the diameter or the radius. The radius is a line segment that connects the center of the circle to any point on its outer edge (circumference). In the first circle, the radius is labeled r.

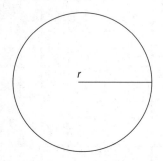

The diameter of a circle is a line segment that passes through the center of the circle and connects two points on either side of the circumference, as shown in the following circle. The diameter d is related to the radius r by the formula $d = 2r$. In other words, the diameter is always twice the length of the radius.

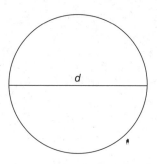

The area of a circle is found with the formula $A = \pi r^2$ where $\pi \approx 3.14$. For example, if a circle has a radius of 3 cm, then the area of that circle will be $\pi(3)^2 \approx (3.14)(9) = 28.26$ cm^2. Similarly, the circumference of a circle can be found with the formula $C = 2\pi r$. Continuing our example, the circle would have a circumference of $2(3.14)(3) = 18.84$ cm.

Triangles

There are three types of triangles:

▶ **Equilateral.** Each angle of an equilateral triangle is equal to 60 degrees, and the lengths of all three sides are equal.
▶ **Isosceles.** An isosceles triangle has two sides and two angles that have the same measure.
▶ **Scalene.** Scalene triangles have no equal sides and no equal angles. If a scalene triangle has an angle of 90 degrees, we can classify it as a "right triangle."

In each type of triangle, two important properties hold:

▶ The sum of the interior angles is always 180 degrees.
▶ The largest angle is opposite the longest side.

To find the area of a triangle, we use the formula $A = \frac{1}{2}bh$, where b represents the length of the base of the triangle and h represents the height of the triangle. In the following triangle, the area is $\frac{1}{2}(12)(5) = \frac{1}{2}(60) = 30$.

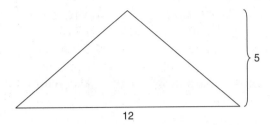

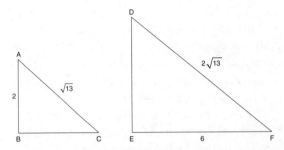

Find the length of *DE* in the triangle shown here.

The Pythagorean Theorem. The Pythagorean theorem states that for any right triangle with legs of length *a* and *b* and hypotenuse (the side opposite the right angle) of length *c*, $a^2 + b^2 = c^2$.

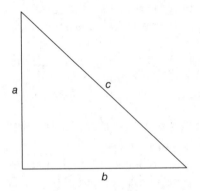

For example, if a triangle has legs of length 3 and 4, then the Pythagorean theorem can be used to find the length of the hypotenuse, as follows:

$$3^2 + 4^2 = c^2$$
$$25 = c^2$$
$$c = 5$$

Congruence and Similarity. Two shapes are congruent if they have the same shape and the same size. Two shapes are similar if they have the same shape but different sizes.

When you know two shapes are similar, you can use the lengths of one shape to find a length with the other shape, using proportions. Example:

We can tell that these two shapes are similar, since they are both right triangles (same shape) and have similar proportions, but have different sizes. This means that the sides are proportional, and we can find the length of *DE* with the following formula, which can be solved by cross multiplying:

$$\frac{2}{DE} = \frac{3}{6}$$
$$3DE = 12$$
$$DE = 4$$

Properties of Parallel Lines

Two lines are parallel if they never cross. If a third line crosses two parallel lines, it is called a transversal. As you can see from the example shown here, several angles are created in this situation.

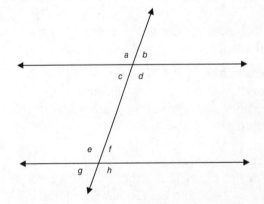

We can categorize the angles in the example in the following way:

▶ **Adjacent angles** are the angle pairs *a* and *b*, *c* and *d*, *e* and *f*, and *g* and *h*. Each pair of adjacent angles adds to 180 degrees.

▶ **Corresponding angles** are the angle pairs *a* and *e*, *b* and *f*, *c* and *g*, and *d* and *h*. Corresponding angles have equal measure.

▶ **Vertical angles** are the angle pairs *a* and *d*, *c* and *b*, *e* and *h*, and *g* and *f*. Vertical angles have the same measure.

▶ **Alternate interior angles** are the angle pairs *c* and *f*, and *d* and *e*. Alternate interior angles have the same measure.

▶ **Alternate exterior angles** are the angle pairs *a* and *h*, and *b* and *g*. Alternate exterior angles have the same measure.

The Metric System

The metric system uses a base measure and the following prefixes to describe length, width, and other measures. Please note that this table provides just a sample of the most commonly used prefixes.

	SYMBOL	FACTOR
kilo-	k	1,000
hecto-	h	100
centi-	c	0.01
milli-	m	0.001

The base measures of the metric system are listed in the following table:

MEASURES	BASE UNIT
length	meter
weight	gram
volume	liter

Suppose we want to convert 150 meters to kilometers. Using the factor of 1,000, we would divide by 1,000 and get 150 meters = 0.150 kilometers. In fact, let's list all of the conversions of 150 meters.

	METHOD	CONVERSION
kilo-	divide by 1,000	0.15 km
hecto-	divide by 100	1.5 hm
centi-	multiply by 100	15,000 cm
milli-	multiply by 1,000	150,000 mm

It is also possible to convert between measures not in their base units. For example, let's convert 19,000 milligrams to kilograms. Converting first to grams, we will divide by 1,000 (since a milligram is 0.001 grams) and get 19 grams. Now to convert to kilograms, we will divide by 1,000 again and get 0.019 kg.

Conversely, to convert to a smaller measure—say, 12 kilograms to centigrams—we multiply. To start, 12 kilograms is equivalent to 12,000 grams. Multiplying again by 1,000 will give us the measure in milligrams: 12,000,000.

Domain 4: Statistics and Data Analysis

Basic Numerical Summaries

The Mean. The mean of a data set is simply the average of all the numbers in that data set. You can find the mean by adding all of the numbers in the data set and dividing by how many there are. Example:

Data set: 1, 7, 9, 12

$$\text{Mean: } \frac{1+7+9+12}{4} = \frac{29}{4} = 7.25$$

The Median. The median is the middle value of an ordered data set. Calculating the median differs depending on whether there is an odd or even number of values.

When there is an odd number of values, we can simply pick the median as the middle number after placing the numbers in order. For instance, the median of the data set 1, 5, 8, 9, 10 is 8. However, if there is an even number of values in the data set, as in the set 1, 5, 7, 10, then the median is found by taking the average of the middle two values:

$$\frac{5+7}{2} = \frac{12}{2} = 6$$

The Mode. The mode is the most commonly occurring value in the data set. It is possible for a data set to have no mode, a single mode, or two modes.

DATA SET	MODE
1, 2, 5, 10	none
1, 1, 1, 2, 2, 5, 7	1
1, 1, 1, 2, 2, 2, 5, 7	1 and 2

The Range. The range is a measure of the overall spread of a data set. It is calculated by taking the largest value and subtracting the smallest value. In our data set 1, 5, 7, 10, the range is 10 – 1 = 9.

Basic Probability

The probability of an event is a measure of the likelihood that the event will occur. This can be written as a fraction, a percentage, or a decimal. Before we discuss exactly how to calculate it, though, we must define some important terms:

▶ **Outcome.** An outcome is a single result of some experiment or activity. For instance, if we flip a coin, one outcome is that tails comes up.
▶ **Event.** An event is a collection of one or more outcomes. If we are rolling a six-sided die, one possible event would be rolling an even number. This could be represented as {2, 4, 6}.
▶ **Sample space.** The sample space represents all of the possible outcomes of a particular experiment or activity. In the die-rolling example, the sample space is {1, 2, 3, 4, 5, 6}.

The probability of an event A is denoted $P(A)$. We can find this value by counting the number of outcomes in event A and then dividing by the number of outcomes in the sample space:

$$P(A) = \frac{|A|}{|S|}$$

This formula can be used only when the outcomes in the sample space are equally likely. Using our example with the die, the probability of rolling an even number on a single roll is $\frac{3}{6} = \frac{1}{2}$, since there are three possible even numbers and six outcomes in the sample space.

Complementary Events. Suppose we have an event A in the sample space S. The complement of event A, denoted $\overline{A}$, is the event that contains all of the outcomes in S that are not in A. For example, if our event is rolling a number larger than 2 on a six-sided fair die, the complement would be rolling a number less than or equal to 2 on a six-sided fair die.

Complementary events have a very useful property:

$$P(A) = 1 - P(\overline{A})$$

This property is useful because it may be difficult to find the probability of A directly. If that is the case, we can instead find the probability of the event A complement and subtract that from 1.

To illustrate that this works, let's look again at our previous example of rolling a die:

▶ A is rolling a number larger than 2 on a six-sided fair die.
▶ A complement is rolling a number less than or equal to 2 on a six-sided fair die.

The probability of A complement is $P(\overline{A}) = \frac{2}{6} = \frac{1}{3}$. By our property, the probability of A must be $P(A) = 1 - \frac{1}{3} = \frac{2}{3}$. We can verify this by calculating the probability of A directly. Since there are four numbers that are larger than 2, and six outcomes in the sample space, $P(A) = \frac{4}{6} = \frac{2}{3}$.

Mutually Exclusive Events. Two events are mutually exclusive if they cannot happen at the same time. Mathematically, this means that $P(A \text{ and } B) = 0$. In the following example, the two events are mutually exclusive:

▶ Event A: Roll a 6 on a six-sided die
▶ Event B: Roll an odd number on a six-sided die

Since 6 is not an odd number, the events are mutually exclusive.

Independent Events. Two events are independent when the occurrence of one event has no effect on the probability that the other event will occur. Successive die rolls, coin flips, and selection with replacement are examples of independent events. Of course, if two events are not independent, then they are said to be dependent.

When we know two events are independent, we can find the probability of them occurring in sequence by multiplying the probabilities of the individual events. For example, the probability of flipping tails on a single coin is $\frac{1}{2}$. Therefore, the probability of flipping two coins and getting tails on both flips can be found by multiplying $\left(\frac{1}{2}\right)\left(\frac{1}{2}\right) = \frac{1}{4}$.

CHAPTER 7

Subtest III

Physical Education, Human Development, and Visual and Performing Arts

Physical Education

The CSET questions on physical education (PE) are divided into three domains: (1) movement skills and movement knowledge, (2) self-image and personal development, and (3) social development. These questions will focus on a wide range of topics related to movement, exercise, development, and characteristics of physical fitness. Questions on the test will not simply entail defining a list of fitness-related terms, but will require you to apply a solid understanding of these ideas to given scenarios and activities. Your answers to the questions will allow you to demonstrate your understanding of the purpose of PE activities, your ability to evaluate students' performance and characteristics, and your capacity for recognizing the needs of your students. The lists in the following sections suggest concepts with which you should be familiar in order to answer the questions correctly on the CSET.

Domain 1: Movement Skills and Movement Knowledge

The concepts that will be addressed in the area of movement skills and movement knowledge include basic movement skills, exercise physiology, and movement forms. Let's take a closer look at the types of information that fall into each of these categories.

BASIC MOVEMENT SKILLS
- Movement concepts and body and space awareness
- Locomotor, nonlocomotor, and manipulative skills and the development and assessment of these skills
- Basic concepts of biomechanics that affect movement
- Critical elements of basic movement skills

EXERCISE PHYSIOLOGY: HEALTH AND PHYSICAL FITNESS
- Benefits and risks to health and fitness
- Designing activities and exercise programs that encourage a physically active lifestyle
- Safety and medical factors
- Exercise principles promoting physical fitness
- Physical fitness components
- Elements of a comprehensive fitness development program
- Benefits of cardiovascular fitness and fitness education
- Basic terms of skeletal and muscular physiology
- *Physical Education Framework for California Public Schools* guidelines for physical education instruction

MOVEMENT FORMS
- Traditional and nontraditional games and activities
- Basic rules and social etiquette for activities
- Games that include all students

- Ability to structure lessons to include all students
- Integration of physical activities with academic content areas

Domain 2: Self-Image and Personal Development

Concepts related to physical growth, development, and self-image also will be addressed on the PE section of the CSET. Take a look at some of the skills and concepts that will be important to understand.

PHYSICAL GROWTH AND DEVELOPMENT

- Development of fine and gross motor skills
- Ability to design activities that are appropriate for given developmental levels
- Influence of growth spurts and body type on movement and coordination
- Factors that affect physical health and well-being
- Focus of the fitness approach to physical education
- Benefits of cardiovascular fitness and fitness education
- Role of play, game, and sports in a physical education program
- Understanding of basic kinesiology
- Importance of safety equipment and safety planning on the prevention of injuries

SELF-IMAGE

- Effect of physical activity on self-image
- Impact of psychological skills on promoting physical activity
- Evaluation of body composition and its impact on health
- Exercise physiology and assessment of the impact of exercise
- Benefits of appropriate nutrition
- Effect of drug, alcohol, and tobacco use on body systems
- Components of a program that promotes positive self-image

Domain 3: Social Development

The social aspects of physical education and the cultural and historical aspects of movement forms will also be addressed on this section of the CSET. Make sure to familiarize yourself with the concepts in the following two lists.

SOCIAL ASPECTS OF PHYSICAL EDUCATION

- Recognition of individual differences
- Understanding of the social and psychological importance of physical education
- Development appropriateness of social behaviors
- Activities promoting enjoyment, self-expression, and personal and social responsibility
- Social approaches to teaching physical education

CULTURAL AND HISTORICAL ASPECTS OF MOVEMENT FORMS

- Significance of cultural and historical influences on various physical activities
- Impact of socioeconomic position on participation in sports-related activities
- Responsibility levels in participation in physical education

Physical Education Vocabulary

The following list includes PE terms and concepts with which you should be familiar. Remember, it will be important not only to know the definitions of these terms, but also to apply them to creating and evaluating an effective PE program.

abdominals: stomach muscles
aerobic: describing exercise that uses oxygen in the blood
agility: the body's ability to change position quickly
asthma: respiratory disease that includes sudden difficulty in breathing
balance: having one's center of gravity directly above its support base in order to maintain equilibrium
bend: use joints to bring parts of the body toward each other
biceps: top muscles found in the upper part of the arm

body composition: proportion of body fat to muscle

bound flow: movement that is halting

cardiorespiratory endurance: ability of the circulatory and respiratory systems to continue supplying the body with oxygen during exercise

clavicle: collarbone

climb: push or pull the body to a higher or lower position while maintaining one's balance

coordination: ability to perform motor skills quickly

court games (divided and shared): games such as tennis or jai alai in which an object is hit so that the opponent is unable to return it

cranium: bones of the head

crawl: move while on the stomach, using the elbow and hips

creep: move using the hands and the knees or feet

deltoids: shoulder muscles

diabetes: medical disorder that occurs when the body cannot regulate blood sugar

dynamic balance: moving balance activities

ecological integration approach: approach to teaching physical education that emphasizes students learning to participate successfully with groups

endurance: ability to sustain physical activity for a period of time

exercise: physical activity, especially intended for fitness and health

femur: bone in the upper leg (thigh)

field games: games such as baseball in which a ball is hit so that opponents are unable to retrieve it

flexibility: ability to move joints and muscles through a range of motion

flow: continuity of a movement

force: body tension used to perform a movement

free flow: movement that is continuous

frequency: how often an activity occurs

friction: resistance of the motion of two objects

gallop: move in a combination of walking and running with one leg remaining in front

gastrocnemius: muscle found in the calf

gluteus maximus: buttock muscles

hamstrings: muscles in the back of the thigh

hang and swing: activity that is usually performed on a bar, which should be not more than twice the height of the child in order to prevent injury, during which the child hangs and swings by his or her hands

high-space activity: movements performed either in the air or while standing on tiptoes

hop: push the body upward on one foot and land on the same foot

humerus: bone in the upper arm

intensity: difficulty of an activity

jump: push the body upward so that both feet leave the ground

kinesiology: study of the motion of the body

leap: jump forcefully with one leg leading, as if running

locomotor skills: abilities to perform movements that cause the body to change location

low-space activity: movements performed while bending or while the body is otherwise close to the ground

manipulative skills: movements that affect or manipulate objects

middle-space activity: movements performed while standing upright

motor control: use of muscular control and the nervous system to coordinate the muscles used to perform a motor skill

motor development: the acquisition of motor skills and their improvement throughout life

motor learning: the process through which children acquire motor skills

muscular strength: amount of force exerted by the muscles

Newton's laws of motion: three laws of physics that are applicable to all forms of movement

nonlocomotor activity: movements that do not cause a change in location

nutrition: the body's process of absorbing nutrients from food and using them to stay healthy and to grow

patella: kneecap

power: ability to generate force quickly

primary rules: well-known, written rules that define a game or activity

quadriceps: muscles found in the front of the thigh

radius: bone in the lower arm

roll: rotate the body around its axis

run: move through space by transferring weight from one foot to the other; both feet are often off of the ground at the same time

scapula: shoulder blade

secondary rules: changes in rules to account for variety in age, ability level, and conditions

self-actualization approach: approach to physical education that focuses on matching the curriculum to what interests and motivates the students

skip: move with a combination of a step and a hop in which the leading foot alternates

slide: move with a sideways gallop

social responsibility approach: approach to physical education that focuses on building strong interpersonal relationships between students

space: location where movements are performed; the relative position of the body

sprain: a stretched or torn ligament

static balancing: stationary balance activities

sternum: breastbone

strain: a stretched or torn muscle

strength: the amount of force a muscle is able to exert

stretch: extend a body part away from the center of the body

substance abuse: pertaining to a minor: use of any alcohol or illegal drugs by a child, the use of any medication not specifically prescribed by a doctor for the child, or the misuse or overuse of prescribed or over-the-counter medication by a child

target games: games such as bowling, golf, or horseshoes that require propelling an object toward a specific goal or target

territory games: games such as basketball, football, and soccer in which a team or player must guard parts of a playing field and attempt to push into the area guarded by the opposing team or player

tibia: inner bone found in the lower leg

time: duration of an activity; speed at which movements are performed

triceps: underneath muscles in the upper arm

turn: rotate the entire body or body parts around the vertical axis of the body

twist: rotate a part of the body around an axis

ulna: bone in the lower arm

walk: move through space by transferring weight from one foot to the other; at least one foot is in contact with the ground at all times

weight transfer: movement of weight of the body from one part of the body to another by such activities as skipping or "bear crawling"

Human Development

The CSET questions relating to human development will address cognitive, social, and physical development, including the educational implications of each. You will be required to apply knowledge in these areas to understand differences in and to explain behavior in children, including those with special needs. The following lists identify concepts with which you should be familiar in order to answer the questions on the CSET correctly.

Domain 1: Cognitive Development from Birth Through Adolescence

The concepts listed here relate to children's cognitive, or mental, development.

COGNITIVE DEVELOPMENT
- Concepts of cognitive and moral development
- Stages of cognitive and language development
- Characteristics of play and how these influence development
- Perspectives on intelligence
- Influential behaviorists and their behavioral theories
- Exceptionalities in children, IQ, and various learning disabilities, and the educational implications of these

Domain 2: Social and Physical Development from Birth Through Adolescence

A child's social development and physical development are important parts of the child's growth. The following lists include some of the important concepts related to these types of development.

SOCIAL DEVELOPMENT
- Development of personality and temperament
- Ability to interact appropriately with other children and adolescents
- Types of play, including their characteristics and their influence on social development
- Changes in the family structure
- Influences on the development of prosocial behavior

- Theories of social learning and the stages of psychosocial and moral development
- Differences in students of various ages, race, and cultures
- Theories of classical and operant conditioning

PHYSICAL DEVELOPMENT
- Stages of physical development in children and adolescents at different ages
- Differences in physical development
- Prenatal factors affecting development
- Implications of human diversity on students' learning
- Gender differences

Domain 3: Influences on Development from Birth Through Adolescence

Many factors influence a child's development. The following list includes many of these factors.

INFLUENCES ON DEVELOPMENT
- Potential impact of sex and gender; genetic, organic, sociocultural, and socioeconomic factors; crime; violence; and ethnicity on development
- Sources of possible abuse and neglect and the influence of these on development
- Effect of cultural and academic diversity on student learning and instructional adaptations for meeting the needs of various students
- Factors influencing successful learning experiences
- Impact of nutrition and obesity on development

Human Development Vocabulary

The following list includes terms and concepts that are related to human development and will be important to understand as you prepare for the CSET.

accommodation: process of children adjusting prior understanding in order to assimilate new experiences or information

assimilation: method by which children incorporate new information with previous knowledge

Bandura, Albert: psychologist known for his social learning theory

behaviorism: first significant development theory; addresses observable behaviors and what actions or events serve as reinforcers

cognitive development: changes in thinking, language, and intelligence as a child grows

concrete operational: Piaget's third stage of cognitive development, occurring from ages 7 to 11, in which children form the ability to reason logically

conservation: concept that the basic properties of an object are unchanging

constructive play: manner of play that involves making objects into something; usually occurs in toddlers through preschool age

Erikson, Erik: psychologist who developed a model of the psychosocial stages of development

extinction: mechanism of operant conditioning through which undesired behaviors are not reinforced and are, therefore, extinguished

extrinsic motivation: motivation that comes from a source other than the student him- or herself

formal operational: Piaget's fourth stage of cognitive development, beginning at about age 11, during which children develop deductive reasoning and the capacity for abstract thought

functional play: repetition of simple muscle movements, which often occurs from birth through age two

giftedness: above-average ability and intelligence

hearing impairment: type of learning disability that limits the ability to perceive sounds

imaginative play: make-believe play, which helps to build imagination, usually from about 18 months through the preschool years

intrinsic motivation: motivation that comes from within the student, rather than from an outside source

Kohlberg, Lawrence: psychologist whose theories outlined the stages of moral development

law of effect: Thorndike's conclusion that rewards strengthen behaviors while punishment weakens behaviors

law of exercise: Thorndike's conclusion that conditioned responses are strengthened through practice and repetition

learning disability: discrepancy between intelligence and performance

mental handicap: significantly below-average ability and intelligence

multiple intelligences: Howard Gardner's theory that children demonstrate various kinds of intelligence and strength

negative reinforcement: mechanism of operant conditioning in which desired responses allow punishment to be escaped

Pavlov, Ivan: behavior theorist noted for his experiments connecting stimulus and response

Piaget, Jean: psychologist who outlined the stages of cognitive development

positive reinforcement: mechanism of operant conditioning in which desired responses are rewarded

preoperational: Piaget's second stage of cognitive development, occurring from ages two to seven, during which time children do not have the capacity for logical reasoning and lack the ability to understand situations from more than one point of view

psychosocial stages: steps in the development of personality that occur during life from infancy to old age, including: basic trust versus mistrust; autonomy versus shame and doubt; initiative versus guilt; industry versus inferiority; identity versus role confusion

punishment: mechanism of operant conditioning in which undesired behaviors are punished

race: a complicated and controversial term meant to describe groups of humans according to ethnicity, familial origin, or physical characteristics

rough-and-tumble play: tag, chasing, and wrestling play, which children engage in from approximately the end of the early childhood years through middle childhood

scaffolding: support provided by the teacher, parent, or peer until the student is able to master a task independently

sensorimotor: Piaget's first stage of cognitive development, occurring from birth through age two, during which time an infant begins to under the world through his or her senses and physical actions

SES: socioeconomic status

Skinner, B. F.: behavior theorist noted for his theory of operant conditioning

substance abuse: abuse of drugs, alcohol, or tobacco, which influences development

symbol manipulation: interpretation and use of intangibles, such as numbers and letters

Thorndike, Edward: psychologist known for his behaviorism theory of instrumental conditioning, in which a desired behavior is positively reinforced by a reward

visual impairment: type of learning disability that involves the sense of sight

Watson, John: behavior theorist who stated that children's behavior can be easily conditioned

zone of proximal development: distance between a child's actual performance and his or her potential performance

Visual and Performing Arts

The visual and performing arts questions on the CSET cover the areas of dance, music, theater, and visual arts. You will be required to interpret and make judgments about the quality of various works based on the elements and principles specific to the art form presented, using criteria for and justifying these statements. You will also need to apply knowledge of related terms and vocabulary. Let's take a look at the types of information from the visual and performing arts domains that will be addressed on the test.

Domain 1: Dance

Since dance and physical education are so closely related, many of the terms and concepts reviewed in that section of the text also apply to this form of movement. It will be important to explain the principles behind the movement of dance, describe dance forms, and discuss the role of dance in society. The following list identifies several other concepts and objectives related to dance with which you should be familiar:

▶ Basic fluency with the elements of dance and the ability to use these elements to make judgments about dance
▶ Ability to use basic techniques to create dance and movement with children
▶ Principles of kinesiology, internal and external force, and range of movement as they relate to dance
▶ Styles of dance from various times, places, and cultures
▶ Dance innovators and styles that have influenced the development of the art form
▶ Integration of dance with other forms of art, and recognition of how other disciplines can be integrated into movement and dance

Dance Vocabulary

The following list includes dance-related terms and concepts. You may notice that some of the terms also relate to other areas of art, as well as to physical education. Be prepared to apply and explain these concepts and terms.

accent: dance that includes two separate sections that have some commonalities
aesthetic criteria: standards by which a dance is judged
alignment: how the body lines up with its base of support
axial movement: nonlocomotor movement in which dancers move around a fixed body part
ballet: graceful dance form developed during the European Renaissance
canon: a dance in which performers demonstrate the same movements but start at different times
choreography: art of composing or planning the movements included in a dance
contrast: dances performed side by side in order to highlight differences
creative movement: children's exploratory dance movement
dance: sequential, rhythmic, intentional movement to express a thought, feeling, or image
dance medium: type of movement while dancing
folk dance: dance form associated with a certain culture
force: the energy that produces a dance
genre: specific dance form
improvisation: art of spontaneously creating a dance
jazz: dance form developed in the United States from syncopated, ethnic forms of music
kinesthetic perception: ability of the human body to sense movement
modern dance: form of theatrical dance based on original movements and expression of feelings
narrative dance: a dance that tells a certain story
phrase: an organizational element of a dance
pirouette: a turn performed while on a single foot while dancing
pulse: the beat of a dance
retrograde: a dance performed first forward, then in reverse
shape: the way one's body is positioned
space: the area or sphere immediately around one's body
tap dance: form of dance in which dancers produce rhythms by striking feet on the floor
technique: skills used by a dancer while performing

tempo: the speed at which a dance is performed

time: the tempo and beat during a dance

Domain 2: Music

The questions on the CSET related to music will require knowledge of musical elements, the ability to respond to and evaluate music, and the ability to integrate music with other forms of art, as well as with other disciplines. You may notice that some of the dance terms previously discussed also relate to music, as these two forms of art often go hand in hand. The following list identifies some of the other skills and concepts that will be important to understand:

▶ Basic fluency with the elements of music and the ability to identify and use these elements to describe and make judgments about music

▶ Basic techniques for creating vocal and instrumental music with children

▶ Ability to group sounds by the way in which they were produced, and to identify ways to change the sound

▶ Capability to arrange, compose, and perform various styles of music, both vocally and instrumentally

▶ Capacity to evaluate and derive meaning from music

▶ Ability to explain, compare, and contrast styles and types of music and instruments from various times, places, and cultures

▶ Integration of music with other forms of art, as well as with other disciplines

Music Vocabulary

The following list includes musical terms and concepts you will need to understand and be able to apply on the CSET. Some of the terms may be familiar from previous vocabulary lists in this chapter; be sure to understand the differences in meaning as the terms relate specifically to music.

a cappella: sung without the accompaniment of instruments

accompaniment: instruments or voices in a musical piece that support a melody

adagio: musical tempo that is very slow

allegro: musical tempo that is fast

aria: a song set off from the rest and sung as a solo or duet in an opera

articulation: the way in which adjacent notes are connected

blues: form of African-American folk music

brass: family of instruments, traditionally created from brass or metal, which produce sounds from the vibration of the player's lips against the mouthpiece

canon: a musical form that repeats the melody in more than one staggered part

chamber music: music played by a small ensemble with one performer for each part

chord: three or more notes played or sung at the same time

clef: symbol at the beginning of each staff of printed music to indicate the pitch

duet: two singers or instrumentalists performing together

duple meter: beats grouped into sets of two

dynamics: the volume of music; how loud or soft the sounds are

elements of music: ways of describing music, including dynamics, form, harmony, pitch, rhythm, texture, and timbre

finale: the final number of a musical work, which brings the composition to an end

flat: a note one half-step lower in pitch than that of a given note; or, a note that is slightly below the intended pitch

form: the structure of a piece of music

forte: loud

genre: certain type of music

harmony: two tones performed at the same time to create a pleasing sound

improvisation: spontaneous, unrehearsed music

libretto: complete spoken and sung text of an opera

melody: sequence of notes that usually have a distinctive rhythm; main or primary tune

movement: one of several parts of a large piece of music

opera: a drama that is highly musical

orchestra instruments: four families of instruments (string, woodwind, brass, and percussion) used for orchestral performances

overture: a musical, orchestral introduction for an opera, play, ballet, or longer musical work

percussion: family of instruments that produce sounds from striking

pitch: the sound-wave frequency of a single musical note

ragtime: style of American piano music that led to the development of jazz

rhythm: the beat of a piece of music

scale: series of sequential musical notes, arranged in order of ascending or descending pitch

sharp: one-half step higher in pitch than that of a given note; or, a note slightly higher in pitch than the intended note

staff: set of five horizontal lines on which musical notes are written

string quartet: four musicians playing a viola, a cello, and two violins

strings: family of instruments that produce sounds when the player plucks or draws a bow across strings

symphony: a musical work that contains between three and five movements, written for an orchestra

syncopation: a rhythm in which the weak beats are emphasized

tempo: the speed of a piece of music

texture: the feel of a piece of music

timbre: unique sounds created by specific instruments or voices

tone: a sound that has a distinctive quality, including pitch, volume, and timbre

woodwinds: family of instruments that produce sounds from the player blowing

Domain 3: Theater

The theater questions on the CSET will require you to evaluate a dramatic work and demonstrate fluency in the basic components of theater. The following list identifies some of the other skills and concepts you will need to understand for this assessment:

▶ Creation of, participation in, and evaluation of various types of productions

▶ Basic fluency in acting, directing, design, and scriptwriting

▶ Ability to apply the elements and principles of theater to create dramatic activities with children and to use these elements to make judgments about dramatic works

▶ Ability to explain styles of theater from various times, places, and cultures, to demonstrate understanding of genres, and to describe the literature of the theater

▶ Evaluation of factors influencing the overall appearance of a production, including details such as light, distance, position, and motion

▶ Integration of theater not only with other art forms, but also with various disciplines

Theater Vocabulary

The following list includes terms and concepts related to theater. It will be important to understand the terms and be able to apply the concepts as they relate to this domain.

acting: speaking and moving to participate in a performance before an audience

action: the external and internal activity between characters, which is used to achieve their objectives in a production

actors: the people participating in a play or performance by playing a role in the work

ad-lib: to speak lines that are not included in the script of a dramatic work

arena stage: a type of stage that has members of the audience on all sides; also known as "theater in the round"

audience: the people who watch a performance

auditorium: the section of a theater that is intended for the audience

black light: ultraviolet light

blocking: the plan for the positions of the actors and scenery in a performance

cast: list of actors and the characters they portray

catwalk: a walkway located above the width of a stage

character: figure portrayed by an actor

characterization: the way a writer or actor portrays and develops a character

cold read: an unrehearsed reading of a script

collaboration: a joint effort in writing a play

conflict: the central feature around which the action of the plot revolves

context: the setting of a play

costume: the clothing worn by the actors while onstage

critique: a commentary regarding a performance

cue: a signal used for an actor

curtain: the beginning or end of a theatrical performance

curtain call: an additional bow by an actor at the end of a play or performance

dialogue: words spoken by actors during a performance

direction: coordination of the activities that occur onstage

director: the person in charge of everything involved in a performance

downstage: the part of the stage that is closest to the audience

drama: literature intended to be performed

drama elements: parts of a performance, including the plot, characters, theme, music, and dialogue

effectiveness: the impact a performance has on an audience

ensemble: a group of performers in a dramatic presentation

flat: a rectangular frame that is covered in canvas and is part of a set for a theater production

flood: a beam of light that is unfocused

footlights: lights located at floor level at the front of the stage

grip: people who are responsible for moving the scenery in a theatrical production

house: the area of the theater where the audience is seated

improvisation: a form of acting in which performers create a spontaneous presentation

intent: the reason, purpose, or objective for presenting a theatrical performance

legs: narrow vertical theater curtains

light board: the console used to control the lighting for a theatrical production

melodrama: a dramatic work that includes exaggerated emotions, stereotyped characters, and interpersonal conflict

monologue: a dramatic presentation or speech, spoken by one person

motivation: the reason for an actor's performance

pantomime: a form of live performance that does not include words

pit: the area of a theater below the front of the stage, which is commonly where the orchestra is seated

playmaking: creating a story and then structuring, performing, and evaluating the performance without including a formal audience

plot: the series of events that compose the action of a dramatic performance

production: the process of arranging for a theater performance

prompt: assistance given to an actor to help the actor recall his or her lines

reprise: repetition of a musical performance that was previously played or sung

script: a written description of a play or other type of performance, including the words and movements to be performed by the actors

spike: a mark used to indicate the intended placement of set pieces

stage: the place where actors present a performance

stage left: the part of the stage to the actors' left when they are facing the audience

stage right: the part of the stage to the actors' right when they are facing the audience

structure: relationship between components of a dramatic piece, such as conflict, contrast, and emphasis, among others

subtext: underlying meaning

theater: a formal presentation that involves an audience and actors

thrust: a stage that has the audience on three of the sides

upstage: (1) the part of the stage that is away from the audience; (2) to outdo and divert attention away from someone else

wings: the sides of the stage that are not visible to members of the audience

worth: the value of a dramatic work

Domain 4: Visual Arts

The questions on the CSET addressing visual arts will relate to a range of artistic forms, including not only paintings and sculptures, but also photos, prints, carvings, and architecture. You will need to understand the visual elements around which visual arts are created and be able to analyze and evaluate representations based on these elements, as well as on the principles of design. The following list identifies some of the concepts and skills you will need to understand in order to do your best on subtest III of the CSET:

▶ Basic fluency with the principles of art
▶ Ability to distinguish between the elements of art and to recognize ways in which these elements are affected by light and shadow
▶ Analysis of the creative process and the impact of artists on thinking and culture
▶ Ability to explain, describe, compare, and contrast styles of visual arts representing various times, places, themes, and cultures
▶ Capability to interpret works of art to derive meaning and make judgments based on the principles of art
▶ Use of design principles to describe art and explain how these affect the quality of a piece
▶ Recognition of the mood of a work of art
▶ Understanding of how to integrate visual art with other art forms and disciplines

Visual Arts Vocabulary

The following list includes terms and concepts related to the four areas of visual arts. It will be important to understand the terms and be able to apply the concepts.

abstract art: composition or piece of art that includes unrecognizable representations of actual objects or thoughts

allegory: symbolic artwork

amphora: a narrow-necked Grecian urn, usually made of clay and having two handles

annealing: the process of heating hardened glass or metal in order to soften it

arabesque: ornate, detailed design that incorporates plant life and geometric patterns

asymmetry: the effect achieved when a piece of work has a sense of balance created by the lightness and color of different parts of the piece

avant-garde: art thought to be innovative, unconventional, or ahead of its time

balance: the sense of visual stability or equilibrium in a piece of art

battens: wooden slats on which plaster or tiles are attached

bevel: a slanted or rounded edge

biscuit: porcelain that has not been glazed

bust: a sculpture that shows only the head and shoulders of the subject

calligraphy: a type of decorative, artistic handwriting

canopy: a covering made of fabric

carvings: designs made by cutting wood or stone

ceramics: objects made from porcelain or hard, fired clay

chalice: ornamental cup used in religious services for Communion or Mass

chancel: area of a church near the altar, which is reserved for the clergy

chroma: the brightness or dullness of a color; also called saturation or intensity

collage: type of art that is created by pasting various types of media, including paper, fabric, wood, photographs, paintings, or drawings, onto a surface

color: the visible light that is reflected off of objects

contrast: the artistic representation of two opposites, used to represent dramatic differences in a composition

course: one layer of stones or bricks that make up a wall

cuneiform: belonging to an ancient writing system that involved making wedge-shaped impressions in soft clay

decoupage: cut-out designs or pieces of paper materials used in a collage, glued to a surface, and then covered with varnish

dominance: use of color, size, and position of objects in a piece of art to draw the viewer's attention to the most essential part of the work

eclectic: involving a variety of styles and sources

emphasis: the center of interest in an artistic composition; used to draw the viewer's eye to the focal point

enamel: powdered glass fused onto metal, glass, or ceramics to create a glassy decorative coating

engraving: inscribing a design or words onto a hard surface such as metal or glass

etching: (1) creating a design by applying acid to initial scratching on metal plates; (2) a print created by using etched plates

filigree: elaborate, lacy designs created from thin gold or silver wire

focal point: the part of an artwork to which the viewer's eye is drawn

foreshortening: the exaggeration of linear perspective by representing the near parts of an object closer to the farther parts of the object

form: a figure with height, width, and depth that helps define the objects contained in a piece of art

fresco: artistic technique that involves painting on damp or wet plaster

genre: category of paintings, such as portraits or landscapes

golden ratio: the artistic proportion that is believed to be the most pleasing: approximately 1.6 to 1

gouache: painting technique that involves mixing opaque watercolors with gum

hieroglyphics: ancient Egyptian symbols that were used to represent letters or words

hue: the point of a particular color on the color spectrum

illustration: a drawing, picture, photograph, or diagram used to represent a written idea

intensity: the brightness or dullness of a color; also called saturation or chroma

line: a continuous mark whose direction, length, or width may vary

linear: a technique used to represent three-dimensional space in two dimensions

linear perspective: an artistic technique used to represent three-dimensional figures in a two-dimensional piece of art by representing objects that are farther away by drawing them smaller

macramé: a type of artwork that is created through the use of knotted fabric or string

method: the artistic medium used to create a piece, such as watercolor or sculpture

monolith: a figure created by sculpting or carving a single piece of stone

mural: a large painting created on or attached to a wall

niche: a recess in a wall, especially used to hold a statue

nonrepresentational art: compositions or pieces of art that represent only themselves and are not related to actual objects, people, or thoughts

obelisk: a rectangular block of stone that is especially built to be a monument, often has a tapered top, and is similar to a pyramid

papier-mâché: paper, especially newspaper, soaked with water and flour and formed into figures

parquet: type of decorative wooden flooring that is made from wooden tiles placed in a pattern

perspective: ways of using two-dimensional space to create the appearance of three dimensions

pigment: substance used to give color to something such as paint

plaster: limestone, sand, and water mixture applied to ceilings and interior walls to create a hard surface when dry

points: the simplest of all visual elements; represented by dots in an artistic composition

projection: image or picture cast on a flat surface

proportion: size of the design elements relative to each other, especially the size of the elements in the foreground relative to those in the background

relief: style of carved or molded artwork in which the figures are elevated from the background

representational art: composition or piece of art in which the people, places, or things are recognizable

rhythm: the repetition of the elements in a piece of art

saturation: the brightness or dullness of a color; also called intensity or chroma

scale: size ratio, often used in the creation of a map or a model

shape: in two-dimensional art, a bounded figure that has height and width and is created by lines that are joined together

sizing: a substance used to stiffen paper or to seal a wall or a canvas

space: the area within the boundaries of an artistic composition

stipple: to paint something by dabbing on paint

style: the way in which an artist expresses his or her ideas; examples include impressionism and baroque

symmetry: the effect achieved by having one side of a piece of art generally reflect the other side

tapestry: fabric with a woven design

tempera: a painting technique that mixes colors from powdered pigments, water or oil, and egg yolk

texture: element of art used to describe how a piece might actually feel or how it appears to feel

unity: the sense that all components of an artistic composition belong with one another, giving the feeling that the piece is complete

value: the amount of lightness or darkness of a color

warp: the thick, fixed threads used in weaving

weft: the thin, horizontal threads that are woven with the warp

CHAPTER 8

CSET Writing Tips

Most of the questions on the CSET: Multiple Subjects Subtest I will be multiple-choice, but four of them—about 30 percent of your score—will be constructed-response assignments. You may also be required to verify your proficiency in basic writing skills by passing the CSET: Writing Skills exam. This test consists of two constructed-response assignments. One will require you to describe or analyze a particular situation or statement, and the other will ask you to express your personal views on an issue or write about a personal experience. The questions on these exams are meant to test your expository and expressive writing skills.

Constructed-Response Assignments

Constructed responses are not like typical essays. They are generally short, open-ended responses that measure specific skills and subject matter. They can range from a few sentences to several paragraphs.

The evaluators for the constructed-response assignments on the Writing Skills exam and the Multiple Subjects Subtest I will score your answers according to different criteria. The Writing Skills constructed-response assignments are meant to test your writing ability, not your knowledge of specific subject matter. The Multiple Subjects constructed-response assignments will be scored primarily on your knowledge of the subject matter and how well you communicate your answers. Consult the test guides for these exams for a list of criteria used to score the constructed-response assignments.

Basic Writing Points

There are a few basic points to keep in mind when writing your constructed responses:

- ▶ Be aware of your audience. You will be given instructions as to the composition of your readers. In the past, CSET has stated that the intended audience was educated adults. Tailor your word choice, tone, and sentence structure to your audience.
- ▶ Be aware of the time constraints.
- ▶ Stay on topic. Your grade will depend on how well you address the specific topic.
- ▶ Structure the points you make in a logical way, and use grammatical devices to show the logical connection between your points.
- ▶ Know your subject matter well.
- ▶ Avoid ambiguity in your words and statements.
- ▶ Support all general statements and assertions with detailed and relevant information.
- ▶ Use the entire space provided for your response.
- ▶ Proofread: check your syntax, paragraph structure, sentence structure, spelling, punctuation, and capitalization before turning in your test.

Expository Writing

Expository writing is often used in writing nonfiction. This style of writing describes, explains, analyzes, discusses, or simply presents factual information. A good expository response will stay focused on the topic throughout every paragraph. This requires strong organizational skills, but the choice of words can help hold your composition together. Use words that will introduce the facts or events in a logical order, such as *first, second, next,* and *furthermore.* Expository writing is more concerned with facts than opinion, so make sure you support your general statements with specific details and facts. Your conclusions should always be supported by these facts.

Expressive Writing

Expressive writing is meant to express your opinions, feelings, or reflections about something you experienced. It seems easier than expository writing, but good expressive writing that can hold the reader's attention requires skill. Use the first-person point of view, and choose your words and tone to best reveal the interior emotional journey you are writing about. Understanding the conventions of narrative and descriptive writing will be useful for this assignment.

Writing Constructed Responses for the CSET: Writing Skills Exam

Constructed responses for the CSET: Writing Skills exam will not require any specialized knowledge, but they will require rigorous attention to writing conventions. Before you begin your response, make a brief outline by jotting down the major points you intend to cover and arranging them in logical order. This outline will be your guide as you write your answers.

Composition

Whether you are writing an expository or expressive essay, follow basic principles of composition. Structure your responses according to the conventional outline for essays: an introductory paragraph, several body paragraphs, and a concluding paragraph. Let's look at each section of the conventional outline for essays.

Introductory Paragraph

The opening paragraph should state your thesis or response to the test question in a succinct way. You can repeat part of the question in your response for cohesion, but paraphrase, rather than using the identical phrasing. Example:

> *Test question:* What historical texts would you use to explain basic American values to a foreigner?

> *Your response:* The U.S. Constitution and the Declaration of Independence, two documents that incorporate American values, may be fine teaching tools for foreigners interested in learning about American culture.

Clarity is the key for your introduction; this is the only section of the essay where you tell your reader exactly what you are writing about. The paragraphs following your introduction will flesh out your answer, but in your initial paragraph, briefly state what you intend to do and how you intend to do it. Limit your introductory paragraph to five or six sentences. Choose your words carefully, and make every word count.

Body Paragraphs

The body paragraphs will provide all the factual or personal information necessary to support the thesis you stated in your introductory paragraph. You can use quotes, statistics, examples, and facts, but make sure you use only relevant, specific supporting data. Avoid general statements that are not backed up with specific examples. For example, do not simply state, "Documents from the Revolutionary War era clearly explain basic American values." Instead, discuss specific documents, and analyze how they explain basic American values.

Evaluators will expect your argument to be coherent throughout the essay. Therefore, the order of your sentences is important. They should be arranged either chronologically or logically, depending on your thesis and the type of essay you're writing. Use transitional words to move from one paragraph to the next, and make sure each paragraph is distinct and recognizable.

Evaluators will look for how well you can maintain your focus on the topic. Avoid the temptation to ramble or to bring in issues or ideas that do not directly relate to or clarify the main topic. Your brief outline of major points will be helpful in keeping you on track. Given the time constraints, two or three well-constructed and information-packed body paragraphs may be sufficient, but you can write more or less if you choose.

Concluding Paragraph

Do not introduce any new issues, ideas, or data in the concluding paragraph. The final paragraph should briefly summarize the essence of the main points in the body paragraphs (not the actual points) and offer a concluding remark that ties back to the introductory paragraph. For example, if, in your body paragraphs, you quoted or paraphrased several notable phrases from the U.S. Constitution and the Declaration of Independence, you can state in the final sentence of the concluding paragraph, "The ringing words from these founding documents clearly convey to foreigners the values that are important to all Americans."

Grammatical Rules

Evaluators for the CSET: Writing Skills exam will grade you on how well you structure your responses and apply grammatical conventions.

Sentence structure is important. Use correct parts of speech and syntax (subject-predicate structure). Vary your sentences to add rhythm and interest to your writing. Short, simple sentences can offset compound and complex sentences.

Use transitional phrases to hold together all paragraphs, and introduce transitional sentences with words that indicate a sequence—for example, *furthermore, consequently, moreover,* and *next.*

Pay attention to the conventions for spelling, capitalization, and punctuation. In expressive writing, punctuation marks are especially important to guide the reader toward understanding your views and feelings.

When you have finished writing, proofread and edit your essay. Look for errors in spelling and punctuation, and make sure you have used clauses and phrases correctly. Also, check that you have answered the question, stayed on topic, and provided supporting details for your general statements. Don't be afraid to eliminate sentences or even entire paragraphs if they are not specific to the topic.

Writing Constructed Responses for the CSET: Multiple Subjects Subtest I

Because of time constraints, your constructed responses for the CSET: Multiple Subjects Subtest I will likely be shorter than those for the CSET: Writing Skills exam. You may have time to write only a single information-packed paragraph and will not be able to follow all of the guidelines for conventional essays.

For the constructed responses on this subtest, here are the most important guidelines to remember:

▶ Understand the question thoroughly before starting to write.
▶ Use outlines, brainstorming, and any other device to help you generate relevant ideas quickly. You may have only 10 to 15 minutes to write your constructed responses. Spending a few minutes on your outline will help you maintain focus under pressure.
▶ Organize your outline points in a logical or chronological order, and keep that order in your response.
▶ Use only the terms, dates, names, and facts that relate to the specific topic.

A final tip to help you get the best score possible on these exams: write legibly. If the evaluator cannot read your handwriting, you may lose points.

PART 4

Practice CSETs

CHAPTER 9

Practice Test 1

Test Directions

The simulated exam in this chapter includes full-length practice tests for each of the three CSET subtests. Each subtest includes two sections:

▶ **Multiple-choice questions.** Each multiple-choice question includes four answer choices. Your goal is to choose the single best answer.
▶ **Constructed-response assignments.** The constructed-response assignments require written responses. Directions appear directly before the assignments.

You may work on the multiple-choice questions and constructed-response assignments in whatever order you choose. Keep in mind, though, that if you take all three CSET subtests, you will have five hours to complete them.

For each section, you will be able to tear out sheets on which to write your answers. For the multiple-choice sections, there are answer sheets before each section. For the constructed-response assignments, pages on which to enter your answers are provided after the directions for each assignment.

Constructed-Response Assignments

You'll write a response for each constructed-response assignment. Be sure to read each assignment closely and consider how you will organize your response. The scoring for the responses to the CSET assignments is based on the following criteria:

▶ **Purpose.** Your response addresses the objectives of the assignment.
▶ **Knowledge.** You successfully apply your knowledge of relevant subject matter to the assignment.
▶ **Support.** Your supporting evidence is of high quality and relevant to the assignment.

While the constructed-response assignments are used to assess your command of the subject matter and not your writing ability, keep in mind that the level of clarity of your responses will affect how your responses are judged. Write your responses as you would address an audience of fellow educators. In the answer key for this practice test, you will find sample responses to which you can compare what you've written.

SUBTEST I

READING, LANGUAGE, AND LITERATURE; HISTORY AND SOCIAL SCIENCE

Multiple-Choice Answer Sheet

Reading, Language, and Literature

QUESTION NUMBER	YOUR RESPONSE
1	
2	
3	
4	
5	
6	
7	
8	
9	
10	
11	
12	
13	
14	
15	
16	
17	
18	
19	
20	
21	
22	
23	
24	
25	
26	

History and Social Science

QUESTION NUMBER	YOUR RESPONSE
27	
28	
29	
30	
31	
32	
33	
34	
35	
36	
37	
38	
39	
40	
41	
42	
43	
44	
45	
46	
47	
48	
49	
50	
51	
52	

Multiple-Choice Questions

1. Some common vowel patterns are associated with more than one pronunciation (e.g., the *oo* in *boot* and *foot*). Which of the following nonsense words illustrates a vowel pattern that is highly consistent in its pronunciation?

   A. Tain

   B. Fead

   C. Lough

   D. Sloot

2. What generally occurs during the period when a child is two to five years old?

   A. Holophrastic speech

   B. Emergent speech and grammar explosion

   C. Increasing literacy

   D. Telegraphic speech, mostly content words without affixes or function words

3. Which of the following word identification strategies is typically learned first?

   A. Learning letter sounds

   B. Using contextual clues

   C. Analyzing word structure

   D. Applying phonics knowledge

4. Marina is having difficulty learning to read. What is the most likely reason that the difficulty exists?

   A. The same letter always has the same sound in English.

   B. She has not learned to recognize phonemes and morphemes.

   C. Different languages have different semantics.

   D. She is not motivated.

5. Why is rhyming an effective scaffolding tool?

   A. It helps develop a large oral vocabulary.

   B. It helps develop phonemic awareness.

   C. It helps a child sound out words.

   D. It helps a child identify the syllables in spoken words.

6. Which of the following statements best explains why an extensive oral vocabulary is most likely to contribute to a reader's decoding skills?

   A. It assists the reader in applying phonics generalizations to sound out a word.

   B. It helps the reader use syntactic cues to determine the meaning of an unfamiliar word.

   C. It helps the reader relate an unfamiliar word to known words with similar spellings.

   D. It assists the reader in recognizing a word after sounding it out.

7. During the phonetic stage of spelling development, a child _____.

   A. understands letter-sound correspondence as a principle and may use a single letter to represent a word or syllable

   B. moves from a dependence on sound and phonology to the use of visual memory and an understanding of word structure

   C. starts to represent speech sounds with letters or groups of letters in a logical way

   D. knows the basic rules of English and the correct spellings of many words by memory

8. English is similar to other languages in that they all _____.

   A. follow the rules of morphology

   B. use the same phonemes and morphemes

   C. have the same social conventions regarding speech

   D. have a logical syntax

9. Which of the following skills will help sixth-graders develop comprehension of nonfiction writing?

   A. Reading the first sentence of each paragraph

   B. Making an outline

   C. Taking notes

   D. Previewing and summarizing

10. In which of the following sentences is the italicized word used correctly?

   A. Just before the class was over, the professor made an *illusion* to a paper about the ancient Greeks.

   B. Sometimes, if the weather is hot and dry, you will see an *illusion* on a roadway as you drive.

   C. The crowd thought that the magician created an *allusion,* but it was totally real.

   D. I thought it was inappropriate for the speaker to make such a positive *illusion* to his own book.

11. Which of the following sentences contains a relative clause?

   A. Scientists have found and studied the remains of mammoths.

   B. The photographs that Lily took of the campus are on display at the library.

   C. After the football game was over, the players went to eat at the new diner.

   D. The conference was held during school hours, but students were allowed to attend.

Read the following passage; then answer the two questions that come after it.

(1) In 1799, Napoleon's troops were at a place called Rosetta on the western side of the Nile River. (2) A soldier found a black stone slab built into a wall of an Arab fort covered with writing. (3) One language was Greek, but the other two were unknown at the time. (4) It was noted by a scholar named Jean-François Champollion that the writing on the stone was in three different languages, and he took a guess that the three of them all said the same thing. (5) Because he could translate the Greek, Champollion was able to decipher the other two inscriptions. (6) The young scholar used Greek to understand the inscriptions of Egyptian hieroglyphics. (7) This resulted in greater knowledge of the ancient Egyptian civilization.

12. Which of the following changes could best improve the logical organization of the passage?

   A. Move sentence 4 so that it follows sentence 1.

   B. Move sentence 4 so that it follows sentence 2.

   C. Move sentence 7 so that it follows sentence 1.

   D. Move sentence 7 so that it follows sentence 3.

13. Which of the following revisions of a sentence would best improve the style of the passage?

    A. Sentence 1: Napoleon's troops, in 1799, reached the western side of the Nile River, where Rosetta is located.

    B. Sentence 4: A scholar named Jean-François Champollion noted that the writing on the stone was in three different languages and guessed that all three said the same thing.

    C. Sentence 5: The other two inscriptions were comprehended by Champollion, who was able to speak Greek and translate the writing.

    D. Sentence 7: All of this resulted in a greater knowledge of the ancient Egyptian civilization being available for scholars.

Read the following paragraph; then answer the question that comes after it.

(1) Many experts say that bananas were the first fruit cultivated by humans. (2) But unfortunately some people fear that bananas may completely disappear in the near future. (3) This is because they are prone to disease. (4) Fungus organisms can infect the banana plant fairly easily. (5) Since all bananas are grown from plants, the disease would likely be transmitted from one to the other very quickly. (6) Scientists are trying to engineer banana plants that are more resistant to disease.

14. Which of the following is the topic sentence of this paragraph?

    A. Sentence 1

    B. Sentence 2

    C. Sentence 3

    D. Sentence 5

15. Which of the following features would be most important to include at the end of a persuasive essay?

    A. An explanation of why the issue is important to the reader

    B. A rebuttal of alternative viewpoints taken by opponents

    C. An appeal to the reader to accept the author's viewpoint

    D. A summary of the various viewpoints about the subject

16. Pausing after a main point in an oral presentation would be most effective for _____.

    A. conveying a feeling of excitement

    B. helping poor listeners catch up

    C. emphasizing the importance of what is being said

    D. allowing time to breathe and relax

17. Variation in rate, pitch, and rhythm is most likely to enhance the delivery of an oral presentation by _____.

    A. making the presentation seem more substantial

    B. increasing the presentation's emotional effect

    C. allowing the audience to participate in the presentation

    D. causing the audience to be less critical

Read the following excerpt from a letter; then answer the two questions that come after it.

(1) The concept of recycling is not new. (2) The reuse of materials has always been a large part of society, particularly when there are not a lot of materials. (3) But today, recycling of computers and electronic equipment has not grown in the way that it should. (4) Although some retailers are willing to accept old electronic equipment, too few people make use of this option. (5) Instead, most electronic equipment finds its way into landfills, where components can leach into the groundwater, causing terrible effects on health. (6) It is imperative that the state take steps to ensure that this does not continue to happen. (7) We need to act now to prevent greater pollution from electronic equipment.

18. Which sentence most strongly suggests that the intent of the letter is persuasive?

    A. Sentence 2

    B. Sentence 4

    C. Sentence 5

    D. Sentence 6

19. Which of the following research questions would be the best for starting an objective investigation of the issue of electronic equipment recycling?

    A. How many computers and other pieces of electronic equipment are sold on an annual basis?

    B. How many computers and other pieces of electronic equipment are dumped in landfills?

    C. What kinds of chemicals are released when electronic equipment is dumped in landfills?

    D. Which retailers have programs that allow consumers to recycle electronic equipment?

20. Which of the following elements does a satire generally include?

    A. A humorous exposé of a situation or person

    B. A story featuring a happy ending

    C. An explanation of the earth's beginnings

    D. A story that includes animals that talk

Read the following excerpt from a Native American myth; then answer the two questions that come after it.

And the Forefathers, the Creators and Makers, who were called Tepeu and Gucumatz said: "The time of dawn has come, let the work be finished, and let those who are to nourish and sustain us appear, the noble sons, the civilized vassals; let man appear, humanity, on the face of the earth." Thus they spoke.

They assembled, came together and held council in the darkness and in the night; then they sought and discussed, and here they reflected and thought. In this way their decisions came dearly to light and they found and discovered what must enter into the flesh of man. It was just before the sun, the moon, and the stars appeared over the Creators and Makers. From Paxil, from Cayalá, as they were called, came the yellow ears of corn and the white ears of corn. These are the names of the animals which brought the food: *yac* (the mountain cat), *utiú* (the coyote), *quel* (a small parrot), and *hoh* (the crow). These four animals gave tidings of the yellow ears of corn and the white ears of corn, they told them that they should go to Paxil and they showed them the road to Paxil. And thus they found the food, and this was what went into the flesh of created man, the made man; this was his blood; of this the blood of man was made.

21. This passage is typical of many myths because _____.

    A. the characters are animals

    B. it is about how humankind was created

    C. it uses dialogue

    D. it has little or no plot

22. The style of the passage is most like a myth because _____.

    A. it recounts what happened a very long time ago

    B. it uses many characters to make a point

    C. it talks about animals

    D. it contains a moral

Read the following poem, "Her Hands" by Anna Hempstead Branch; then answer the two questions that come after it.

My mother's hands are cool and fair,
Like water in the May,
They can do anything.
Delicate mercies hide them there
Like flowers in the spring.

When I was small and could not sleep,
She used to come to me,
And with my cheek upon her hand
How sure my rest would be.

For everything she ever touched
Of beautiful or fine,
Their memories living in her hands
Would warm that sleep of mine.

Her hands remember how they played
One time in meadow streams, —
And all the flickering song and shade
Of water took my dreams.

Swift through her haunted fingers pass
Memories of garden things; —
I dipped my face in flowers and grass
And sounds of hidden wings.

One time she touched the cloud that kissed
Brown pastures bleak and far; —
I leaned my cheek into a mist
And thought I was a star.

All this was very long ago
And I am grown; but yet
The hand that lured my slumber so
I never can forget.

For still when drowsiness comes on
It seems so soft and cool,
Shaped happily beneath my cheek,
Hollow and beautiful.

23. The images used in the poem help to reinforce _____.

   A. the anger that the poet feels toward the death of her mother

   B. the ambivalence that the poet feels about her mother

   C. the anxiety the poet feels about losing her mother

   D. the joy the poet feels when remembering her mother

24. The last two stanzas of the poem most clearly support which of the following themes?

   A. A daughter will grow to be an image of her mother.

   B. Mothers and children enjoy having time one-on-one.

   C. Sleepiness comes more easily when a child grows into an adult.

   D. A mother can still comfort her child, even in adulthood.

Read the following poem, "Hats" by Carl Sandburg; then answer the two questions that come after it.

Hats, where do you belong?
What is under you?
On the rim of a skyscraper's forehead
I looked down and saw: hats: fifty thousand
   hats:
Swarming with a noise of bees and sheep,
   cattle and waterfalls,
Stopping with a silence of sea grass, a silence
   of prairie corn.
Hats: tell me your high hopes.

25. In this poem, the image of the hats most clearly symbolizes _____.

   A. bees

   B. people

   C. hopes

   D. ideas

26. The narrator of the poem most likely thinks that _____.

   A. buildings should not be tall

   B. people are very much the same

   C. nature is difficult to contain

   D. individuals should strive for their dreams

Use the map shown here to answer the following question.

27. The unshaded land area on the map shows the extent of the empire associated with which of the following rulers?

   A. Julius Caesar

   B. Alexander the Great

   C. Charlemagne

   D. Genghis Khan

28. In the Chinese philosophy of Taoism, the Tao is considered to revolve around which of the following?

   A. The emphasis of correctness of social relations

   B. Stressing mindfulness and awareness of thoughts

   C. The possibility of being reborn into a higher caste

   D. The encompassing of all opposite and complementary

29. During the Middle Ages, the Roman Catholic Church grew very powerful. Which of the following was true of the church during that time?

   A. The church issued a decree that accepting gifts was immoral.

   B. The church tolerated other sects as long as they paid taxes to the church.

   C. The kings and rulers of Europe cooperated with the laws of the church.

   D. Opposition to the Roman Catholic Church would result in excommunication.

30. Which of the following works from ancient Greece serves today as the basis for beginning high school mathematics courses?

   A. Aristotle's *Physics*

   B. Zeno's *Parmenides*

   C. Euclid's *Elements*

   D. Plato's *Phaedo*

31. The Roman Empire reached its height of grandeur and power under which of the following rulers?

   A. Augustus Caesar

   B. Marcus Tullius Cicero

   C. Julius Caesar

   D. Constantine I

Use the following list to answer the question that comes after it.

> ► The document was signed at Runnymede.
> ► It was a series of written promises between the king and his subjects.
> ► Many of the clauses concerned the legal system of the time.

32. The facts listed best describe which of the following historical documents?

   A. Mayflower Compact

   B. Augsburg Confession

   C. Magna Carta

   D. Hammurabi's Code of Laws

33. Which of the following was a contributing factor to the end of the expansion of the Ottoman Empire?

   A. Battle of Vienna

   B. Congress of Paris

   C. Sharia

   D. Battle of Varna

34. Which line in the following table best matches an archaeological period on the African continent with a characteristic of that period?

Line	Archaeological Period	Characteristic
1	Iron Age	development of farming
2	Paleolithic age	implements hammered into shape
3	Bronze Age	development of writing
4	Neolithic age	use of stone tools

   A. Line 1

   B. Line 2

   C. Line 3

   D. Line 4

35. Which of the following events was a reason for European nations to finance seagoing expeditions during the age of exploration beginning in the fifteenth century?

   A. Fall of Constantinople

   B. Rise of European nation-states

   C. Discovery of the Americas

   D. Establishment of Macao

36. Which of the following was an impact of the Italian Renaissance?

   A. The rise of city-states and nation-states

   B. The growth in power of the Medici family

   C. The beginning of the Reformation

   D. The rise of the money economy

37. Which of the following is an argument on which the Kentucky and Virginia Resolutions were based?

   A. The right of the Supreme Court to renounce acts of Congress

   B. The right of states to renounce acts of the federal government

   C. The right of the president to renounce rulings of the Supreme Court

   D. The right of Congress to renounce acts of the states

38. Which of the following statements best describes the importance of Pinckney's Treaty, also called the Treaty of San Lorenzo?

   A. It allowed Lewis and Clark to reach the Pacific Ocean.

   B. It laid the groundwork for the United States to purchase Florida from Spain.

   C. It opened up the Mississippi River to American ships.

   D. It ended the Mexican-American War of 1846–1848.

39. Which of the following statements best describes William Penn?

   A. He actively advocated for the end of slavery.

   B. He established relations with the New England Puritans.

   C. He worked tirelessly on the Articles of Confederation.

   D. He made sure Lenape Indians were fairly paid for their lands.

40. An impact of the Battle of New Orleans in 1815 was to ____.

    A. nullify the Treaty of Ghent

    B. enhance the reputation of Andrew Jackson

    C. force Britain to resume its policy of impressments

    D. encourage opposition to the Louisiana Purchase

Use the map shown here to answer the following question.

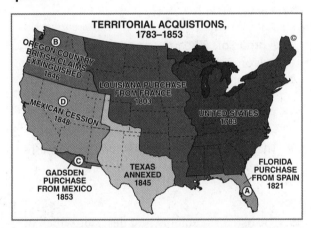

41. Which of the following statements matches a region on the map with an accurate description of how the region became a part of the United States?

    A. Region A: The United States acquired the region during the American Revolutionary War.

    B. Region B: The United States obtained the region in an 1803 treaty with France.

    C. Region C: The United States purchased the region in the Gadsden Purchase of 1853.

    D. Region D: The United States obtained the region from Mexico in the Adams-Onis Treaty of 1819.

42. Which of the following actions resulted in the abolition of slavery in the United States?

    A. Kansas-Nebraska Act of 1854

    B. Ratification of the Thirteenth Amendment in 1865

    C. *Dred Scott* case in 1864–1865

    D. Civil Rights Act of 1866

43. When the Chinese Exclusion Act of 1882 expired, which of the following laws replaced it?

    A. Johnson-Reed Act

    B. Naturalization Act

    C. Anti-Coolie Act

    D. Geary Act

Use the following excerpt to answer the question that comes after it.

Joint Resolution of Congress H.J. RES 1145
August 7, 1964
Resolved by the Senate and House of Representatives of the United States of America in Congress assembled,

   That the Congress approves and supports the determination of the President, as Commander in Chief, to take all necessary measures to repel any armed attack against the forces of the United States and to prevent further aggression.

44. Which of the following statements best describes the effect this joint resolution of Congress had in Southeast Asia?

    A. It gave the president the authority to declare war.

    B. It limited the powers of Congress during times of war.

    C. It authorized the president to use military force.

    D. It limited the power of the president to use U.S. troops overseas.

45. Which of the following statements best describes King Carlos III's decision to build settlements in Alta California?

   A. He was looking for a trade route across the Pacific to China.

   B. He needed Native American laborers to work on the farms.

   C. He was pursuing legendary and fabled lands of mystery and wealth.

   D. He was concerned about Russian seal hunters off the coast.

46. In 1812 the Russian-American Company (RAC) established Fortress Ross north of present-day San Francisco. Which of the following best describes its primary function until 1841?

   A. To serve as a garrison for conflicts with the Tlingit Indians

   B. To supply New Archangel with food supplies

   C. To develop a center for fur trading

   D. To act as a barrier to stop expansion of the Spanish to the south

47. Which of the following statements best describes a result of the Franciscan padres' management of the missions in California until the rancho period?

   A. Native Americans were given land of their own after a set time.

   B. A twenty-second mission was founded and constructed in Santa Rosa.

   C. There was a decline in the Native American population.

   D. The measles epidemic of 1806 decimated the Native American population.

48. Which of the following statements best describes the effect the Compromise of 1850 had on California?

   A. It outlawed slavery in California.

   B. It extended slave territory into southern California.

   C. It regulated the influx of foreigners pouring into California seeking gold.

   D. It allowed California into the union undivided.

Use the following list to answer the question that comes after it.

- A group of 33 heavily armed men took over a Californian Mexican garrison.
- General Mariano Vallejo was taken prisoner and signed a letter of surrender.
- The men included settlers, mountain men, and explorers.
- They invited citizens who wished to establish a "republican government" to join.

49. The listed statements best describe which of the following military actions?

   A. Siege of La Paz

   B. Battle of Churubusco

   C. Battle of Palo Alto

   D. Bear Flag Revolt

50. When many midwestern farmers lost their farms during the dust bowl of the 1930s, they immigrated to California. Which of the following statements best describes the way many Californians felt about them?

    A. They were resented because they added to the number of the unemployed.

    B. They were welcomed because they were willing to work for low wages.

    C. They were viewed as a source of badly needed capital investment.

    D. They were given a warm reception as a new market for local businesses.

Read the following excerpt from the California Food and Agricultural Code, and use it to answer the question that comes after it.

Pursuant to subdivision (d) of Section 821, it is the intent of the Legislature that programs at the University of California designed to promote research on, and facilitate adoption of, sustainable agricultural practices, including, but not limited to, research, teaching, and outreach in the areas of sustainable farming systems, biologically integrated farming systems, organic agriculture, small farms, agro ecology systems, bio intensive integrated pest management, and biological pest control shall be adequately funded through the annual budget process to ensure the programs' ongoing ability to respond to the needs of all sectors of California's agricultural industry.

51. Which of the following groups would benefit the most from this provision of section 821 of the code?

    A. American Federation of Teachers (AFT)

    B. United Farm Workers (UFW)

    C. Floriculture growers

    D. California State Beekeepers Association (CSBA)

Use the following list to answer the question that comes after it.

> ▶ Ranks first by employment in all 50 states
> ▶ Average annual wage in 2001: $53,900
> ▶ More than 2,800 separate establishments
> ▶ Provides hundreds of thousands of indirect and support jobs

52. The statistical data listed best describe which of the following employer categories in California?

    A. Film and moviemaking

    B. Agriculture and farming

    C. Aviation and aerospace

    D. State and local government

Constructed-Response Assignment 1

Read the following passage from *Anne's House of Dreams,* by L. M. Montgomery; then complete the exercise that comes after it.

It was a happy and beautiful bride who came down the old carpeted stairs that September noon—the first bride of Green Gables, slender and shining-eyed, with her arms full of roses. Gilbert, waiting for her in the hall below, looked up at her with adoring eyes. She was his at last, this long-sought Anne, whom he won after years of patient waiting. It was to him she was coming. Was he worthy of her? Could he make her as happy as he hoped? If he failed her—if he could not measure up to her standards . . . But then, their eyes met and all doubt was swept away in a certainty that everything would be wonderful. They belonged to each other; and, no matter what life might hold for them, it could never alter that. Their happiness was in each other's keeping and both were unafraid.

Write a response in which you describe how the author creates a sense of mounting tension followed by resolution in the passage. Be sure to cite specific evidence from the text.

Constructed-Response Sheet—Assignment 1

_____

_____

_____

_____

_____

_____

_____

_____

_____

_____

_____

Constructed-Response Assignment 2

Explain the relationship of phonemic awareness to the process in which a child learns to read, including how a lack of this awareness affects early readers.

Constructed-Response Sheet—Assignment 2

_____

_____

_____

_____

_____

_____

_____

_____

_____

_____

_____

_____

_____

_____

_____

_____

Constructed-Response Assignment 3

Complete the exercise that follows.

In 1954, after nearly 60 years of legally sanctioned racial segregation, the Supreme Court ruled, in *Brown v. Board of Education*, that "separate educational facilities are inherently unequal."

Using your knowledge of U.S. history, prepare a response in which you:

▶ Identify two important effects of the Supreme Court ruling;
▶ Select one of the effects you have identified; and
▶ Explain why that effect has had an impact on American society.

Constructed-Response Sheet—Assignment 3

_____

_____

_____

_____

_____

_____

_____

_____

_____

_____

_____

_____

_____

Constructed-Response Assignment 4

Complete the exercise that follows.

Between 1848 and 1864, about 500,000 people came to California in search of gold.

Using your knowledge of California history, prepare a response in which you:

▶ Identify the social, economic, and cultural effects of this migration;
▶ Select one of the effects you have identified; and
▶ Explain how that effect shaped California history.

Constructed-Response Sheet—Assignment 4

_____

_____

_____

_____

_____

_____

_____

_____

_____

_____

_____

_____

_____

_____

SUBTEST II

SCIENCE, MATHEMATICS

Multiple-Choice Answer Sheet

Science

QUESTION NUMBER	YOUR RESPONSE
1	
2	
3	
4	
5	
6	
7	
8	
9	
10	
11	
12	
13	
14	
15	
16	
17	
18	
19	
20	
21	
22	
23	
24	
25	
26	

Mathematics

QUESTION NUMBER	YOUR RESPONSE
27	
28	
29	
30	
31	
32	
33	
34	
35	
36	
37	
38	
39	
40	
41	
42	
43	
44	
45	
46	
47	
48	
49	
50	
51	
52	

Multiple-Choice Questions

1. In the periodic table, which elements will have the most similar properties?

   A. Elements in the same row

   B. Elements in the same column

   C. Elements with similar prefixes

   D. Elements in the middle three columns

2. Which of the following is the best example of a physical change in matter?

   A. A piece of iron is left outside and rusts over time.

   B. An ice cube placed in a hot cup of tea melts.

   C. A teaspoon of salt is dissolved in a glass of water.

   D. A dozen cookies left in an oven too long burn.

3. Of the isotopes listed, which has the largest number of protons?

   C_6^{14} Li_3^7 Ne_{10}^{16} Mg_{12}^{19}

   A. The carbon isotope

   B. The lithium isotope

   C. The neon isotope

   D. The magnesium isotope

4. Which of the following liquids will have the highest pH?

   A. Water

   B. Vinegar

   C. Tomato juice

   D. Ammonia

5. Newton's first law of motion states that a body at rest will remain at rest and a body in motion will remain in motion unless an outside force acts on it. Which of the following is the best example of this law?

   A. A ball on a perfectly flat surface will stay where it is placed until someone pushes it forward.

   B. If two different balls are placed on a flat surface, the heavier ball requires more force than the lighter ball before it will move.

   C. If two balls are dropped at the same time, a ball dropped from 5 feet above the ground will hit the ground before a ball dropped from 10 feet.

   D. A ball placed on an incline will immediately begin to roll down that incline.

6. Which of the following examples best describes the concept of acceleration?

   A. A vehicle is measured to be traveling at 61.5 miles per hour.

   B. A plane is traveling at a due-north heading and then turns to a due-west heading.

   C. A track runner who is running at 13 mph at the 100-meter mark increases his speed to 20 mph over the next 10 meters.

   D. An object is moving at 4.2 meters per second along a vector in the xy-plane that passes through the point (1, 1).

7. Given the information shown about two elements, which of the following statements most accurately describes a difference between atoms of these elements?

91.22	32.06
Zr	**S**
40	16

   A. A zirconium atom has a total of 40 neutrons and protons in its nucleus, while a sulfur atom has a total of 16.

   B. A zirconium atom has 40 neutrons in its nucleus, while a sulfur atom has 16.

   C. A zirconium atom has 40 protons and 40 electrons, while a sulfur atom has 16 protons and 16 electrons.

   D. A zirconium atom has a total of 40 protons and electrons, while a sulfur atom has a total of 16 protons and electrons.

8. Which of the following is the best example of heat transfer by conduction?

   A. A person uses a heated compress to warm her muscles.

   B. A microwave oven heats a glass of water.

   C. A person holds her hands over a fire to warm them.

   D. A pot of water is boiled on a stovetop.

9. A major role of the endocrine system is to _____.

   A. control organs, control movements, and process sensory information

   B. transport nutrients and oxygen throughout the body

   C. remove excess water, toxins, and other waste from the body

   D. store, produce, and secrete hormones into the bloodstream

10. Biologists have observed a small liparid fish attaching itself to the legs of crabs as a means of transport toward areas with food and possibly to protect itself from predators. This attachment appears to cause no harm to the crabs. This is an example of which type of relationship?

    A. Predation

    B. Parasitism

    C. Mutualism

    D. Commensalism

11. Which organelle in a cell is responsible for the production of adenine triphosphate (ATP)?

    A. Mitochondria

    B. Cell wall

    C. Smooth endoplasmic reticulum

    D. Nucleus

12. In photosynthesis, organisms produce food molecules in the presence of light energy. What is the waste product in this reaction?

    A. Carbon dioxide

    B. ATP

    C. Oxygen

    D. Proteins

13. Which of the following events is part of the metamorphosis stage of a frog's life cycle?

    A. The laying of eggs by a female frog

    B. The hatching of eggs into tadpoles

    C. The development of lungs and legs

    D. The development of terrestrial habitats

14. Which of the following phrases describes primary consumers in an ecosystem?

    A. Mostly herbivores, which subsist on plant life

    B. Mostly plants, which convert sunlight into organic molecules through photosynthesis

    C. Mostly carnivores that feed on herbivores

    D. Mostly carnivores that feed on other carnivores

15. In Central and South America, some species of tropical birds have been found to follow large swarms of army ants as they move through the jungle. Which of the following is most likely to be an advantage of this behavior?

    A. The birds are able to make nests more easily by using the twigs and leaves broken by the swarm of ants.

    B. Any predator of the bird will be attracted to the area in which the birds are located and then likely be eaten by the ants.

    C. Since the ants are marching toward food, the birds can simply follow them instead of searching for food on their own.

    D. The birds can easily feed on insects and small animals that rush away from the ant swarm.

16. Which of the following statements best describes the distribution of biomass in an ecosystem?

    A. Biomass is evenly distributed among the producers, primary consumers, and secondary consumers.

    B. Biomass is most concentrated among the producers, with less biomass for each group following them (primary consumers, secondary consumers, etc.).

    C. Biomass is most concentrated among the consumers, with the producers accounting for the least biomass.

    D. Biomass is most concentrated among the tertiary consumers and the producers.

17. Which of the following phrases best describes igneous rocks?

    A. Rocks that are the result of the cooling of magma

    B. Rocks that are composed of fragments of other eroded rocks

    C. Rocks that were formed from other types of rocks under heat and pressure below the earth's surface

    D. A mixture of rock debris and mineral fragments

18. The primary distinction between minerals and rocks is that ____.

    A. minerals are much older than rocks and were mostly deposited on earth by meteorites

    B. minerals are homogenous, while rocks are made up of possibly many types of minerals

    C. minerals occur only beneath the earth's surface, while rocks occur only on the earth's surface

    D. minerals are made up primarily of eroded rocks and some organic materials

19. Of the following observations, which is commonly recognized as evidence of plate tectonics?

    A. Measurements from the oceans that show the age of the sediment near ridges is much older than the age of sediment near the continents

    B. Fossil records that show clearly distinct species lived on the different continents during the Cretaceous period

    C. The regular intervals in which the earth's magnetic field has changed

    D. Studies of glacial deposits indicating movement of glaciers that would be impossible otherwise

20. In general, which of the following conditions has the greatest influence on the strength of a hurricane?

    A. The amount of sunlight that reaches the area near the hurricane

    B. The part of the world in which the hurricane develops

    C. The temperature of the ocean near the hurricane

    D. The number of hurricanes that have recently developed in the area

21. An anemometer is used to measure _____.

    A. wind speed

    B. humidity

    C. temperature

    D. air pressure

22. If the current time is noon at a location of latitude 42 degrees north and longitude 90 degrees west, then it is also noon at _____.

    A. latitude 90 degrees north, longitude 42 degrees west

    B. latitude 42 degrees north, longitude 65 degrees west

    C. latitude 25 degrees north, longitude 90 degrees west

    D. latitude 42 degrees south, longitude 90 degrees east

23. Most of the time, which planet is closest to Earth, on average?

    A. Venus

    B. Mercury

    C. Mars

    D. The moon

24. Which of the following statements best describes the manner in which comets travel through our solar system?

    A. Comets are on an elliptical orbit around our sun.

    B. Comets follow the same type of orbit as planets in the solar system and are concentrated in a belt between Mars and Jupiter.

    C. Comets follow a straight-line path through our solar system.

    D. Comets follow irregular paths through the solar system, making them difficult to predict.

25. In the diagram shown here, which location or locations on Earth will be experiencing high tide?

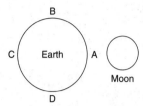

    A. Location A

    B. Locations A and C

    C. Location B

    D. Locations B and D

26. A moderate to large drop in barometric pressure is usually associated with _____.

    A. the approach of a storm system

    B. a period of calm and mostly clear weather

    C. a heat wave

    D. early-morning fog

Use the equation provided to answer the question that follows it.

$$5x - 4(x + 5) = 3x + 1$$

27. Which of the following equations could occur as a step in solving the equation for x?

    A. $4x = -19$

    B. $4x = 6$

    C. $2x = -21$

    D. $2x = 4$

28. The prime factorization for 588 is of the form $a^2 \cdot b \cdot c^2$. What is the product of a, b, and c?

    A. 6

    B. 14

    C. 21

    D. 42

29. Which of the following questions would be answered with the operation $2\frac{1}{2} \times \frac{1}{4}$?

    A. Bob has $2\frac{1}{2}$ pounds of apples. He wants to divide them equally among 4 people. How many pounds of apples should each person get?

    B. A recipe requires $2\frac{1}{2}$ pounds of flour for a large batch of biscuits. Marsha wishes to make four batches of biscuits. How many pounds of flour should she use?

    C. A flight is usually $2\frac{1}{2}$ hours long. A delay causes the flight time to increase by $\frac{1}{4}$ hour. How long will the flight be?

    D. The area of a circle is $2\frac{1}{2}$ square feet. If there are four circles, what is the total area of all the circles?

30. To add the following numbers, Steve first rounds each to the nearest ones digit and then adds the rounded values. By how much will Steve's result differ from the actual sum?

   100.2

   257.8

   302.5

   46.9

   18.0

   A. 0.6

   B. 0.8

   C. 2

   D. 3

31. Which of the following numbers is larger than 1.2×10^{-8}?

   A. 1.2×10^{-9}

   B. 3.2×10^{-9}

   C. 4.1×10^{-6}

   D. 5.0×10^{-10}

32. In a group of 1,200 people, 5% are evenly divided among those with one to two years' experience in a full-time job, those with less than one year's experience in a full-time job, and those with no experience in a full-time job. How many of the 1,200 have no experience in a full-time job?

   A. 3

   B. 10

   C. 20

   D. 60

33. If the rectangle shown here represents one unit, then which of the following fractions is equivalent to the fraction of the rectangle that is shaded?

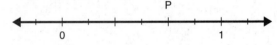

   A. $\dfrac{24}{60}$

   B. $\dfrac{1}{2}$

   C. $\dfrac{32}{48}$

   D. $\dfrac{2}{3}$

34. On the number line shown here, which of the following numbers would be located to the right of the point P?

   A. $\dfrac{152}{301}$

   B. $\dfrac{19}{187}$

   C. $\dfrac{185}{291}$

   D. $\dfrac{110}{163}$

35. A recipe for 30 chocolate cookies requires 2 cups of white sugar and $\frac{1}{2}$ cup of butter. To make a larger batch of cookies, Josephine adjusted the recipe and used 9 cups of sugar. How many cups of butter should she use?

A. $2\frac{1}{2}$ cups

B. $2\frac{1}{4}$ cups

C. $3\frac{1}{2}$ cups

D. $7\frac{1}{2}$ cups

36. In the following division problem, what is the value of X?

$$
\begin{array}{r}
2\ 1\ X \\
8\ \overline{)\ 1\ \square\ 0\ \square} \\
\underline{1\ 6} \\
1\ 0 \\
\underline{8} \\
2\ 4 \\
\underline{2\ 4} \\
0
\end{array}
$$

A. 0

B. 3

C. 4

D. 7

37. In the diagram shown here, triangle ABC is similar to triangle DEF. What is the approximate length of side DF?

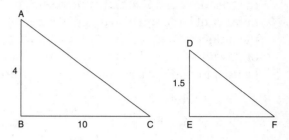

A. 3.75

B. 4.04

C. 12.50

D. 16.31

38. The algebraic expression $-4(x+2)-5x$ is equivalent to _____.

A. $-x-8$

B. $-x+2$

C. $-9x-8$

D. $-9x+2$

39. The data in the following table most likely represent a _____.

x	y
–2	–8
–1	–5
0	–4
1	–5
2	–8

A. linear function with a positive slope

B. linear function with a negative slope

C. quadratic function with a graph that opens down

D. quadratic function with a graph that opens up

40. To raise money for a charity, Bob and Joe sell two sizes of T-shirts: $10.50 for large and $12.50 for extra-large. After selling 150 shirts, the friends raised $1,625. If x represents the number of large shirts sold and y represents the number of extra-large shirts sold, which of the following systems of equations could be used to find the price of each size of shirt?

A. $x + y = 150$
   $x + y = 1{,}625$

B. $10.5x + 12.5y = 150$
   $x + y = 1{,}625$

C. $x + y = 150$
   $10.5x + 12.5y = 1{,}625$

D. $10.5x + 12.5y = 150$
   $10.5x + 12.5y = 1{,}625$

41. Which of the following graphs represents a linear equation with a positive slope?

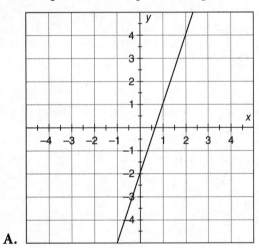

A.

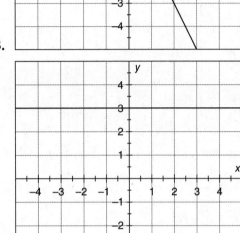

B.

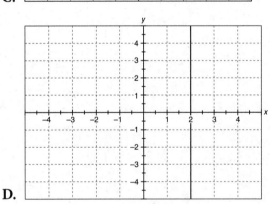

C.

D.

42. Triangle *ABC* is a right triangle, and angle *B* is 15 degrees. If angle *C* is the right angle, what is the measure of angle *A*?

    A. 90 degrees

    B. 75 degrees

    C. 60 degrees

    D. 30 degrees

43. The points (1, 2) and (4, 5) lie on line *L*. Line *M* is parallel to line *L*, and the point (2, 5) lies on it. Which of the following points would also lie on line *M*?

    A. (5, 8)

    B. (4, 5)

    C. (8, 5)

    D. (5, 4)

44. The scale on a map is 1 inch = 25 miles. On the same map, Springfield is 6 inches from Lawson. If Fairfield Beach is half the distance from Springfield that Lawson is, how long will it take to drive from Springfield to Fairfield Beach traveling at 55 mph, on average?

    A. 1 hour 22 minutes

    B. 1 hour 36 minutes

    C. 2 hours 44 minutes

    D. 3 hours 12 minutes

45. The volume of a cube is 27 cu. ft. If four cubes are places together in the shape of a square, as shown in the figure, what is the area of the square that is formed?

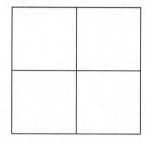

    A. 36 sq. ft.

    B. 81 sq. ft.

    C. 144 sq. ft.

    D. 324 sq. ft.

46. A phone company charges a flat fee of $18 a month for its most basic service plan. Under this plan, long-distance calls are charged at 33 cents per minute. Which of the following expressions best represents the charge for someone who used *n* long-distance minutes?

    A. $18n + 0.33$

    B. $(18 + 0.33)n$

    C. $18 + 0.33n$

    D. $18 + 0.33 + n$

47. What is the median of the following set of numbers?

    0, 1, 1, 1, 1, 2, 3, 6, 8, 9

    A. 1

    B. 1.5

    C. 2

    D. 3.2

48. If the probability of an event A is 26%, then the probability of the event's complement must be ____.

    A. 6.8%

    B. 26%

    C. 52%

    D. 74%

49. Which of the following statements best describes two mutually exclusive events?

    A. The fact that one of the events has occurred has no effect on the probability the other event will occur.

    B. The events cannot happen at the same time.

    C. Together, both events represent the entire sample space.

    D. Both events have multiple outcomes in common.

50. Which of the following statements best describes the role of randomness in selecting a sample from a population?

    A. Randomness is used to reduce bias by making it equally likely to pick any individual from the population.

    B. Using randomness, we are able to prevent selecting the same individual more than once for our sample.

    C. Randomness helps us recognize important patterns in the population that we would want to include in our sample.

    D. Randomness is used so that individuals in the sample will not know they were selected for the sample, thus reducing bias.

51. In some countries, a "stone" is used as a measurement of weight. Two men, one of which weighs twice what the other man weighs, weigh a total of 30 stone. If the lighter man weighs 140 pounds, how many pounds is 1 stone?

    A. 5

    B. 9

    C. 10

    D. 14

52. A right triangle has legs of lengths $5x$ and 2. Which of the following expressions represents the length of the hypotenuse in terms of x?

    A. $\sqrt{4 + (5x)^2}$

    B. $(2 + 5x)^2$

    C. $x\sqrt{7}$

    D. $49x$

Constructed-Response Assignment 1

Complete the following exercise.

A chemist needs to dilute 100 milliliters of a 10-molar salt solution before mixing it with 40 milliliters of a 5-molar sugar solution.

Using your knowledge of chemistry:

▶ Determine how many milliliters of water the chemist needs to add to the salt solution to dilute it to a concentration of 2 molar.
▶ If she adds 80 milliliters of the diluted salt solution to all of the sugar solution, what is the final concentration of the two together?
▶ If she heats the solution until all of the water boils away, how many moles of sugar and salt are left in the bottom of the beaker?

Constructed-Response Sheet—Assignment 1

_____

_____

_____

_____

_____

_____

_____

_____

_____

_____

_____

_____

_____

Constructed-Response Assignment 2

Complete the following exercise.

Two years ago, you conducted field observations of a newly discovered insect species in a secluded cave habitat. While you didn't directly observe the insects eating anything, you found several centipede exoskeletons in the moist, sandy areas where the insects make their nests. The centipedes mostly eat cave crickets. Although you spied several cave crickets eating fungus and a dead rat, you didn't notice any of the novel insects doing the same.

When you return to the cave two years later, you discover that it has been colonized by a shrew-like mammal. You see only a few individuals from the novel insect species that you studied during your previous trip. And you find several mammal nests in the moist, sandy areas where you previously saw the novel insect. You observe several members of the new mammal species eating fungus, but there is no evidence to suggest that it eats anything else.

Using your knowledge of ecology:

▶ Describe the trophic levels occupied by each of the organisms mentioned, including the trophic level that the novel insect species most likely occupied before the shrew-like mammal arrived.
▶ If the shrew-like mammal is not eating the novel insect species, provide an alternative hypothesis to explain how the mammal's arrival in the cave coincided with the insect population's decline.

Constructed-Response Sheet—Assignment 2

_____
_____
_____
_____
_____
_____
_____
_____

Constructed-Response Assignment 3

Use the diagram shown here to complete the following exercise.

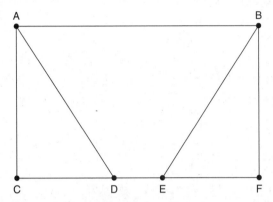

In the rectangle *ABFC*, side *AC* has length *x*, while side *CF* has length *y*. Triangles *ACD* and *BEF* are of the same size, and the leg *CD* has a length of 2.

Use your knowledge of algebra and geometry to:

▶ Express the area of triangle *ACD* in terms of *x* and *y*.
▶ Express the area of trapezoid *ABED* in terms of *x* and *y*.
▶ Express the perimeter of trapezoid *ABED* in terms of *x* and *y*.

Constructed-Response Sheet—Assignment 3

_____

_____

_____

_____

_____

_____

_____

_____

Constructed-Response Assignment 4

Complete the following exercise.

Consider the quadratic equation $x^2 - 5x - 14 = 0$.

Use your knowledge of algebra to:

▶ Find two different methods to solve the equation.
▶ Explain what the solutions represent in the graph of the equation.

Constructed-Response Sheet—Assignment 4

_____

_____

_____

_____

_____

_____

_____

_____

_____

_____

_____

_____

_____

_____

_____

SUBTEST III

PHYSICAL EDUCATION, HUMAN DEVELOPMENT, AND VISUAL AND PERFORMING ARTS

Multiple-Choice Answer Sheet

Physical Education		Human Development		Visual and Performing Arts	
QUESTION NUMBER	YOUR RESPONSE	QUESTION NUMBER	YOUR RESPONSE	QUESTION NUMBER	YOUR RESPONSE
1		14		27	
2		15		28	
3		16		29	
4		17		30	
5		18		31	
6		19		32	
7		20		33	
8		21		34	
9		22		35	
10		23		36	
11		24		37	
12		25		38	
13		26		39	

Multiple-Choice Questions

1. Which of the following is an example of a low-space activity?

   A. Hula hooping

   B. Doing seated hamstring stretches

   C. Playing volleyball

   D. Running relay races

2. A class of students practices bouncing, throwing, kicking, and hitting balls with a bat. Which types of skills are these?

   A. Competitive

   B. Locomotor

   C. Manipulative

   D. Nonlocomotor

3. Which of the following is NOT true about alcohol?

   A. Alcohol is the most lethal and most abused drug today.

   B. Approximately 25 percent of traffic deaths are alcohol related.

   C. The human nervous system can be disabled by alcohol use.

   D. Many health problems leading to premature death are caused by alcohol.

4. A physical education teacher asks the students what they are interested in learning during class, and then she plans her instruction around the students' input. Which approach is she using?

   A. Self-actualization approach

   B. Curriculum-based approach

   C. Social responsibility approach

   D. Ecological integration approach

5. Students in an elementary-school physical education class are instructed to walk laps around the field for 25 minutes. Which component of the FITT guidelines should be altered in order to make the activity more appropriate?

   A. Frequency

   B. Intensity

   C. Time

   D. Type

6. Which skill will a child most likely develop after learning to gallop?

   A. Jumping

   B. Leaping

   C. Running

   D. Skipping

7. During a physical education class period, second-grade students performed calisthenics, received step-by-step instruction on basketball dribbling and passing, and then rotated through three noncompetitive activity stations. Which of the following activities should the students participate in next?

   A. Soccer game

   B. Timed sprints

   C. Light walking

   D. Return to class

8. Students are instructed to bend their arm and then use a strong movement to connect with an object. Which skill is being practiced?

   A. Throwing

   B. Striking

   C. Pushing

   D. Pulling

9. Which is a benefit of cardiovascular fitness?

   A. Increased heart rate

   B. Lower LDL cholesterol levels

   C. Lower HDL cholesterol levels

   D. Eliminated risk of heart attack

10. Which of the following does NOT describe the order in which children develop motor skills?

    A. From the head to the toes

    B. From the waist to the extremities

    C. From the gross-motor to the fine-motor areas

    D. From the dominant to the nondominant side

11. What is the main objective of the fitness approach to physical education?

    A. Build muscle strength

    B. Increase physical endurance

    C. Encourage participation in sports

    D. Improve cardiovascular performance

12. Polymetric exercise refers to _____.

    A. an activity that involves lengthening a muscle and then immediately shortening the same muscle

    B. activities that are considered to be of moderate intensity and require sustained rhythmic movements

    C. light to moderate movements, performed for 5 to 10 minutes, to help the body recover from more-intense exercise

    D. strenuous movements performed for a short duration, which are intended to increase muscle mass and improve the ability to move quickly

13. Which would be an effective sports adaptation for students who have special needs?

    A. Use a longer racket when playing tennis.

    B. Increase the playing area of a soccer field.

    C. Allow two hands for dribbling a basketball.

    D. Use a smaller ball when playing volleyball.

14. A student becomes anxious about losing his library book. This feeling of irresponsibility is an indication that the student has entered which of Erikson's stages of psychosocial development?

    A. Identity versus identity confusion

    B. Identity versus inferiority

    C. Initiative versus guilt

    D. Intimacy versus isolation

15. Which of the following is a true statement about modern families?

   A. Approximately 50 percent of children now live in single-parent homes.

   B. Approximately 15 percent of children currently live with a stepparent.

   C. More than 90 percent of women who have children are in the paid workforce.

   D. Less than 10 percent of children have a stay-at-home mother and a working father.

16. A teacher is planning activities for a group of students who have learning disabilities. Which of the following strategies would NOT be effective in lessons for these students?

   A. Offer brief but highly structured assignments.

   B. Include experiences that involve manipulative materials.

   C. Present repeated opportunities that include auditory learning.

   D. Provide materials that have a reading level one year below grade level.

17. In what ways should instruction be differentiated for students coming from various socioeconomic backgrounds?

   A. Less structure should be provided for low-SES students.

   B. Competitiveness should be minimized for high-SES students.

   C. Teacher expectations should be lowered for low-SES students.

   D. A decreased amount of material should be presented to high-SES students.

18. A teacher uses Skinner's extinction approach to operant conditioning as a part of his behavior plan. According to this approach, the students _____.

   A. are punished for undesired behaviors

   B. are rewarded for repeating desired behaviors

   C. escape punishment by repeating desired behaviors

   D. are not reinforced for exhibiting undesired behaviors

19. Which accurately describes changes or differences that are present during the middle childhood years?

   A. Children grow about three inches annually until they reach 11 years old.

   B. The leg and arm strength of boys and girls is comparable at this age.

   C. Girls display more highly developed fine-motor skills than boys.

   D. Children lose most of their baby fat during these years.

20. Which of the following actions is NOT a characteristic of functional play?

   A. Repeated, or practiced, behaviors

   B. Repetitive muscular movements

   C. Sensorimotor movements to manipulate objects

   D. Sensorimotor movements used to create something

21. A teacher notices that one of her students has been losing weight and consistently arrives at school with strong body odor. These factors could be a sign of _____.

    A. emotional maltreatment

    B. physical neglect

    C. physical abuse

    D. sexual abuse

22. All of the following are effective strategies for promoting positive self-image EXCEPT _____.

    A. setting exceptionally challenging goals for personal fitness

    B. developing stronger communication and cooperation skills

    C. working with a group of peers to make decisions

    D. demonstrating traits of positive sportsmanship

23. A student demonstrates egocentric thinking and has difficulty with conservation-of-number tasks. In which of Piaget's stages of cognitive development is the child operating?

    A. Concrete operational

    B. Formal operational

    C. Preoperational

    D. Sensorimotor

24. During which of Kohlberg's stages of moral development do students comply with rules as a result of the consequences?

    A. Conventional morality

    B. Law-and-order morality

    C. Preconventional morality

    D. Postconventional morality

25. Which is an accurate statement about prenatal influences on the development of an unborn child?

    A. The mother's drug use during pregnancy use can lead to neurological problems, learning disabilities, and impaired motor development.

    B. Older mothers face a greater risk of birth complication, while adolescent mothers face the least risk of complications.

    C. Environmental factors have the greatest impact on the child's development between 8 and 12 weeks gestation.

    D. Alcohol use by pregnant mothers can cause mental retardation and respiratory problems in the child.

26. A child took a jump rope from a classmate on the playground. Soon it began to rain, and the students had to go inside. The child believed that taking the jump rope caused the rain. This is an example of _____.

    A. hypothetical-deductive reasoning

    B. transductive reasoning

    C. transitive inference

    D. metacognition

27. A painting is created using shades of blue. Which statement is true about the piece?

    A. The colors create a cold mood and appear to contract the size of the piece.

    B. The colors create a cold mood and appear to expand the size of the piece.

    C. The colors create a warm mood and appear to contract the size of the piece.

    D. The colors create a warm mood and appear to expand the size of the piece.

28. Which of the following is NOT a property of color?

    A. Hue

    B. Pigment

    C. Saturation

    D. Value

29. The two-step and grapevine are examples of which element of dance?

    A. Space

    B. Time

    C. Levels

    D. Force

30. In a symphony orchestra, which instruments are directly in front of the conductor, closest to where he or she is standing?

    A. Cellos

    B. Flutes

    C. Oboes

    D. Violas

31. During the eighteenth and nineteenth centuries, _____.

    A. dances were in circle form

    B. folk dances grew from earlier ritual dances

    C. many dances were formal and lacked spontaneity

    D. the emphasis of dance was on fantasy and emotion

32. Which technique can raise the value of a color?

    A. Adding a dark color

    B. Adding white

    C. Adding a primary color

    D. Adding a secondary color

33. In an orchestra, which instrument is NOT considered part of the string section?

    A. Bass

    B. Cello

    C. Harp

    D. Viola

34. Processing, analyzing, and responding to sensory information by using language skills unique to music, theater, dance, and visual arts is _____.

    A. artistic perception

    B. creative expression

    C. aesthetic valuing

    D. art appreciation

35. In dance, an axial movement _____.

    A. is a type of dance movement that is spontaneous

    B. is a nonlocomotor movement performed around a fixed body part

    C. refers to a movement that occurs while the body is aligned with the base

    D. refers to part of a sequence that is performed first forward and then in reverse

36. A word that could be used to describe the timbre of a piece of music is _____.

    A. adagio

    B. bright

    C. forte

    D. motif

37. Which phrase best describes the characteristics of music during the baroque period?

    A. Homophony and simple texture

    B. Ornate style and the use of counterpoint

    C. Use of the lute and introduction of the clavichord

    D. Introduction of sonatas, symphonies, and dissonance

38. Which type of dance is often taught to primary-school children?

    A. Folk dance

    B. Social dance

    C. Cultural dance

    D. Modern dance

39. Which characteristic creates a feeling of informality in a painting?

    A. Asymmetry

    B. Balance

    C. Proportion

    D. Unity

Constructed-Response Assignment 1

Complete the exercise that follows.

A physical educator is preparing a lesson to teach object manipulation skills to primary-grade students.

Using your knowledge of movement skills:

▶ List and define two examples of object manipulation skills, and explain how these skills could be taught to the targeted students; and

▶ Discuss why these activities are important precursors to later development of object manipulation skill

Constructed-Response Sheet—Assignment 1

_____

_____

_____

_____

_____

_____

_____

_____

_____

_____

_____

Constructed-Response Assignment 2

Complete the exercise that follows.

Physical education activities must be adapted to meet the needs of students with disabilities.

Using your knowledge of human development:

▶ Discuss the components that should be included in planning an adapted physical education program; and

▶ Suggest adaptations that could be made to a traditional team sport in order to include students with special needs.

Constructed-Response Sheet—Assignment 2

_____

_____

_____

_____

_____

_____

_____

_____

_____

_____

_____

_____

_____

Constructed-Response Assignment 3

Complete the exercise that follows.

The role of electronic technology in visual and performing arts instruction is increasing in importance.

Using your knowledge of visual and performing arts:

▶ Briefly explain reasons why technology is important to visual and performing arts; and

▶ Give examples of how electronic technology can be integrated into visual and performing arts instruction in elementary, middle, and high school classrooms.

Constructed-Response Sheet—Assignment 3

_____

_____

_____

_____

_____

_____

_____

_____

_____

_____

_____

_____

_____

_____

CHAPTER 10

Practice Test 1 Results

Domain Answer Sheets

As with the diagnostic test, on the following pages you'll find Domain Answer Sheets that will help you evaluate your answers. The first two columns show the correct answer for each question. Use the other two columns to indicate whether you answered a specific question correctly. After the columns, there is a space where you can enter the total number of questions you answered correctly for that particular domain. After the Domain Answer Sheets, you'll have the chance to look over explanations for each question, which will help clarify which topics you've mastered and those you may need to review more.

SUBTEST I:
DOMAIN ANSWER SHEET

READING, LANGUAGE, AND LITERATURE

QUESTION NUMBER	CORRECT ANSWER	YOUR ANSWER Correct?	YOUR ANSWER Incorrect?
1	A		
2	B		
3	A		
4	B		
5	B		
6	D		
7	C		
8	D		
9	D		
10	B		
11	B		
12	A		
13	B		
14	B		
15	C		
16	C		
17	B		
18	D		
19	C		
20	A		
21	B		
22	A		
23	D		
24	D		
25	B		
26	D		

You answered _____ out of 26 questions correctly.

SUBTEST I:
DOMAIN ANSWER SHEET

HISTORY AND SOCIAL SCIENCE

QUESTION NUMBER	CORRECT ANSWER	YOUR ANSWER Correct?	YOUR ANSWER Incorrect?
27	C		
28	D		
29	D		
30	C		
31	A		
32	C		
33	A		
34	C		
35	A		
36	C		
37	B		
38	C		
39	D		
40	B		
41	C		
42	B		
43	D		
44	C		
45	D		
46	B		
47	C		
48	D		
49	D		
50	A		
51	D		
52	C		

You answered _____ out of 26 questions correctly.

SUBTEST II:
DOMAIN ANSWER SHEET
SCIENCE

QUESTION NUMBER	CORRECT ANSWER	YOUR ANSWER Correct?	YOUR ANSWER Incorrect?
1	B		
2	B		
3	D		
4	D		
5	A		
6	C		
7	C		
8	A		
9	D		
10	D		
11	A		
12	C		
13	C		
14	A		
15	D		
16	B		
17	A		
18	B		
19	D		
20	C		
21	A		
22	C		
23	A		
24	A		
25	B		
26	A		

You answered _____ out of 26 questions correctly.

SUBTEST II:
DOMAIN ANSWER SHEET
MATHEMATICS

QUESTION NUMBER	CORRECT ANSWER	YOUR ANSWER Correct?	YOUR ANSWER Incorrect?
27	C		
28	D		
29	A		
30	A		
31	C		
32	C		
33	A		
34	D		
35	B		
36	B		
37	B		
38	C		
39	C		
40	C		
41	A		
42	B		
43	A		
44	A		
45	A		
46	C		
47	B		
48	D		
49	B		
50	A		
51	D		
52	A		

You answered _____ out of 26 questions correctly.

SUBTEST III:
DOMAIN ANSWER SHEET
PHYSICAL EDUCATION

QUESTION NUMBER	CORRECT ANSWER	YOUR ANSWER	
		Correct?	Incorrect?
1	B		
2	C		
3	B		
4	A		
5	B		
6	D		
7	C		
8	B		
9	B		
10	D		
11	D		
12	A		
13	C		

You answered ＿＿ out of 13 questions correctly.

SUBTEST III:
DOMAIN ANSWER SHEET
HUMAN DEVELOPMENT

QUESTION NUMBER	CORRECT ANSWER	YOUR ANSWER	
		Correct?	Incorrect?
14	C		
15	D		
16	D		
17	B		
18	D		
19	C		
20	D		
21	B		
22	A		
23	C		
24	C		
25	A		
26	B		

You answered ＿＿ out of 13 questions correctly.

SUBTEST III:
DOMAIN ANSWER SHEET

VISUAL AND
PERFORMING ARTS

QUESTION NUMBER	CORRECT ANSWER	YOUR ANSWER	
		Correct?	Incorrect?
27	A		
28	B		
29	A		
30	D		
31	D		
32	B		
33	C		
34	A		
35	B		
36	B		
37	B		
38	A		
39	A		

You answered _____ out of 13 questions correctly.

Subtest I Explanations

READING, LANGUAGE, AND LITERATURE; HISTORY AND SOCIAL SCIENCE

1. A The *ai* vowel pattern is associated with the long-*a* sound in words such as *pain, rain,* and *train*. Studies have shown there are very few exceptions to this rule (notably, *said*). Choices B, C, and D are associated with multiple pronunciations: the *ea* in *fead* is found in *lead, read,* and *beam*; the *ou* in *lough* is found in *ought, rough,* and *through*; the *oo* in *sloot* is found in *hoop, look,* and *proof.*

2. B While this may not always be completely true, this is the usual linguistic development during this period. Choice A is associated with the period of one to two years. Choice C does not occur until seven years and later. Choice D is associated with ages 18 months to 30 months.

3. A This is the first strategy a child learns in order to begin to read and is the easiest to learn. Choices B, C, and D would come much later.

4. B This is the reason children have difficulty learning to read. They must first recognize phonemes and morphemes. Choice A is not correct because in English, the same letter can have different sounds (for example, the letters *c* and *y*). Nor is choice C correct. Research has found that choice D is not the reason most children have difficulty reading.

5. B Rhyming helps a child recognize similar sounds and develops phonemic awareness. It does not help develop a large oral vocabulary. Talking to adults would improve that. It does not help a child sound out words or identify the syllables of spoken words, so choices C and D are incorrect.

6. D This is how an extensive oral vocabulary contributes to a reader's decoding skills. Knowing more words allows the child to recognize a word after sounding it out. Choice A does not explain why a large oral vocabulary is important. An oral vocabulary certainly does not help with using syntactic clues to determine the meaning of unfamiliar words (choice B) or with relating an unfamiliar

word to known words with similar spellings (choice C).

7. C During the phonetic stage of spelling, a child begins to understand how to represent letters or groups of letters, such as writing *dun* for *done* or *kom* for *come*. Choice A occurs during the semiphonetic stage. Choice B occurs in the transitional stage. Choice D occurs during the correct stage.

8. D Choice D describes the way in which all languages are similar. Choice A is not correct, since not all languages form a plural by adding the letter *s*. Choice B is incorrect because languages have different and arbitrary phonemes and morphemes. Choice C is incorrect because all languages have different social conventions.

9. D Previewing and summarizing new nonfiction writing is the most effective way to develop comprehension, since it draws attention to the main idea and supporting details. Choice A would not yield greater comprehension and could be confusing. Choice B is useful for breaking down information, but not necessarily comprehending it. Choice C would allow a student to remember details but would not improve comprehension.

10. B The word *illusion* means a false perception of reality. The word *allusion* means an indirect reference. Choice B is the only sentence that is correct; it uses the word *illusion* correctly. The other choices confuse the words *allusion* and *illusion.*

11. B Choice B is the only sentence to contain a relative clause, "that Lily took of the campus." Choice A has only a main clause; it is a simple sentence with a compound predicate. Choices C and D are complex sentences that contain a main clause and a subordinate clause.

12. B Choice B creates a logical flow of ideas in the passage. The other choices would not make sense.

13. **B** Choice B changes the verb from the passive to the active and also uses more succinct language to express the meaning of the sentence. Choice A is written in an awkward manner. Choice C changes the verb to a passive form and is overly wordy. Choice D is wordy and not as direct as the original sentence 7.

14. **B** This choice is the best topic sentence. It is what the passage is mostly about. Sentence 1 (choice A) gives a detail about the history of the banana plant. Choice C relates more information about the main idea. Choice D also gives supporting information about the main topic.

15. **C** An appeal to the reader would most likely come at the end of a persuasive essay. Choice A would most likely come at the beginning of the essay. Choices B and D would most likely be found in the middle of the essay.

16. **C** Pausing after an important point allows listeners to think about what was just said and realize that it is important. Pausing does not convey a feeling of excitement (choice A), nor does it act as a chance for poor listeners to catch up (choice B). Choice D is not correct either because it implies that you have made them uneasy to the point of holding their breath, which is usually not a tactic employed in an oral presentation.

17. **B** Variation in rate, pitch, and rhythm is most likely to increase the presentation's emotional effect, since it provides the audience with some variety of tone. It will not, however, make the presentation seem more substantial (choice A). It will not allow the audience to participate (choice C), nor will it allow choice D to occur.

18. **D** Sentence 6 most strongly suggests that the intent of the letter is persuasive, since it reveals the author's opinion of dumping electronic equipment in a landfill. Sentence 2 gives background information, so choice A is not correct. Choices B and C give information about what is happening to electronic equipment but do not convey a sense of persuasion.

19. **C** Choice C is the best research question, since it would yield the kinds of chemicals that are released and tell their toxicity.

Choice A would yield interesting information, but it is not the best research question to address the issue. Choice B would be a good addition to an objective study of the issue but would not yield the most important information. Choice D is not vital to the issue.

20. **A** Choice A is what a satire generally includes. It is a piece that uses humor to expose a situation or person; although it is not directly critical, it is inherently critical. Choice B would apply to a romance. Choice C would be consistent with a mythological passage. Choice D is a component of fairy tales or fables.

21. **B** Creation is a major theme in myths, including this one. Choice A might be true, but there are many other forms of fiction that use animals as characters. Choice C is incorrect; myths do not necessarily include dialogue. There could also be a strong plot in a myth, as there is in this one.

22. **A** This is the style element that is most like a myth. Using many characters is not typical of a myth, nor is talking about animals. Choice D is incorrect because fables, not myths, contain morals.

23. **D** All of the images stress the joy the poet feels toward her mother and the way that she helped her fall asleep. Choice A is not suggested by the poem; there is no sense of anger. Choice B is not correct; the poet is not ambivalent. There is also no sense of anxiety on the part of the poet (choice C).

24. **D** Choice D represents the theme that the two stanzas support. There is nothing in the stanzas to indicate that choice A is correct. Choice B may be true, but it is not the theme supported by the two stanzas. Choice C is incorrect also because, though sleeping is mentioned, there is no mention in the poem of sleeping in adulthood.

25. **B** The hats are symbols of the people who are wearing them. The poem likens the hats to bees, but the hats are not symbols of them. Nor are the hats symbols of hopes or ideas.

26. **D** The last line of the poem suggests this is what the poet thinks. There is no basis for choices A, B, and C.

27. **C** From the age of 29 in 771, when his brother Carloman died and he became ruler

of the Frankish domains, Charlemagne made many annexations through military victories. In 800 he was crowned emperor of the Holy Roman Empire. He is known for his educational reforms. Aachen, the capital, became a center of learning and art. Caesar's empire (choice A) was much larger at its height. Alexander the Great (choice B) did not annex present-day Italy in his empire. The empire of Genghis Khan (choice D) was in Asia.

28. **D** A basis of Taoism is the concept of yin and yang, light and dark, masculine and feminine, a unity from which all existence comes into being. Choice A is incorrect because correct social relationship is a foundation of the philosophy of Confucius. Mindfulness is a tenet of Buddhism, so choice B is incorrect. Hinduism (choice C) revolves around the caste system and the possibility of being reborn into a higher caste.

29. **D** The threat of excommunication stifled any opposition; it meant that a person could no longer attend church services and would not have a place in heaven. Contrary to choice A, the Catholic Church accepted all sorts of gifts and favors from those who wanted to be assured of going to heaven. The church did not tolerate any other sect and viewed them as heretics; hence choice B is wrong. The Middle Ages were a time of constant conflict between secular laws and the laws of the pope, making choice C incorrect.

30. **C** For centuries, Euclid's 13-volume work *Elements* has been an introduction for high school students to plane geometry and algebraic geometry. Aristotle's work *Physics* (choice A) is a treatise on logic and not the basis for high school math. Zeno laid out his doctrine of multiplicity in *Parmenides* (choice B). And Plato defined his theory of forms in *Phaedo* (choice D).

31. **A** Augustus Caesar, who ruled from 27 BCE until 14 CE, was Rome's first emperor. He strengthened the army and expanded the empire enormously, building a network of roads and collecting taxes. He rebuilt much of Rome; he was also friend to poets, scholars, and artists. Contrary to choice B, Cicero (106–43 BCE) was not a ruler, but a philosopher, orator, and statesman. Choice

C is incorrect because Julius Caesar, the last ruler of the Roman Republic, was assassinated in 44 BCE, after which Rome fell into civil strife. Constantine I (choice D), who ruled from 306 to 337 CE, was the founder of the Eastern Roman Empire, building a palace at Byzantium, naming it Constantinople. He was the first emperor to convert to Christianity.

32. **C** Signed in 1215, the Magna Carta was an agreement between King John and English barons to protect feudal rights. It inspired numerous future documents, including the U.S. Constitution. The Mayflower Compact (choice A) was the first document about governing the new colony at Plymouth when the ship *Mayflower* landed in Massachusetts in 1620. Choice B is incorrect, since the Augsburg Confession was written in 1530 by Martin Luther; it was a manifesto of the Protestant religion. Choice D is not correct because the Babylonian king Hammurabi's Code of Laws promised to treat conquered peoples justly and to honor their gods.

33. **A** The defeat of the Ottoman Empire at the Battle of Vienna in 1683 at the hands of the armies of the Holy Roman Empire and the Polish-Lithuanian Commonwealth marked a turning point in the 300-year conflict between the Ottomans and the Hapsburgs. The Congress of Paris (choice B) in 1856 after the end of the Crimean War maintained the integrity of the Ottoman Empire. Sharia (choice C) is the religious law of Islam, following principles set forth in the Qur'an. The Ottomans defeated Hungary at the Battle of Varna (choice D) in 1444.

34. **C** The Bronze Age was noted for the beginning of writing in Egypt and the Near East, as well as for the use of bronze and copper to make tools and weapons. During the Iron Age (choice A), implements were hammered into shape, rather than being cast, as they were in the Bronze Age. Choice B is incorrect because during Paleolithic times, stone tools and weapons were used. The Neolithic age (choice D) is noted for the development of farming in the Fertile Crescent.

35. **A** The fall of Constantinople to the Ottoman Empire in 1453 closed the trade routes to

Asia, North Africa, and the Red Sea, so Europeans were forced to look for other trade routes. Choice B is not correct, since the rise of European nation-states occurred at the same time as the age of exploration began. Choice C, the discovery of the Americas, did not occur until the end of the fifteenth century. Choice D is incorrect, since the establishment of Macao by the Portuguese—the first European colony in China—occurred in 1557, after the age of exploration had begun.

36. **C** The Reformation (Protestantism) could not have happened without the spirit of intellect and humanism fostered by the Italian Renaissance. Choice A is wrong, since city-states and nation-states prospered at the same time as the Italian Renaissance and grew as a result of the decline in power of the Catholic Church. The Medicis (choice B) invested their wealth in art and architecture and were a part of, but not an impact on, the Italian Renaissance. The money economy (choice D) grew as a result of the decline of agrarian and feudal societies and the growth of cities.

37. **B** Written by Thomas Jefferson and James Monroe, the Kentucky and Virginia Resolutions were passed by the two states in 1798 and 1799 in response to the Alien and Sedition Acts, declaring them unconstitutional and arguing for states' rights. The resolutions were very controversial; no other state accepted the Kentucky and Virginia Resolutions. The Supreme Court did not rule that the acts contradicted the constitution. President Adams signed the acts, which were passed into law by Congress.

38. **C** Pinckney's Treaty played a large role in the expansion of a young nation, opening up the Mississippi River to American navigation and allowing western settlers to conduct transactions in New Orleans. The Lewis and Clark expedition (choice A) of 1804 to 1806 opened up territory from the recently completed Louisiana Purchase. Choice B is not correct because the Adams-Onis Treaty of 1819 approved the purchase of Florida from Spain and set a boundary with New Spain, now Mexico. The Treaty of Guadalupe

Hidalgo (choice D) in 1848 ended the Mexican-American War.

39. **D** Penn befriended local Indians, learned their dialects, and paid for their land instead of taking it as other colonists did. Although Quakers would eventually come out against slavery, Penn did not; in fact, he owned and traded slaves, so choice A is incorrect. Contrary to choice B, Puritans were just as negative toward Quakers as the English were. While many of the ideas in the Articles of Confederation were similar to those of William Penn, the articles were drafted in Philadelphia in 1776–1777, long after Penn had died in 1718, which makes choice C incorrect.

40. **B** Jackson's victory in New Orleans enhanced his reputation in the United States and prepared the way for his presidency in 1829. The Treaty of Ghent (choice A) ending the War of 1812 was approved in December 1814, but the news traveled slowly; in any case, it was ratified in February 1815. Britain's policy of impressments, or taking men by force to serve in its navy, was one of the causes of the War of 1812 and had been abandoned by 1815, so choice C is incorrect. Choice D is incorrect because President Thomas Jefferson decided to go ahead with the Louisiana Purchase in 1803 despite criticism by some who said it was not constitutional.

41. **C** The Gadsden Purchase involved 29,000 square miles along the Mexican border and was the last territorial acquisition in the contiguous United States. Region A, Florida, was acquired in 1819 in the Adams-Onis Treaty with Spain. Region B was acquired in an 1846 treaty with Great Britain. Region D represents the Mexican Cession, land that Mexico ceded to the United States in 1848 after the Mexican-American War.

42. **B** When Congress ratified the Thirteenth Amendment in December 1865, slavery was abolished. The Kansas-Nebraska Act (choice A) allowed settlers in the new territories to determine through popular sovereignty if slavery would be allowed, resulting in widespread violence between antislavery and proslavery factions known as "Bloody

Kansas." In the *Dred Scott* case (choice C), the Supreme Court ruled that Congress had no authority to prohibit slavery in the new territories and that the Missouri Compromise of 1820, which banned slavery north of the southern border of Missouri, was unconstitutional. The Civil Rights Act of 1866 (choice D) stated that all persons born in the United States, including former slaves, are citizens, regardless of race.

43. **D** The Geary Act of 1892 extended the Chinese Exclusion Act for an additional 10 years and added the requirement that all Chinese immigrants carry a certificate of residency. The law was made permanent in 1902 and upheld by the Supreme Court in 1903 in *Fong Yue Ting v. United States*. Choice A is not correct: the Johnson-Reed Act of 1824 limited immigration totals to 2 percent of the people of that origin living in the United States in 1890. The Naturalization Act (choice B), one of the four Alien and Sedition Acts of 1798, extended the residency of aliens to become U.S. citizens from 5 years to 14 years. The Anti-Coolie Act of 1862 (choice C), formally known as An Act to Protect Free White Labor Against Competition with Chinese Coolie Labor, was passed by the California Legislature to deal with the large numbers of Chinese immigrants at the height of the gold rush.

44. **C** Congress authorized President Johnson to use force after the Tonkin Gulf incident in Vietnam, where Vietnamese gunboats attacked U.S. ships in international waters. Choice A is incorrect, since the Constitution states that Congress has the authority to declare war. The Vietnam War was fought without a formal declaration of war. The resolution did not limit the powers of Congress or the president with regard to war, so choices B and D are incorrect.

45. **D** Spain had the right of discovery to Alta, or Upper, California, and Carlos wanted to establish a Domain of Spain there, so he sent missionaries to establish settlements in 1769 because he was afraid Russia would gain dominance in the region. Choice A is incorrect because at that time the upper Pacific was uncharted. Choice B is incorrect because the Franciscan padres were the ones who sent missionaries to convert Native Americans and at the same time conscript them to work on the farms. Although there were many rumors in Spain about a legendary "Island of California" where riches abounded (choice C), this was not the reason that King Carlos III decided to build settlements in Alta California.

46. **B** The Russian-American Company used Fortress Ross, now called Fort Ross, to raise food for the capital of Russian America, New Archangel, now called Sitka, in Alaska. Choice A is incorrect because the Tlingit tribe was in Alaska, not California. Although New Archangel was originally planned as a fur-trading center, by 1817 the sea otter were almost all gone, so choice C is not correct. After the Mexican War of Independence in 1821, Spanish missions went into decline, so choice D is incorrect.

47. **C** Population declined because of the Franciscan policy of cloistering Native American women in the *convento* and controlling their sexuality during their childbearing years, so there was a decline in the Native American population. Although Native Americans were regularly promised their own land to farm, none was ever given, so choice A is incorrect. Plans to start a twenty-second mission (choice B) were abandoned in 1827. The outbreak of the measles epidemic (choice D), which killed a quarter of the Native American population, occurred because the native people had no natural immunity to the disease, but it was not related to the padres' management of the missions in California.

48. **D** The Compromise of 1850 had five statutes; the third allowed California to be admitted into the union as a free state, undivided by the 36-degree 30-minute line of the Missouri Compromise, which would have called for a free and a slave state. Choice A is incorrect because slavery was unanimously outlawed by the delegates to the California Constitutional Convention in 1849. Choice B is incorrect as well, since it was the South that wanted to extend slave territory into southern California. In response to the

reality of the state's burgeoning population as a result of the gold rush, there was a demand for a better government, resulting in the Constitutional Convention of 1849, so choice C is not correct.

49. **D** The Bear Flag Revolt took place on June 14, 1846; there was no fighting. General Vallejo realized Mexico was not administrating California properly and agreed to the group's claims. The group painted a flag with a bear and a star along with the words *Republic of California*. The republic was short-lived; shortly afterward the Mexican-American War broke out, and California became a state. Vallejo would go on to be a state senator. The Siege of La Paz was a minor skirmish the Mexicans lost just before the Treaty of Guadalupe Hidalgo, ending the war, was signed, so choice A is incorrect. In the Battle of Churubusco (choice B) in 1847, the Americans, under General Scott, forced Santa Anna's forces to flee after heavy causalities. The Battle of Palo Alto in Texas (choice C) was the first major battle of the Mexican-American War, with the Americans victorious.

50. **A** The immigrants were not viewed kindly in California, for they strained the already-swollen ranks of the unemployed during the Depression. There was not very much work available in those times at any wage, so choice B is incorrect. Because they had lost everything back home, they certainly had little if any capital to invest, and similarly would not represent a new market for business owners, making choices C and D wrong as well.

51. **D** The code specifically mentions food, agriculture, and farming, which would include beekeeping and producing honey. It is unlikely that a teacher's union would gain any benefit, so choice A is incorrect. The United Farm Workers (choice B) advocates for the rights of farmworkers, especially migrant workers, so the code would not be applicable to them. Floriculturists raise flowers, not food, so choice C also is incorrect.

52. **C** The aviation and aerospace sector provides over 283,000 jobs in California, the most in the nation, with a median wage of $53,900 at more than 2,800 employers, according to a study commissioned by Congress in 2002. That is about twice the number of employees in the moviemaking business, according to the California Film Commission, so choice A is wrong. Agriculture provides twice as many jobs because of its labor-intensive nature, but wages are much less, making choice B incorrect. And the government sector employs about half that number, according to the state comptroller's office, so choice D is incorrect as well.

Constructed-Response Assignments—Sample Responses

1. The author creates a sense of mounting tension by the use of rhetorical questions that Gilbert asks himself about Anne, the woman he loves and is about to marry. At first, the author sets the scene describing how beautiful Anne is with her "adoring eyes." The passage has Gilbert talking to himself about how long he has waited to win her. Then the author suggests that Gilbert is losing his confidence when she has him ask himself if he was "worthy of her." Gilbert's inner thoughts continue, and he becomes even more worried, asking himself if he could make Anne happy. The resolution comes when Anne's and Gilbert's eyes meet and all uncertainty is "swept away." Gilbert regains his confidence because he realizes that they "belonged to each other."

2. To become a good reader, a child must develop phonological or phonemic awareness. Phonemic awareness is the knowledge that there are repeated sounds that form the basis of language. Without this awareness, a child will not be able to learn to read. There are many strategies that can help build phonemic awareness. One of the most important and basic is to learn rhyming patterns. After the child has learned to rhyme sounds, he or she will be better prepared to distinguish different beginning sounds in words while understanding that a part of the word has the same sound, as in the case of *can* and *tan* or *hat* and *cat*. This skill will allow the child to

begin segmenting words into their component phonemes. After mastering this skill, the child will be prepared to develop the ability to combine phonemes into words.

3. *Brown v. Board of Education* was not just one case; it was a combination of separate cases filed in South Carolina, Delaware, Virginia, and the District of Columbia, as well as *Brown* in Topeka, Kansas. The ruling ended de jure (i.e., mandated by law) segregation enforced by the *Plessy v. Ferguson* Supreme Court ruling of 1896, which held that as long as separate facilities were equal, they did not violate the Fourteenth Amendment.

    The Supreme Court's mandate forced Americans to look at each other and decide if they could live up to the concept that "All men are created equal," as Thomas Jefferson wrote in the Declaration of Independence. Despite those words, the framers of the Constitution did not deal with the issue of slavery. When the Emancipation Proclamation freed the slaves, the concept of racial segregation became the law in southern states.

    The decision also had a global impact. Other nations that had long criticized the United States for racial segregation saw that black Americans could be integrated into American democracy. The Soviet Union, which had long used the race card in its propaganda, began to lose ground in black Africa, whose nations were beginning the struggle for independence, and the balance in the Cold War shifted.

4. The population boom brought people from all over the world, which resulted in enormous social changes that often led to racial conflicts that caused much bloodshed. Economically, the merchants, hotel and saloon owners, and other entrepreneurs benefited from selling the services that the gold miners needed. Culturally, the Native Americans suffered; they were attacked by the miners and decimated by disease from exposure to the newcomers. Native Americans numbered more than 150,000 in the 1840s; by 1870, they had dwindled to less than 30,000.

    Among those who made a fortune from the gold rush were Collis Huntington, Leland Stanford, Charles Crocker, and Mark Hopkins Jr. These men, who were referred to as the Big Four, went on to found the Central Pacific Railroad. On May 10, 1869, the tracks of the Central Pacific were joined with those of the Union Pacific Railroad, and the transcontinental railroad was born. It meant that California farmers could sell their produce on the East Coast, opening up a huge new market.

Subtest II Explanations

SCIENCE, MATHEMATICS

1. **B** Groups appear as columns in the periodic table and are organized such that they have similar properties.

2. **B** The ice cube only changes state, so this represents a physical change.

3. **D** The upper number represents the mass number of the isotope (number of protons plus number of neutrons), while the lower number represents the atomic number, which is the number of protons in the nucleus. Therefore, the magnesium isotope has 12 protons, the largest number among the elements shown.

4. **D** A higher pH means the liquid is more basic, and ammonia is the most basic of the listed liquids.

5. **A** In this example, the ball does not move until the outside force (pushing it) causes it to move forward. The ball will continue in motion until forces such as gravity and friction cause it to slow down and eventually stop.

6. **C** Acceleration is a change in velocity over time. In this example, a runner increases his speed over time and distance.

7. **C** In the periodic table, the number below the symbol is the atomic number of the element (the number of protons). Since both elements are neutral, they have the same number of electrons as protons.

8. **A** The heat from the compress is transferred to the person's muscles though direct contact with a heated surface.

9. **D** The endocrine system includes glands that regulate and release hormones throughout the body (among other functions).

10. **D** In the relationship, the crab has no benefit or loss from the liparid fish, while the fish gains a simple transport mechanism. When one of those in the relationship receives no loss or gain while the other gains, the relationship is described as commensalism.

11. **A** ATP is created in the mitochondria.

12. **C** Photosynthesis converts carbon dioxide to energy in the presence of light energy. The by-product of this reaction is oxygen.

13. **C** The frog's development of lungs and legs represents a large change in its body's form. By definition, this is a metamorphosis.

14. **A** Primary consumers subsist by eating the primary producers in an ecosystem. In the described situation, the grasses would be primary producers, so the primary consumers are the herbivores that eat the grasses.

15. **D** Many of the described situations—including the ants and the birds sharing the same food source (and the birds not searching for their own food) and ants killing predators—are unlikely. Finally, it is unlikely that the birds would use twigs and leaves broken by the ants, as these are already easily available in their environment.

16. **B** The available energy decreases as the distance from the primary producers increases. This means less energy is available for the consumers, resulting in less supportable biomass.

17. **A** By definition, igneous rocks are formed through the cooling of magma.

18. **B** The primary difference between rocks and minerals is their makeup. Rocks are made of many different substances, while minerals are thought of as purer substances.

19. **D** Glacial deposits on Earth occur in patterns that would not be possible unless there was originally one large continent.

20. **C** The strength of a hurricane is strongly affected by the surface temperature of the ocean. The other listed factors have little if any effect on a hurricane's strength.

21. **A** An anemometer measures wind speed. Humidity (choice B) is measured by a hygrometer, temperature (choice C) by a thermometer, and air pressure (choice D) by a barometer.

22. **C** It will be noon along the entire line of 90 degrees west longitude.

23. **A** Mercury is between the sun and Venus, while Venus and Mars are adjacent to Earth. On average, Venus is closer to Earth than Mars is.

24. **A** In general, comets follow elliptical orbits around the sun. Answer choice B is describing the asteroid belt, although it does not describe all asteroids in the solar system.

25. **B** The side closest to the moon will experience high tide due to the gravitational pull toward the moon, while the side directly opposite will experience high tide due to centrifugal force.

26. **A** In general, barometric pressure is lower around storm systems that are associated with cloudy and rainy or even stormy weather.

27. **C** Distributing the −4 and combining like terms on the left side will yield the equation $x - 20 = 3x + 1$. Subtracting 1 and x from both sides yields the equation in answer choice C.

28. **D** $588 = 2^2 \cdot 3 \cdot 7^2$, and $2(3)(7) = 42$.

29. **A** Division by 4 is equivalent to multiplication by $\frac{1}{4}$.

30. **A** When rounding, Steve will decrease the first value by 0.2, increase the second by 0.2, increase the third by 0.5, increase the fourth by 0.1, and leave the fifth unchanged: $-0.2 + 0.2 + 0.5 + 0.1 = 0.6$.

31. **C** These numbers are in scientific notation, and a more negative exponent represents a smaller number. Answer choice C is the only choice with a less negative exponent.

32. **C** In the group, $0.05(1,200) = 60$ are evenly divided among three subgroups: those with one to two years' experience, those with less than one year, and those with none.

Therefore, each group contains 60/3 = 20 people.

33. **A** The portion shaded is 4/10, which is equivalent to (4 × 6)/(10 × 6) = 24/60.

34. **D** Numbers to the right of P are larger than P, and P represents $\frac{2}{3}$. By converting the fractions to decimals, it can be determined that only answer choice D is larger than $\frac{2}{3}$.

35. **B** The ratio of white sugar to butter is 2 to $\frac{1}{2}$. Since 9 cups of sugar were used and this ratio must be maintained, we can set up an equation where x is the number of cups of butter to use:

$$\frac{2}{\frac{1}{2}}=\frac{9}{x}$$
$$2x=\frac{9}{2}$$
$$x=\frac{9}{4}=2\frac{1}{4}$$

36. **B** The X is the third number in the long division, so it must be from the third step within the long division. This step is where 24/8 = 3 is calculated. Therefore, $X = 3$.

37. **B** Since the triangles are similar, the length of each side of the first triangle is the same multiple of the length of each side of the second triangle. The length of AC can be found using the Pythagorean theorem:

$$4^2+10^2=AC^2$$
$$116=AC^2$$
$$AC=10.77$$

The ratio of DE to AB must match the ratio of DF to AC:

$$\frac{1.5}{4}=\frac{DF}{10.77}$$

Cross multiplying yields $DF = 4.04$.

38. **C** Distribute the −4 and combine like terms: $-4(x+2)-5x=-4x-8-5x=-9x-8$.

39. **C** As x increases by 1, there is not a constant rate of increase in y. Therefore, this can't be a linear function. Since the y values are at their highest at −4 and are then the same on both sides of −4 (and decreasing), this must be a quadratic function, which is graphed as a parabola opening down.

40. **C** The total number of shirts sold was 150, which can be represented as $x + y = 150$. Additionally, for each large shirt sold, the pair makes \$10.50, while each extra-large shirt brings in \$12.50. The total amount brought in for each size was $10.50x$ and $12.50y$. Since the total of all shirt sales was \$1,625, we can express this as $10.5x + 12.5y = 1,625$.

41. **A** A linear equation with positive slope will be a line that rises from left to right.

42. **B** The angles within a triangle must add to 180 degrees, and by definition, a right angle is 90 degrees. Therefore the remaining angle is 180 − 15 − 90 = 75.

43. **A** The slope of line L is $\frac{5-2}{4-1}=\frac{3}{3}=1$, and since line M is parallel to line L, line M also has a slope of 1. Using the given point (2, 5) in the point slope formula, line M has the following equation:

$$y-y_1=m(x-x_1)$$
$$y-5=1(x-2)$$
$$y-5=x-2$$
$$y=x+3$$

Of the points given in the answer choices, only (5, 8) satisfies this equation.

44. **A** Springfield is 6 × 25 = 150 miles from Lawson, and Fairfield Beach is half that far, or 75 miles from Springfield. Traveling at 55 mph, it will take 75/55 = 1.36 hours, or 1 hour and 0.36 × 60 = 22 minutes.

45. **A** Cubes have sides that are all the same length, so to find the volume, take that length to the third power. Therefore, the length of one side of this cube is $\sqrt[3]{27}=3$ feet long. Based on the picture, the square must have sides of 6 each, giving an area of 6 × 6 = 36 square feet.

46. **C** Every minute costs \$0.33. If n represents minutes, this will be a cost of $0.33n$. After this is calculated, a fee of \$18 is added. This yields the equation $0.33n + 18$.

47. **B** The median represents the middle value of a set of ordered numbers. In this case, both 1 and 2 could be thought of as the middle numbers, so the average of these two numbers (or 1.5) is said to be the median.

48. **D** The probability of an event and its complement will always add to 1.

49. **B** Two events that are mutually exclusive cannot both occur. In other words, $P(A \text{ and } B) = 0$.

50. **A** By using randomness, we try to ensure that no particular segment of the population is overrepresented.

51. **D** If x represents the weight of the lighter man and y represents the weight of the heavier man (in stone), then $x + y = 30$. Since the heavier man is twice the weight of the lighter man, $y = 2x$. Solving this system of equations, we find that $x = 10$. That is, the lighter man weighs 10 stone. Given that this is equivalent to 140 pounds, then each stone must be $140/10 = 14$ pounds.

52. **A** By the Pythagorean theorem, $(5x)^2 + 2^2 = c^2$, where c is the length of the hypotenuse. Solving for c yields the expression of answer choice A.

Constructed-Response Assignments—Sample Responses

1. Find the amount of water needed for dilution by using the following formula:

   Concentration 1 × Volume 1 = Concentration 2 × Volume 2
   $$C_1 \times V_1 = C_2 \times V_2$$
   $$10 \text{ M} \times 100 \text{ mL} = 2 \text{ M} \times V_2$$
   $$500 \text{ mL} = V_2$$

   Find the final concentration of salt and sugar by using the same formula ($C_1 \times V_1 = C_2 \times V_2$). First, the salt concentration:

   $$2 \text{ M} \times 80 \text{ mL} = C_2 \times (80 \text{ mL} + 40 \text{ mL})$$
   $$1.33 \text{ M} = C_2$$

   Then the sugar concentration:

   $$5 \text{ M} \times 40 \text{ mL} = C_2 \times (80 \text{ mL} + 40 \text{ mL})$$
   $$1.67 \text{ M} = C_2$$

To find the number of moles of salt and sugar, multiply the solution's final volume by the concentration of each component before the water is removed. The final solution has a volume of 120 mL.

Salt:
   1.33 M = 1.33 M/1 L
   Number of Moles = (1.33 moles/1,000 mL) × 120 mL = 0.16 mole

Sugar:
   1.67 M = 1.67 moles/1 L
   Number of Moles = (1.67 moles/1,000 mL) × 120 mL = 0.20 mole

2. Producers are species that grow without consuming other species, although other species often consume *them*. On the earth's surface, plants are among the most common producers. In this exercise, the cave fungus is a producer.

   Centipedes are typically predators and in this exercise serve as secondary consumers. The novel insect species appears to eat only centipedes, which are predators, so the species can be classified as a tertiary consumer.

   Since both the shrew-like mammal and the cave crickets eat fungus but apparently don't hunt other animals, these two species can be considered primary consumers. But since the cave crickets eat dead animals, this species is probably better described as a scavenger.

   The shrew-like mammal and the novel insect do not seem to consume each other, and they do not seem to compete for food. However, the two species do appear to compete for one resource: space. If the mammal is taking prime nesting spots, the insect may have difficulty hatching and raising its young, which might have caused the novel insect's population decline.

3. Express the area of triangle ACD in terms of x and y: Labeling the diagram with the given lengths, as shown here, and using the formula for the area of a triangle ($\frac{1}{2} \times \text{base} \times \text{height}$), we find the area of ACD to be $\frac{1}{2} \times 2 \times x$. Simplifying this expression gives the area: x square units.

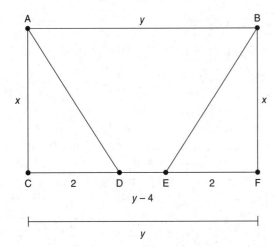

Express the area of the trapezoid in terms of x and y: To find the area of the trapezoid, subtract the area of the two triangles from the area of the larger rectangle. The rectangle has sides of length x and y, respectively, so the rectangle has an area of xy square units. The triangles each have an area of x square units, and there are two of them, resulting in a total area of $2x$ for both of the triangles together. Therefore, the trapezoid will have an area of $xy - 2x = x\left(y - 2\right)$ square units.

This area could also be found using the formula for the area of a trapezoid. In general, the area of a trapezoid is one half the sum of the bases times the height. Substitute the known values and solve:

$$\frac{1}{2}\left[(y-4)+(y)\right]\times x = \frac{1}{2}(2y-4)\times x$$
$$= (y-2)\times x$$
$$= x\left(y-2\right)$$

Express the perimeter of the trapezoid in terms of x and y: The perimeter is the sum of the length of the sides. Here, sides AD and BE represent the hypotenuse of a triangle with legs of length 2 and x. Since these are right triangles, we can find the length of each of these sides by using the Pythagorean theorem ($a^2 + b^2 = c^2$, where a and c are the legs of the triangle and c is the hypotenuse):

$$c^2 = 2^2 + x^2$$
$$c = \sqrt{4 + x^2}$$

Therefore, the perimeter is:

$$y + (y-4) + \sqrt{4+x^2} + \sqrt{4+x^2} = 2y - 4 + 2\sqrt{4+x^2}$$

It is important to note that the perimeter would not be expressed in square units.

4. This quadratic equation can be solved using the quadratic formula or by factoring. Each method will result in the same solution since they are equivalent.

Here is the quadratic formula:

$$x = \frac{-b \pm \sqrt{b^2 - 4ac}}{2a}, \text{ where the quadratic}$$
equation is $ax^2 + bx + c = 0$

We are given $a = 1$, $b = -5$, and $c = -14$. Substitute and solve:

$$x = \frac{-(-5) \pm \sqrt{(-5)^2 - 4(1)(-14)}}{2(1)}$$
$$= \frac{5 \pm \sqrt{25 + 56}}{2}$$
$$= \frac{5 \pm \sqrt{81}}{2}$$
$$= \frac{5 \pm 9}{2}$$
$$= -2, 7$$

Factoring: Since the coefficient of the squared term is 1, we need only look for factors of –14 that add to –5. These factors would be –7 and 2. Using these factors, we can rewrite the quadratic equation and use the zero product rule to solve it:

$$x^2 - 5x - 14 = 0$$
$$(x-7)(x+2) = 0$$
$$x - 7 = 0$$
$$x + 2 = 0$$
$$x = 7, -2$$

Explain what these solutions represent on a graph: The solutions to the quadratic equation are the x-coordinates of the x-intercepts of the resulting parabola. Were there no real solutions, the parabola would not touch the x-axis; if there were only one solution to the equation, the graph would touch the axis only at that single point. In this case, there are two solutions, and the graph passes through the x-axis at each of these points.

Subtest III Explanations

PHYSICAL EDUCATION, HUMAN DEVELOPMENT, AND VISUAL AND PERFORMING ARTS

1. **B** Low-space activities are those which are done while close to the ground, such as bending, kneeling, crouching, or crawling. Middle-space activities are performed while standing. High-space activities are performed while on tiptoe or in the air.

2. **C** Manipulative skills have an effect on another thing; examples are pushing, pulling, and bouncing. Locomotor skills move the body from one place to another, as in the case of walking, crawling, or galloping. Nonlocomotor skills are body movements done without changing location, such as stretching or bending.

3. **B** Approximately half of traffic deaths are alcohol related. Alcohol is also a major factor in a large percentage of other types of accidental deaths.

4. **A** Using the self-actualization approach, the teacher matches the students' interests and motivation to the curriculum. The ecological integration approach focuses on teaching PE as a way to prepare students for future successful group participation. The emphasis of the social responsibility approach is teaching students to work together and building strong interpersonal relationships.

5. **B** The intensity of the activity should be increased in order to challenge students' performance and increase their fitness levels. Aerobic activity should occur for a minimum of 8 to 10 minutes out of each hour; however, 20 or more minutes would be ideal. The difficulty level of the activity is low and is not likely to provide the optimal amount of cardiorespiratory exertion.

6. **D** Children develop locomotor skills in this order: crawl, creep, walk, run, jump, leap, gallop, hop, slide, and skip.

7. **C** An appropriate sequence of activities includes warm-up, instruction, physical activity, cooldown, and evaluation. Light walking is a cooldown activity that would prevent injuries and could follow the main physical activity during a class period.

8. **B** Striking involves using a bent arm and a strong movement to connect with or hit something. It can include an object, such as a bat or racket, which will connect with the object. Throwing involves using hands, rather than arms, to propel an object. Pulling moves an object toward oneself. Pushing moves an object away from oneself.

9. **B** LDL is the bad type of cholesterol. Cardiovascular fitness lowers LDL levels, while increasing HDL, or good, cholesterol levels. Another benefit of cardiovascular fitness is lower heart rate. And while the risk of heart attack is reduced, it is not eliminated completely.

10. **D** Motor skill development patterns are not influenced by left-right dominance.

11. **D** This approach focuses on cardiovascular performance and endurance. Other benefits include increases in strength, flexibility, and endurance; however, these are not the main objective.

12. **A** Polymetric exercises involve muscular activities that lengthen and then immediately contract, or shorten, the same muscle. Such movements are performed to increase power.

13. **C** In addition to allowing the use of two hands, altering the size of the equipment used can be an effective strategy for adapting sports. Allow larger balls in games such as tennis, golf, or volleyball, as well as shorter golf clubs, tennis rackets, or baseball bats. Decreasing the field size, lowering or eliminating nets, and allowing walking rather than running are other ways to include all students.

14. **C** Erikson developed a model that posits eight stages of psychosocial development over the course of a lifetime. Of these eight stages, four occur during a child's years in school. Students encounter the initiative-versus-guilt stage between the ages of four

and five. During this time, they develop a sense of responsibility, which increases their initiative. Conversely, if the child feels a sense of irresponsibility, it can lead to feelings of anxiety and guilt.

15. **D** The nature of families in the United States has changed over time. Today, less than 10 percent of children are living in "traditional" families, which include a stay-at-home mother and a working father. The answer choices for the other trends misstate the percentages. Approximately 70 percent of mothers are employed. About 30 percent of children live with a stepparent, and about 25 percent of children are raised by a single parent.

16. **D** Students with learning disabilities perform a minimum of two years below grade level. Materials one year below their grade level would generally be too difficult. Presenting material orally, providing repeated opportunities to practice the same skill, and teaching with manipulative materials are often successful strategies to use with these students.

17. **B** Low-SES students may exhibit behaviors that cause teachers to lower their academic expectations; however, these students are capable of learning, and reducing expectations can be counterproductive. These students need encouragement and a higher amount of structure. High-SES students require less structure and are often higher-achieving academically, so they are able to handle an increased amount of material. Minimizing competitiveness is an effective strategy to use with these students.

18. **D** Behaviorist B. F. Skinner's approach to behavior is known as operant conditioning. This approach relies on four basic responses to behavior: (1) extinction, which does not reinforce students' undesired responses; (2) negative reinforcement, which allows students to escape punishment by repeating desired responses; (3) positive reinforcement, which rewards students' desired responses; and (4) punishment, which punishes students' undesired behaviors.

19. **C** Between the time they are seven and eleven years old, boys display stronger leg and arm muscle strength, while girls display more-advanced fine-motor skills. Contrary to choice A, students typically grow about *two* inches each year until about the age of 11. Baby fat is lost during the early childhood years.

20. **D** Infants engage in functional play. This is followed by constructive play, in which movements are used to build or create something.

21. **B** Emotional maltreatment, physical neglect, and physical or sexual abuse are all types of child abuse. Lack of hygiene, weight loss, and hunger can be signs of neglect and, under California state law, must be reported.

22. **A** Goal setting is an important aspect of developing a positive self-image, but goals should be realistic and attainable.

23. **C** Sensorimotor is the earliest in Piaget's stages of cognitive development. In this stage, children demonstrate poor verbal and cognitive development skills, and they develop the concept of object permanence. In the preoperational stage, language and some problem-solving skills develop, thinking is egocentric, but some concepts such as conservation of number are difficult to develop. During the concrete operational stage, thinking becomes operational, concepts built around concrete materials become organized and logical, and conservation tasks are mastered, but symbolic concepts are not generally understood. During the final stage, formal operational, children develop concepts without the use of concrete materials, think symbolically, and reason effectively and abstractly.

24. **C** Kohlberg's stages of moral development include preconventional morality, conventional morality, and postconventional morality; each of these broad levels is subdivided into two smaller categories. The earliest stage, preconventional morality, is generally demonstrated during preschool and primary elementary grades. At this stage, children view their actions in light of the consequences and often behave well in order to avoid punishment.

25. **A** Prenatal drug use can lead to neurological problems, learning disabilities, and impaired

motor development. Prenatal use of alcohol can lead to several negative results, including mental retardation, low birth weight, and fetal alcohol syndrome; nicotine use can lead to poor respiratory functioning. These agents pose the greatest risk between two and six weeks gestation, since the major organs and body parts are forming during this time. Other factors affecting development include the mother's age; older mothers and adolescent mothers both face the risk of complications.

26. **B** Transductive reasoning is a characteristic of children in Piaget's preoperational stage of cognitive development. Children connect experiences, whether or not one logically causes the other.

27. **A** Color affects the mood and appearance of a piece of art. Blue is a cold color and appears to contract the size of the piece. Yellow, in contrast, is a warm color, which appears to expand the size of the work.

28. **B** The three properties of color are hue, saturation, and value. Hue refers to the shade of the color. Saturation describes the brightness or dullness of a color. Value describes the amount of lightness or darkness in a color.

29. **A** Combined locomotor movements, such as the two-step, grapevine, step-hop, and spinning, are examples of the element of space. Space includes locomotor, nonlocomotor, and combined locomotor movements.

30. **D** Violas are positioned immediately in front of the conductor of a symphony orchestra. Flutes and oboes are behind the violas; cellos are to the conductor's right of the violas. Violins are to the conductor's left.

31. **D** The early eighteenth century brought the era of Romanticism, which emphasized emotion and fantasy in dance. Circle form dances were characteristic of early dance. During the Middle Ages, folk dances developed from the ritual dances of earlier eras. During the Renaissance, one characteristic of dance was its lack of spontaneity.

32. **B** The value of a color is the amount of lightness or darkness. Low-value shades are dark; high-value shades are light. The value of a color can be raised, or made lighter, by adding white. The value can be lowered by adding a dark color.

33. **C** The string section of an orchestra includes the cello, double bass, viola, and violin. While the guitar and the harp are actually string instruments, they are not part of this section of the orchestra.

34. **A** Creative expression involves applying skills to communicate meaning and intent within one's own artistic works. Aesthetic valuing is the analysis or critique of various types of art.

35. **B** Axial movements are performed around a body part that does not change location, such as a foot. Spontaneous dances are called improvisation. The way a dancer's body aligns with a base of support is alignment. Retrograde dance movements are those which are performed forward and then in reverse.

36. **B** The timbre is the tonal quality, or color, of the music; it affects the mood of a piece. Each instrument can have a different timbre than the others. Words such as *shrill*, *harsh*, and *light* also could be used to describe the timbre.

37. **B** Music during the baroque era was very ornate. Opera, the orchestra, and ballet were developed during this period as well.

38. **A** London Bridge, Ring Around the Rosie, and Hokey Pokey are examples of folk dances.

39. **A** Asymmetrical works create a sense of informality.

Constructed-Response Assignments—Sample Responses

1. Throwing and catching are two object manipulation skills that should be taught to primary-grade students. Throwing is the act of propelling an object, such as a ball, away from the body through space. Catching is using the hands to stop an object that is moving.

   Primary-grade students should practice tossing a variety of objects, including balls, beach balls, and bean bags, which will help them develop an understanding of how size and weight affect the force used to throw each object, as well as the speed at which these objects travel. Students should begin with an underhand movement and then move to an overhand movement, since underhand is simpler. Around third grade, students will be able to advance their throwing skills to have more accuracy.

Since hand-eye coordination is needed to catch an object, this skill can be more difficult for students than throwing. Primary-grade students are also afraid of being hit by the object they are supposed to catch, so it is important to begin practicing this skill with objects such as beach balls and balloons. Practicing catching objects that have bounced up from the floor also is important. Students should begin by moving toward the object and catching with both hands. After the students' motor skills have developed further, they will be ready to practice catching smaller objects, such as baseballs, which require more highly developed perception abilities. They will also be able to catch with a single hand later.

2. An adapted physical education program should include an assessment of the students' abilities and areas of delay. The students' Individualized Education Program (IEP) goals also should be considered. The physical education teacher should write IEP goals for PE that are objective and measurable and that reflect the content of the program. Students' progress toward these goals should be evaluated regularly. The adapted physical education program should also consider the least restrictive environment (LRE) for the student. Students should be given the opportunity to be successful in the safest environment possible.

The premise behind adapted physical education is to allow students of all ability levels to participate in the activities. To help students with special needs succeed in volleyball, for example, a bright-colored ball that is larger, lighter, and softer than a traditional volleyball could be used. Allowing students to catch the ball rather than hitting it back could also help these students play the game successfully. Other ways of adapting the activity include lowering the net, using a smaller court, and allowing the students to serve the ball from a location closer to the net.

3. Technology offers students opportunities for creating, displaying, sharing, and communicating their ideas in all areas, including visual and performing arts. Digital photography and video, animation, photo software, and digital recording equipment can help students produce and enhance their artistic products. Electronic technology also offers the opportunity to create more-professional works.

At the elementary level, students can use digital cameras and video cameras to record photos and videos of projects and performances and then upload these to the school website to share with other students and parents. At the middle school level, students can use animation software to develop three-dimensional figures and blueprints to use for creating clay models and sculptures. At the high school level, students can use technology to design sets and scenery for plays and to computerize stage lighting. They can then use technology to record, review, and evaluate performances as a tool for self-improvement.

CHAPTER 11

Writing Skills Practice Test 1

Each of the constructed-response questions in the CSET Writing Skills section is graded on a scale of 1 to 4. At the end of each writing section, you'll find four sample responses for each question, with each sample response illustrating the level of work that would receive a score of 4 (highest), 3, 2, or 1 (lowest).

Expository Writing

Complete the exercise that follows.

You have begun an e-mail correspondence with a pen pal who lives in Bahrain. She is curious about American holidays. In an essay to be read by an audience of educated adults, state which holiday is your favorite and what you feel that holiday tells about the American people.

1. Provide your answer in the space allotted.

Expressive Writing

Complete the exercise that follows.

As children grow up, they need role models to guide them during the process of becoming adults. In an essay to be read by an audience of educated adults, identify a role model you had as a child, and explain how you feel that role model gave you guidance.

2. Provide your answer in the space allotted.

_____

_____

_____

_____

_____

_____

_____

_____

_____

_____

_____

_____

_____

_____

_____

_____

_____

_____

_____

Writing Skills Practice Test 1 Sample Answers

Expository Writing

Question 1 (Score: 4 points)

Thanksgiving is my favorite holiday. It is celebrated on the fourth Thursday of November, and it is a day when Americans gather with their families and reflect on the blessings they have had over the past year. Traditionally, roasted turkey is served. President Abraham Lincoln proclaimed Thanksgiving to be a national holiday in 1863. When he did that, the United States was in the midst of a dark Civil War, and the president felt a need to acknowledge what was good about America as a nation despite the specter of the battlefields, and to give thanks for the good things the country had.

Thanksgiving reminds us of the Pilgrims who fled England for religious freedom and came to this land before it was a country. They established Plymouth Colony in what is now Massachusetts and celebrated their first harvest in the New World with their Native American friends, who had helped the Pilgrims survive the long first winter and plant crops. They dined on fish and lobster, wild turkey, berries, and pumpkins and corn. It was a day of sharing. Even though it was not officially called Thanksgiving at that time, it created the atmosphere that survives in today's Thanksgivings.

This spirit of sharing is what Thanksgiving is all about. It allows all Americans to come together, despite differences in politics, religion, or other issues, and join hands in thankfulness. Thanksgiving is indeed a family holiday, but in a sense, it is about the extended family of humanity, with people opening up their homes and hearts to others.

Thanksgiving is extremely important for children to experience. It is a time when children can be reminded how important it is to respect everyone they know. It is also an ideal time for parents to remind their children that there are many who are not so lucky and don't have enough to eat. Many Americans donate food or give of their time to serve those who are less fortunate in soup kitchens and church halls on this special day. Thanksgiving, then, is a day that makes Americans proud, a day to leave behind our prejudices and petty opinions and to recognize the generosity that is so common in this country.

Score Note: This essay earns a 4 because it is well structured and its arguments are supported by specific detail. It directly addresses the prompt, and it is free of grammatical and punctuation errors.

Question 1 (Score: 3 points)

I love the Fourth of July. It represents so much of our history and all the intelligent choices that the founding fathers made to create our great country. It all started in 1776, when representatives from the 13 colonies decided to draft a resolution declaring their independence from Great Britain with which they were engaged in a revolutionary war. The Fourth of July, also known as Independence Day, is a holiday celebrating the birth of the United States.

Thomas Jefferson wrote the Declaration of Independence. It declared America's independence. Jefferson wrote that "all men are created equal." It is a symbol of liberty and gives inspiration to people all over the world who yearn for freedom. It's my favorite holiday because there are picnics and parades, concerts and fireworks. Families get together for food and barbecues to remember the early patriots.

July Fourth has meaning for Americans because it reminds us of the freedom and liberty that our citizens enjoy. So it is fitting that people show off their patriotism on this holiday. Red, white, and blue decorations are put up on people's houses, and there are many American flags to be seen. July Fourth is also important because it awakens the memory of how hard our forefathers worked to achieve freedom.

Score Note: This essay earns a 3 because it is reasonably well structured, free of glaring grammatical errors, and directly addresses the prompt; however it is fairly repetitive (note how often "freedom" and "liberty" are mentioned), so it gives the impression the writer did not have many concrete details to offer in support of the thesis.

Question 1 (Score: 2 points)

Veterans Day is my favorite holiday. It honors our soldiers who showed heroic in the battles the United States fought. Veteran's Day always falls on November the 11. Because that was the day that World War I ended in 1918.

World War I was a war in which a lot of American soldiers died. There were lots of other wars too, so it is important to remember them on a special day set aside for them and we watch parades on Veterans Day. There are soldiers with medals. There are marching bands and the spectators wave flags and cheer when they go by.

That is why it is important that you show how much thanks we feel for these brave soldiers who defended the United States.

Score Note: This essay earns a 2 because, although it addresses the prompt, it has grammatical and construction errors (note the fragment in the first paragraph). It is very short and poorly organized. The details given do not directly support the argument.

Question 1 (Score: 1 point)

Christmas is a day of giving gifts to others to enjoy and getting some too. It is the most popular holiday of the year. I can shop at the mall for presents because there are a wide variety of stores to choose from. Christmas is a holiday celebrated by Americans and others.

Children like Christmas the most. Since I live in San Diego there is not much chance I can enjoy a "White Christmas" like the popular song goes. Even so, I think Christmas is the holiday that most people enjoy the most.

Score Note: This response receives a 1 because it fails to satisfy the requirements of the prompt. It does not adequately describe the holiday or what it says about American people. Responses that do not directly answer the prompt will always receive low scores. Further, the essay is inappropriately short and its structure is disjointed.

Expressive Writing

Question 2 (Score: 4 points)

My role model is my grandmother, Julia. I always remember when my grandmother came to our house just outside of San Diego every year for Thanksgiving. I was a young girl, and I looked up to her a lot. We always took long walks together every day when she stayed with us. I never tired of hearing her stories of how she had become a daredevil pilot. She was one of only a handful of women pilots in the country. She would tell me about what it felt like to be flying. It was exciting to hear her talk. I wanted to be just like her.

Julia became a pilot because her father was a crop duster. He often took her with him as he worked up and down the Central Valley, going from farm to farm. He taught her to fly, and when she was 14, she made her first solo flight. For her eighteenth birthday, he gave Julia her very own plane. They would go barnstorming during the winter months with two or three other pilots, but she was the only woman. They would land in a farmer's field, negotiate with him to use it as a landing and take-off point, and then go and buzz the town, dropping leaflets offering plane rides for two dollars. Sometimes they would do a show, thrilling the spectators below with loop-the-loops and barrel rolls, pushing their planes to the limit.

When Julia's father passed away, she decided to become a daredevil pilot. She performed in air shows all over the country, competed in air races, and did daring aerobatic feats like dancing on the wing of a plane going 150 mph. She did parachute stunts and stall turns and aerial combat maneuvers. Her shows were always sold out.

Now my grandmother's eyes aren't what they used to be, and her hands tremble. She only flies on commercial airlines. But her example has taught me that it is good to be different and to do what you want. She taught me that if you think you can do something, keep trying until you can. She taught me never to be afraid of anything and to do what you love. I don't want to be a pilot like my grandmother, but I think I will be able to use what she taught me in my work as a teacher.

Score Note: This essay earns a 4 because it is well structured and its arguments are supported by specific detail. It directly addresses the prompt, and it is free of grammatical and punctuation errors.

Question 2 (Score: 3 points)

My seventh-grade English teacher, Mrs. Grey, was a role model for me. When I was younger, I was very shy. My father always read to me at night. And he passed his love of books onto me. When the school year started and Mrs. Grey told us that the class would have weekly book discussions, I was terrified. The first book we had to read was *Where the Red Fern Grows.* I liked the story, and I identified with Billy because I love dogs, and I thought it was very sad.

When we had the class book discussion and Mrs. Grey called on me, I froze. I couldn't say anything. After class Mrs. Grey talked to me and I told her I was afraid to speak in front of others. She worked with me after school for a few minutes every day. She coached me and helped me get the words out.

The last book of the year was *To Kill a Mockingbird.* When it was my turn, I rose and I spoke about how the book portrayed adult prejudice in the Deep South in the 1930s. I talked for 10 minutes, and when I sat down, everybody clapped! Because Mrs. Grey took time and helped me, I had overcame my fear.

That is why I decided I wanted to become a teacher.

Score Note: This essay earns a 3 because it is reasonably well structured and directly addresses the prompt; however it does have some grammatical problems and includes extraneous details that distract the reader from the central point.

Question 2 (Score: 2 points)

My role model is my uncle Arthur who is a doctor that specializes in young people called a pediatricsian. It is important that children go to see the doctor every year, so they can get all their shots. When I go to the doctor they put the children that are sick in a different room so they can't spread illness.

My uncle once let me listen to my own heart with a device called a stethascope that attach to your ears. He had it with him when he came to our house. It was very interesting listening to my heart and a little scary too. He also has a device like a metal spoon and he taps on your knee and your leg moves.

My father says his brother is very smart. He was first in his class at medical school at UCLA. My goal is to go to college and then to medical school so I can take care of kids too.

Score Note: This essay earns a 2 because it addresses the prompt only indirectly, it is inappropriately short, and it features spelling and grammatical errors. It also includes extraneous details that do not support the central argument.

Question 2 (Score: 1 point)

When I was younger the person that I wanted to be alike was coach Johnson my little league coach who helped my game very much by telling me what I was doing wrong. My father had told me that I was a natural athelete and I should try out for a sport so I chose baseball I like to watch baseball games on TV.

Coach put me in the outfield and told me to keep watching for the ball. I was always better catching than hitting. But he told me I was swinging too hard to just try to hit the ball up the middle. And it worked. This is why I want to be like coach Johnson.

Score Note: This essay receives a score of 1 because although it addresses the prompt, it is inappropriately short, includes few details to support the central thesis, and features spelling and grammatical mistakes.

CHAPTER 12

Practice Test 2

Test Directions

The simulated exam in this chapter includes full-length practice tests for each of the three CSET subtests. Each subtest includes two sections:

▶ **Multiple-choice questions.** Each multiple-choice question includes four answer choices. Your goal is to choose the single best answer.
▶ **Constructed-response assignments.** The constructed-response assignments require written responses. Directions appear directly before the assignments.

You may work on the multiple-choice questions and constructed-response assignments in whatever order you choose. Keep in mind, though, that on the day you take all three actual CSET subtests, you will have five hours to complete them.

For each section, you will be able to tear out sheets on which to write your answers. For the multiple-choice sections, there are answer sheets before each section. For the constructed-response assignments, pages on which to enter your answers are provided after the directions for each assignment.

Constructed-Response Assignments

You'll write a response for each constructed-response assignment. Be sure to read each assignment closely and consider how you will organize your response. The scoring for the responses to the CSET assignments is based on the following criteria:

▶ **Purpose.** Your response addresses the objectives of the assignment.
▶ **Knowledge.** You successfully apply your knowledge of relevant subject matter to the assignment.
▶ **Support.** Your supporting evidence is of high quality and relevant to the assignment.

While the constructed-response assignments are used to assess your command of the subject matter and not your writing ability, keep in mind that the level of clarity of your responses will affect how your responses are judged. Write your responses as you would address an audience of fellow educators. In the answer key you will find sample responses to which you can compare what you've written.

SUBTEST I

READING, LANGUAGE, AND LITERATURE; HISTORY AND SOCIAL SCIENCE

Multiple-Choice Answer Sheet

Reading, Language, and Literature

QUESTION NUMBER	YOUR RESPONSE
1	
2	
3	
4	
5	
6	
7	
8	
9	
10	
11	
12	
13	
14	
15	
16	
17	
18	
19	
20	
21	
22	
23	
24	
25	
26	

History and Social Science

QUESTION NUMBER	YOUR RESPONSE
27	
28	
29	
30	
31	
32	
33	
34	
35	
36	
37	
38	
39	
40	
41	
42	
43	
44	
45	
46	
47	
48	
49	
50	
51	
52	

Multiple-Choice Questions

1. Some common vowel patterns are associated with more than one pronunciation (e.g., *ea* in *team* and *tread*). Which of the following nonsense words illustrates a vowel pattern that is highly consistent in its pronunciation?

   A. Drook

   B. Proan

   C. Drow

   D. Sough

2. Which of the following lists reflects the order of study from largest units of a language to the smallest units?

   A. Semantics, syntax, morphemes, phonemes

   B. Morphemes, phonemes, syntax, semantics

   C. Syntax, semantics, phonemes, morphemes

   D. Morphemes, syntax, morphemes, semantics

3. During the transitional stage of spelling, a child _____.

   A. begins to use visual memory and an understanding of word structure

   B. has many words committed to memory and has learned the basic rules of orthography

   C. understands letter-sound correspondence as a principle

   D. begins to systematically represent speech sounds with letters or groups of letters

4. What is the most likely reason that Bobby, a first-grader, cannot read the word *crow*?

   A. The word cannot be sounded out.

   B. The word is not a cognate.

   C. The word has a variable vowel sound.

   D. The word is not in his oral vocabulary.

5. Miss Grey is using a scaffolding tool with Jimmy, a first-grader. She gives Jimmy cards with the letter *d* on them and asks him to put a card on anything he sees that starts with that letter. This scaffolding tool would support _____.

   A. improved morphemic awareness

   B. improved oral vocabulary

   C. improved language acquisition

   D. improved sounding out of words

6. The zone of proximal development is determined by _____.

   A. testing the child's oral vocabulary

   B. having the child identify beginning sounds of objects

   C. having the child sound out words at various levels

   D. observing the child in creative play

7. What is the best way to help children enhance their vocabularies?

   A. Reading aloud to children

   B. Assigning vocabulary words

   C. Having the child do independent reading

   D. Speaking to children about the meaning of words

8. Why is learning English easier for a Spanish-speaking person than for a person who speaks Polish?

   A. Most of the prefixes and suffixes are the same in Spanish and in English.

   B. Many of the words and roots in Spanish have similar spellings and meanings in English.

   C. English and Spanish both have a logical syntax.

   D. English and Spanish have similar cultural conventions regarding language.

9. Which of the following prereading exercises would help sixth-graders' comprehension of a difficult chapter in a content-area text?

   A. Copying the heads and subheads in the chapter into a notebook

   B. Reading aloud the introductory sentences of the first five paragraphs of the chapter

   C. Finding key vocabulary words in the chapter and discussing them

   D. Scanning the text's table of contents

10. In which of the following sentences is the italicized word used correctly?

    A. The soccer team had arrived at the game with a full *compliment* of equipment.

    B. You will probably want to *complement* the director for the way she handled the art project.

    C. I thought about giving the dance troupe a *complement* after the performance was completed.

    D. I have a tendency to blush when you *compliment* me on how well I skate.

11. Which of the following is a compound sentence?

    A. Nina went to the concert, and she heard her friend Elena sing a solo.

    B. The afternoons that were the rainiest were when Michael stayed inside.

    C. Following the lecture, a group of us went for coffee and pie at the new restaurant.

    D. The movie, which many people believed was fiction, was actually a documentary.

Read the following passage; then answer the two questions that come after it.

(1) For thousands of years, the camel has helped people live in the deserts of Asia and Africa. (2) It can travel for days over hot sands without needing water. (3) It is strong and can carry its driver, plus large loads of supplies, on its back. (4) Since its hide can be used for making many other articles as well as sandals and water bags, people say the animal is useful because of this. (5) Camel bites are painful and are often delivered with no warning, so a camel trainer must be careful and skilled. (6) A camel can be trained to kneel on command. (7) However, it is a stubborn, independent, and ill-tempered animal.

12. Which of the following changes could best improve the logical organization of the passage?

    A. Move sentence 5 so that it follows sentence 6.

    B. Move sentence 5 so that it follows sentence 7.

    C. Move sentence 7 so that it follows sentence 1.

    D. Move sentence 7 so that it follows sentence 3.

13. Which of the following revisions of a sentence would best improve the style of the passage?

    A. Sentence 1: The camel, for thousands of years, has helped people live in the deserts of Asia and Africa.

    B. Sentence 4: The camel is very useful, since it can be used for making sandals, water bags, and many other articles.

    C. Sentence 5: Camel bites are often painful and often delivered with no warning, so a camel trainer must be careful and skilled.

    D. Sentence 7: It is stubborn, however, and independent, and an ill-tempered animal.

Read the following paragraph; then answer the question that comes after it.

(1) The gray whale is one of nature's most majestic creatures. (2) Their migration habits are unique as well. (3) From April to November, gray whales live in the Arctic waters of the Bering and Beaufort Seas. (4) The whales then travel to the warm waters off the coast of Baja California, Mexico, where they mate. (5) The females birth and nurse their young in Baja. (6) The baby whales, which are called calves, grow very quickly. (7) The whales return north after the young have become strong, in late winter.

14. Which of the following is the topic sentence of this paragraph?

    A. Sentence 1

    B. Sentence 2

    C. Sentence 3

    D. Sentence 5

15. Which of the following ideas would be most important to include at the start of a persuasive essay?

    A. A summary of the various viewpoints about the subject

    B. An argument against alternative viewpoints taken by opponents of the issue

    C. An overview of the issue and why it is important

    D. A request to the reader to support the author's viewpoint

16. A news commentator and a writer of general material are most similar because _____.

    A. they convey a feeling of excitement

    B. they employ idioms to keep what they say casual

    C. they use the conventions of Standard English

    D. they allow their audience to have input

17. What technique could a speaker employ to keep an audience's attention most effectively?

    A. Varying the rate, pitch, and rhythm of the speech

    B. Pausing until the audience is attentive

    C. Raising the pitch of the voice

    D. Giving a PowerPoint presentation

Read the following excerpt from a letter; then answer the two questions that come after it.

(1) The idea of school uniforms is not new. (2) Faculty, administrators, and students all have concerned themselves with this issue at one time or another. (3) Yet few conclusions have been adopted on whether such a requirement is beneficial to the education process. (4) The pros and cons have been bandied about, but there is no clear-cut answer. (5) But a growing number of people, including me, feel that in today's world, the idea of school uniforms is an anachronism that has outgrown its usefulness. (6) That is why we are coming together as a group to oppose the latest attempt to regulate the clothes that students wear to school. (7) To be sure, we are in favor of dress that is within the guidelines of good taste, but we refuse to approve the notion that all students should look alike. (8) So please consider joining us in our pledge to put an end to this initiative.

18. Which sentence most strongly suggests that the intent of the letter is persuasive?

   A. Sentence 2

   B. Sentence 4

   C. Sentence 7

   D. Sentence 8

19. Which of the following research questions would be best for starting an objective investigation of the issue of the usefulness of requiring school uniforms?

   A. How many schools have adopted school uniform requirements?

   B. What is the academic average of schools with uniform requirements compared with those lacking such requirements?

   C. What kind of uniforms is preferred by schools that require them?

   D. How do students who are required to wear uniforms in school feel about this requirement?

20. Which of the following elements does a fairy tale generally include?

   A. A dramatic soliloquy

   B. A story featuring a sad ending

   C. Magical events happening

   D. An extended metaphor

Read the following excerpt from an fable by Aesop; then answer the two questions that come after it.

An Ant went to the bank of a river to quench its thirst, and being carried away by the rush of the stream, was on the point of drowning. A Dove sitting on a tree overhanging the water plucked a leaf and let it fall into the stream close to her. The Ant climbed onto it and floated in safety to the bank. Shortly afterwards a bird catcher came and stood under the tree, and laid his lime-twigs for the Dove, which sat in the branches. The Ant, perceiving his design, stung him in the foot. In pain the bird catcher threw down the twigs, and the noise made the Dove take wing.

21. This passage is typical of a fable because _____.

   A. there are elements of magic

   B. it has a message or moral

   C. it does not use any dialogue

   D. it has a happy ending

22. The style of the passage is most like a fable because _____.

   A. its plot suggests something about life

   B. it has a complicated plot

   C. its characters are in opposition to one another

   D. it talks about creation

Read the following poem, "Composed on Westminster Bridge" by William Wordsworth; then answer the two questions that come after it.

Earth has not anything to show more fair:
Dull would he be of soul who could pass by
A sight so touching in its majesty:
This City now doth, like a garment, wear
The beauty of the morning: silent, bare,
Ships, towers, domes, theaters, and temples
    lie
Open unto the fields, and to the sky:
All bright and glittering in the smokeless air,
Never did sun more beautifully steep
In his first splendor, valley, rock, or hill;
Never saw I, never felt, a calm so deep!
The river glideth at his own sweet will:
Dear God! The very houses seem asleep;
And all that mighty heart is lying still!

23. The images used in the poem help to reinforce _____.

   A. the feelings of joy when the poet sees the city

   B. the desire to remain innocent in spite of the sophistications of the city

   C. the enjoyment the poet feels by escaping the city

   D. the ambivalence the poet feels toward the city

24. The poem most clearly supports which of the following themes?

   A. It is an amazing sight to experience something so vibrant and quiet.

   B. Early mornings are times when it is easy to be philosophical.

   C. Life cannot be completely enjoyed without pain.

   D. Things that seem quiet at times are really not at peace at all.

Read the following poem, "The House and the Road" by Josephine Preston Peabody; then answer the two questions that come after it.

The little Road says, Go,
The little House says, Stay:
And O, it's bonny here at home,
But I must go away.

The little Road, like me,
Would seek and turn and know;
And forth I must, to learn the things
The little Road would show!

And go I must, my dears,
And journey while I may,
Though heart be sore for the little House
That had no word but Stay.

Maybe, no other way
Your child could ever know
Why a little House would have you stay,
When a little Road says, Go.

25. In this poem, the image of the road most clearly suggests _____.

   A. a person's need to be happy

   B. a person's desire to be alone

   C. a person's desire to see new things

   D. a person's need to break off relationships

26. The narrator of the poem most likely thinks that _____.

   A. choosing what to do is complex

   B. people are by nature lovers of habit

   C. individuals should concentrate on good deeds

   D. it is better to be conservative in life's choices

Use the map shown here to answer the question that follows.

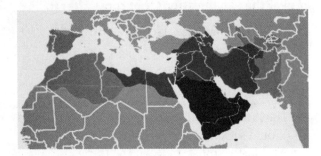

27. The darkest land area on the map shows the extent of which of the following empires?

    A. Ottoman Empire in 1699 CE

    B. Empire of Islam in 732 CE

    C. Phoenician Empire in 950 BCE

    D. Empire of the Han Dynasty in 235 BCE

28. Which of the following statements describes a characteristic of the caste system of feudal Japan in the twelfth century?

    A. Samurai warriors made up a quarter of the population.

    B. Farmers had a higher status than merchants.

    C. The shogun protected the feudal lords and their homes.

    D. Samurai sword makers had their own caste.

29. The Kingdom of Kush exerted control over a wide area of the upper Nile from 2000 to 1500 BCE. Which of the following statements describes a characteristic of this society?

    A. The Kush exported copper to Egypt.

    B. The Kush people resembled their Egyptian neighbors.

    C. The Kush did not have a writing system.

    D. The Kush built ships for long-distance sea voyages.

30. Which of the following best describes the inspiration for Virgil's Latin epic poem *The Aeneid*?

    A. "Hymn to Aphrodite"

    B. *The Iliad*

    C. The Seven Sages

    D. *The Birds*

31. Which of the following is the Roman consul Gaius Marius (157–86 BCE) best known for?

    A. Reforms to benefit the plebeians

    B. Reform of the Roman legion

    C. First Punic War

    D. Leadership in Germania

Use the following excerpt from the Council of Clermont to answer the question that comes after it.

From the confines of Jerusalem and the city of Constantinople a horrible tale has gone forth and very frequently has been brought to our ears, namely, that a race from the kingdom of the Persians, an accursed race, a race utterly alienated from God, a generation forsooth which has not directed its heart and has not entrusted its spirit to God, has invaded the lands of those Christians and has depopulated them by the sword, pillage and fire.

32. Which of the following reasons best describes why the author employed the language used in the excerpt?

    A. To counter the demands of the Eastern Holy Roman Empire

    B. To demand that the invaders leave Jerusalem

    C. To remind the faithful to entrust their spirit to God

    D. To urge the princes of Europe to rescue the Holy Land

Use the following list to answer the question that comes after it.

> ▶ It is one of the oldest deciphered documents.
> ▶ It has been described as an early constitution.
> ▶ It dealt with contracts and transactions.
> ▶ It addressed family matters.

33. The facts in the list best describe which of the following historical documents?

   A. Hippocratic Oath

   B. Augsburg Confession

   C. Magna Carta

   D. Hammurabi's Code

34. Which line in the following table best matches an explorer with what he discovered?

Line	Explorer	What He Discovered
1	Henry the Navigator	Cape of Good Hope
2	Hernando Cortés	West coast of Florida
3	Amerigo Vespucci	Coast of Brazil
4	Ferdinand Magellan	Island of Dominica

   A. Line 1

   B. Line 2

   C. Line 3

   D. Line 4

35. Which of the following is a major historical event of the seventeenth century?

   A. Protestant Reformation

   B. Scientific revolution

   C. Voyage of the *Golden Hind*

   D. Crimean War

36. Which of the following positions was omitted from the Declaration of the Rights of Man and of the Citizen?

   A. The principle of sovereignty resides in the nation.

   B. Law is the expression of general will.

   C. There shall be civil and political rights for women.

   D. Free communication of ideas and opinions is allowed.

Use the following excerpt from a treaty between the United States and Spain to answer the question that comes after it.

TREATY
OF
Friendship, Limits and Navigation,
BETWEEN THE
UNITED STATES OF AMERICA,
AND THE
King of Spain.

His Catholic Majesty and the United States of America deferring to consolidate, on a permanent basis, the friendship and good correspondence which happily prevails between the two parties have determined to establish, by a convention, several parts, the settlement whereof will be productive of general advantage and reciprocal utility to both parties.

37. Which of the following terms best describes the tone of the passage?

   A. Conciliatory

   B. Amicable

   C. Flattering

   D. Obsequious

38. Which of the following statements best summarizes the opinion of Chief Justice John Marshall in *Marbury v. Madison*?

   A. The Supreme Court has jurisdiction to issue writs of mandamus.

   B. The Supreme Court has the authority to review acts of Congress.

   C. The Supreme Court has the authority to establish circuit courts in each judicial district.

   D. The Supreme Court's jurisdiction can be expanded by Congress.

39. Which of the following best describes the doctrine of the Native American Tenskwatawa, known as the Shawnee Prophet?

   A. Rejection of the colonists

   B. Assimilation into white society

   C. Relocation of the Shawnee west of the Mississippi River

   D. Redefinition of the borders of the Indiana Territory

40. Which of the following statements best summarizes the premise of the *South Carolina Exposition and Protest*?

   A. It was meant to resolve strife over slavery in the new territories.

   B. It previewed Calhoun's doctrine of nullification.

   C. It was a tract denouncing abolitionists from the North.

   D. It was a defense of the caning of Senator Charles Sumner.

41. The Mormon Trail, which stretched from Nauvoo, Illinois, to the Salt Lake region of Utah, was used in the 1846 trek because of which of the following events?

   A. The founder of the Mormons, Joseph Smith, had a vision.

   B. The Mormons were told that there was land suitable for farming in Utah.

   C. The Wilmot Proviso excluded slavery in the new western territories.

   D. Brigham Young led 3,000 Mormons to escape persecution.

Use the map shown here to answer the question that follows.

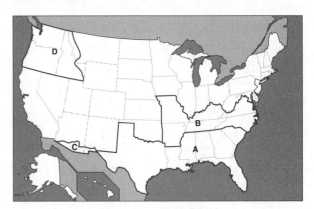

42. Which of the following accurately matches a region on the map with a description of that region?

   A. Region A: states that seceded after the election of Abraham Lincoln in 1860

   B. Region B: land given by the Pawnee native tribe to the United States in 1857

   C. Region C: territory ceded by Mexico after the Mexican-American War in 1848

   D. Region D: land purchased by the United States from France in 1803

43. Which action by the Japanese caused the United States to decide to drop atomic bombs on Hiroshima and Nagasaki in World War II?

    A. Japan began killing American prisoners of war.

    B. Japan captured the island of Guam.

    C. Japan ignored the warning of the Potsdam Declaration.

    D. Japan formed a secret alliance with the Soviet Union.

44. Which of the following best represents a highlight of the presidency of John F. Kennedy?

    A. Bay of Pigs Invasion

    B. Alliance for Progress

    C. Voting Rights Act

    D. U-2 incident

45. When Juan Rodríguez Cabrillo landed in California in what is now San Diego Bay in 1542, the Gabrielino/Tongva Native Americans who rowed out in plank canoes to greet him were a ____.

    A. society in which artisans made soapstone carvings

    B. society that domesticated herds of animals for food and clothing

    C. society that cultivated a number of crops for food

    D. society where people hunted, fished, and gathered wild plants and nuts

46. Which line in the following table accurately matches an important development in California with an event during the era of Mexican rule, 1821–1848?

Line	Development	Event
1	Alta and Baja California are included as territory.	Mexico gains independence from Spain.
2	Cattle ranches are established.	Mission lands are secularized.
3	Citizens of Los Angeles revolt.	Spain establishes formal pueblo government.
4	Cattle herds rapidly expand.	Manuel Micheltorena is appointed governor.

    A. Line 1

    B. Line 2

    C. Line 3

    D. Line 4

47. Which of the following statements best describes the reason the Central Pacific Railroad began hiring Chinese workers to work on the transcontinental railroad in 1865?

    A. Chinese workers were more knowledgeable about railroad-building techniques.

    B. Management considered Irish workers to be too unreliable.

    C. Chinese workers did not have any vices.

    D. There were too many delays, and work was proceeding too slowly.

48. Which of the following statements best describes the effect of World War II on the aircraft industry in California?

    A. Howard Hughes founded Hughes Aircraft Company.

    B. The iconic image of Rosie the Riveter was created.

    C. Many specialized aircraft parts companies were established.

    D. The Boeing Company developed the Boeing Model 1.

49. What was a major ramification of the City of Los Angeles's diversion of water from the tributaries that flow into Mono Lake, beginning in 1941?

    A. The California Supreme Court ruled in favor of the Mono Lake Committee.

    B. The level of salinity in the lake dropped significantly.

    C. Parts of the aqueduct running to Los Angeles were sabotaged.

    D. Aquifers in the area disappeared, and farming and ranching were affected.

50. Governor Ronald Reagan, in a speech before the California Council of Growers on April 7, 1970, is quoted as saying, "If it takes a bloodbath, let's get it over with, no more appeasement." Which of the following events was Governor Reagan referring to?

    A. My Lai Massacre in Vietnam in 1968

    B. Demonstration in People's Park in Berkeley in 1969

    C. Antiwar rioting at the Democratic National Convention in 1968

    D. Shooting at Kent State University in 1970

Use the following excerpt from California Proposition 187 to answer the question that comes after it.

The People of California find and declare as follows:
That they have suffered and are suffering economic hardship caused by the presence of illegal aliens in this state.
That they have suffered and are suffering personal injury and damage caused by the criminal conduct of illegal aliens in this state.
That they have a right to the protection of their government from any person or persons entering this country unlawfully.

51. Which of the following statements best describes a result of Proposition 187?

    A. The law was challenged in the U.S. Supreme Court.

    B. The Republican Party tried to court Latinos.

    C. Latino voters across the state were energized.

    D. The Latino population grew.

Use the following list to answer the question that comes after it.

> ▶ It attracted 40 percent of U.S. venture capital in 2009.
> ▶ It goes through a recurring cycle of boom and bust.
> ▶ Nearly 50 percent of its population speaks a language other than English at home.
> ▶ It is responsible for 50 percent of the new patents issued in California each year.

52. This list of statistical business data best describes which region of California?

    A. San Fernando Valley

    B. San Francisco Bay Area

    C. Sacramento

    D. Silicon Valley

Constructed-Response Assignment 1

Read the following passage from *The Sheik,* by Edith Maude Hull; then complete the exercise that comes after it.

She was totally unembarrassed and completely un-self-conscious. And as they sat silent, her thoughts far away in the desert, and his full of vain longings and regrets, a man's low voice rose in the stillness of the night. "Pale hands I loved beside the Shalimar. Where are you now? Who lies beneath your spell?" he sang in a passionate, vibrating baritone. He was singing in English, and yet the almost indefinite slurring from note to note was strangely un-English. Diana Mayo leaned forward, her head raised, listening intently, with shining eyes. The voice seemed to come from the dark shadows at the end of the garden, or it might have been further away out in the road beyond the cactus hedge. The singer sang slowly, his voice lingering caressingly on the words; the last verse dying away softly and clearly, almost imperceptibly fading into silence. For a moment there was utter stillness, then Diana lay back with a little sigh. "The Kashmiri Song. It makes me think of India. I heard a man sing it in Kashmere last year, but not like that. What a wonderful voice! I wonder who it is?"

Write a response in which you describe how the words the author uses affect the mood of the scene. Be sure to cite specific evidence from the text.

Constructed-Response Sheet—Assignment 1

_____

_____

_____

_____

_____

_____

_____

_____

Constructed-Response Assignment 2

What effect do creative learning methods and playmates have on language acquisition during early to middle childhood?

Constructed-Response Sheet—Assignment 2

_____

_____

_____

_____

_____

_____

_____

_____

_____

_____

_____

_____

_____

_____

_____

_____

_____

Constructed-Response Assignment 3

Complete the exercise that follows.

On June 15, 1215, King John of England agreed to a document that later became known as the Magna Carta.

Using your knowledge of world history, prepare a response in which you:

▶ Identify two important consequences of the Magna Carta;
▶ Select one of the consequences you have identified; and
▶ Explain how the Magna Carta has affected history.

Constructed-Response Sheet—Assignment 3

_____

_____

_____

_____

_____

_____

_____

_____

_____

_____

_____

_____

_____

Constructed-Response Assignment 4

Complete the exercise that follows.

Between the 1920s and the 1940s, the Harlem Renaissance flourished in New York City.

Using your knowledge of U.S. history, prepare a response in which you:

▶ Identify three effects (social, economic, cultural) that affected the Harlem Renaissance;
▶ Select one of the effects; and
▶ Explain how the effect you have selected shaped modern American society.

Constructed-Response Sheet—Assignment 4

_____

_____

_____

_____

_____

_____

_____

_____

_____

_____

_____

_____

SUBTEST II

SCIENCE, MATHEMATICS

Multiple-Choice Answer Sheet

Science

QUESTION NUMBER	YOUR RESPONSE
1	
2	
3	
4	
5	
6	
7	
8	
9	
10	
11	
12	
13	
14	
15	
16	
17	
18	
19	
20	
21	
22	
23	
24	
25	
26	

Mathematics

QUESTION NUMBER	YOUR RESPONSE
27	
28	
29	
30	
31	
32	
33	
34	
35	
36	
37	
38	
39	
40	
41	
42	
43	
44	
45	
46	
47	
48	
49	
50	
51	
52	

Multiple-Choice Questions

1. A barometer is used to measure ____.

   A. temperature

   B. wind speed

   C. humidity

   D. air pressure

2. In the prairie provinces of central Canada, the sarcophagid fly has been observed depositing burrowing larvae on Packard grasshoppers. These larvae will feed on the live grasshopper and leave once fully developed. This describes which of type of relationship?

   A. Commensalism

   B. Parasitism

   C. Predation

   D. Mutualism

3. Which of the following is the best example of a chemical change in matter?

   A. A long piece of wood is carved into the shape of a baseball bat.

   B. The snow in a yard melts as the sun rises.

   C. A vegetable left on a grill becomes charred.

   D. Using a roller, bread dough is flattened to a thickness of ½ inch.

4. In terms of plate tectonics, what name is given to the portion of the earth that is divided into large and small plates?

   A. The atmosphere

   B. The asthenosphere

   C. The hydrosphere

   D. The lithosphere

5. In which of the following organelles does photosynthesis occur?

   A. Nucleus

   B. Ribosomes

   C. Chloroplast

   D. Golgi complex

6. A ball is held on an incline, as shown in the diagram. If the ball is released, what will occur?

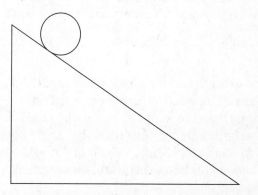

   A. The ball will remain in the same position.

   B. The ball will travel down the incline with a constant speed.

   C. The ball will travel down the incline with increasing speed.

   D. The ball will travel down the incline with decreasing speed due to friction.

7. Mercury and Venus can be seen from Earth near sunset or sunrise. Which of the following statements best explains this phenomenon?

A. It is during these times that the least amount of light is in the sky.

B. At these times, the moon is at its farthest point from Earth.

C. Mercury and Venus are closer to the sun than Earth is.

D. Mercury and Venus have smaller diameters than Earth does.

8. The atomic number of strontium is 38. Which of the following statements must be true?

A. The nucleus of a single atom of strontium contains 38 protons.

B. The nucleus of a single atom of strontium contains 19 neutrons and 19 protons.

C. The total amount of protons and neutrons in the nucleus of a single atom of strontium is 38.

D. The total number of electrons and protons in a single atom of strontium is 38.

9. A cylindrical wax candle and a small rock are each placed in separate one-gallon containers of water. Although the candle weighs more than the rock, the candle floats while the rock sinks. Which of the following statements best explains this observation?

A. The candle has a larger surface area than the small rock.

B. The candle is more porous than the small rock.

C. The small rock is denser than the candle.

D. The small rock weighs more than the gallon of water.

10. Which of the following planets is largest in terms of equatorial diameter?

A. Saturn

B. Venus

C. Earth

D. Mars

11. What process results in the production of gametes?

A. Photosynthesis

B. Meiosis

C. Endocytosis

D. Mitosis

12. Across rows (from left to right), the periodic table is organized by _____.

A. increasing atomic numbers

B. alphabetical order of the chemical symbols

C. similar properties

D. decreasing atomic mass

13. Which of the following phrases best describes what is the epicenter of an earthquake?

A. The point at which the S waves created by the earthquake converge

B. The point at which the earthquake was measured using a seismograph

C. The point within the earth where the motion that caused the earthquake occurred

D. The point on the surface of the earth directly above the point within the earth where the motion that caused the earthquake occurred

14. At a particular location, each of the following conditions can influence the height of high tide EXCEPT ____.

   A. the sun's gravitational pull

   B. the recent air temperature

   C. the moon's gravitational pull

   D. the shape of the immediate coastline

15. A grassland ecosystem consists of short and tall grasses, insects, small rodents that feed on the insects, and large mammals that feed on the grass. Which of the following terms best describes the role of the grasses in the ecosystem?

   A. Primary producers

   B. Primary consumers

   C. Secondary consumers

   D. Tertiary consumers

16. Which of the following statements is true about two different isotopes of the same element?

   A. The two isotopes contain the same number of protons.

   B. The two isotopes contain the same number of neutrons.

   C. The two isotopes have the same atomic weight.

   D. The two isotopes contain different numbers of electrons.

17. On a weather map, isobars connect points of equal barometric pressure. Suppose the isobars over Kansas City, Missouri, are closer together than the isobars over Minot, North Dakota. Which of the following statements would best describe the difference in weather conditions at the two locations?

   A. The temperature in Kansas City is warmer.

   B. There is a greater chance for precipitation in Kansas City.

   C. The winds over Kansas City are stronger.

   D. There is less cloud cover over Kansas City.

18. Quartzite is formed over a long period of time from sandstone under high pressure and temperatures. Quartzite is an example of ____.

   A. a metamorphic rock

   B. an element

   C. a sedimentary rock

   D. a natural glass

19. Which of the following statements does NOT describe the given concept?

Line 1	Velocity is the rate of change in the position of an object along with the direction of the change in position.
Line 2	Speed is the rate of change in position of an object.
Line 3	Acceleration is the difference in the speed of an object at the beginning and the end of its movement.
Line 4	Weight is the magnitude of the force of gravity acting on an object.

   A. Line 1

   B. Line 2

   C. Line 3

   D. Line 4

20. In Brazil, a pod of dolphins has helped fishers for more than 100 years. As the fishers wait, the dolphins corral the fish close to the shore and then signal the fishers to throw their nets. Which of the following statements may explain this behavior?

    A. The dolphins hope the fishers will share some of the total catch.

    B. Dolphins in general have been trained to work for the praise of humans.

    C. The dolphins can easily eat the fish that escape from the nets.

    D. The dolphins eat different types of fish than those the fishers catch.

21. Which of the following is the best example of heat transfer by convection?

    A. The cooler end of a metal rod held in boiling water slowly gets warmer.

    B. A radiator placed in the center of a room warms a bedroom.

    C. An iron pan placed on a stove burner gets warmer.

    D. A person rubs her hands to warm them.

22. A liquid with a high pH can best be described as ____.

    A. neutral

    B. an acid

    C. a base

    D. either a base or an acid, depending on the composition of the liquid

23. In general, the highest wind speed associated with a hurricane is inversely proportional to its ____.

    A. distance from land

    B. diameter

    C. average cloud height

    D. central pressure

24. The prime meridian is the line at which ____.

    A. the longitude is defined to be 0 degrees

    B. the longitude is defined to be 180 degrees

    C. the latitude is defined to be 0 degrees

    D. the latitude is defined to be 180 degrees

25. As an ice cube sits in a freezer, it slowly diminishes in size. This is an example of ____.

    A. osmosis

    B. evaporation

    C. dialysis

    D. sublimation

26. As the overall global temperature increases, the ice caps around the North and South Poles decrease in average size (with seasonal variation). Each of the following is a consequence of this EXCEPT ____.

    A. less carbon dioxide is absorbed by ice at the North and South Poles

    B. the habitats of native polar life shrink, resulting in displacement of populations

    C. there is less ice to reflect heat from the sun, resulting in accelerated warming

    D. the oceans are desalinated, affecting marine life

27. The line $y = -3x + 2$ passes through the point (1, –1). If line l is perpendicular to this line and has a y-intercept of 6, then which of the following points would line l pass through?

    A. (3, 7)

    B. (–1, 1)

    C. (3, 5)

    D. (–1, 4)

28. Combined, the total cost of purchasing a baseball bat and a baseball is $15.50. The baseball bat costs $11.50 more than the baseball. How much does the baseball cost?

    A. $1.00

    B. $2.00

    C. $3.00

    D. $4.00

Use the following equation to answer the question after it.

   $2(x + 5) = 24$

29. Which of the following equations could occur as a step in solving the equation for x?

    A. $2x = 19$

    B. $2x = 14$

    C. $x + 5 = 22$

    D. $x + 5 = 48$

Use the following graph to answer the question after it.

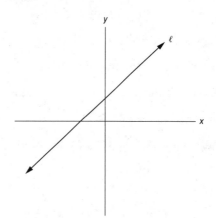

30. Which of the following descriptions is most accurate for line l ?

    A. A line with a positive slope and a positive x-intercept

    B. A line with a negative slope and a positive x-intercept

    C. A line with a positive slope and a negative x-intercept

    D. A line with a negative slope and a negative x-intercept

31. What is the median of the following set of numbers?
    4, 1, 0, 1, 7

    A. 0

    B. 0.5

    C. 1.0

    D. 3.5

32. Of the workforce at a company, $\frac{3}{4}$ are women. Of the women working at the company, $\frac{1}{2}$ have worked there for more than five years. Which of the following questions about the workforce is best answered using multiplication?

   A. What fraction of the workforce are men?

   B. What fraction of the women have less than five years of experience?

   C. What percentage of the workforce are women?

   D. If 25,000 people work at the company, how many are women?

33. The triangle pictured here is a right triangle. What is the area of the triangle in terms of x?

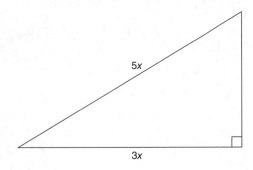

   A. $6x^2$

   B. $9x^2$

   C. $12x^2$

   D. $18x^2$

34. The ages of those attending a small Christmas party are 17, 18, 24, 21, 20, 19, and 81. Which of the following statistics is the best measure of central tendency for this data set?

   A. Mean age

   B. Median age

   C. Mode age

   D. First-quartile age

35. A scale drawing is made of a building such that 1 inch represents 100 feet. If the antenna on the top of the building measures 20 feet, what should it measure in the scale drawing?

   A. 0.2 inch

   B. 0.5 inch

   C. 2 inches

   D. 5 inches

36. If $\frac{1}{3} < x < \frac{3}{8}$, then which of the points on the number line shown here could be x?

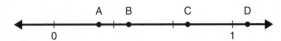

   A. Point A

   B. Point B

   C. Point C

   D. Point D

37. A test contains geometry, algebra, and arithmetic questions. Of the problems on the test, 10 percent are word problems, and half of those require two equations. If there are 100 problems on the test, how many are word problems that require two equations?

   A. 1

   B. 2

   C. 5

   D. 10

38. A factory manufactures two types of items: type X and type Y. Type X items can only be manufactured to be blue, and type Y items can only be manufactured to be red. If an item is randomly selected, then the events "the item is blue" and "the item is type Y" are _____.

   A. mutually exclusive

   B. independent

   C. complementary

   D. opposite

39. Each of the following expressions is a possible prime factorization EXCEPT _____.

   A. $2^2 \cdot 3$

   B. $5^2 \cdot 7^4 \cdot 11$

   C. $4^2 \cdot 7^2$

   D. 7^3

40. A salesperson is paid a flat rate of $500 each month plus a commission of 2 percent of the value of his total sales in a month. If s represents the dollar value of his total sales in a month, which of the following expressions represents his monthly pay?

   A. $500s + 0.02$

   B. $0.02s + 500$

   C. $s(500.02)$

   D. $s(502)$

Use the following multiplication problem to answer the question after it.

$$
\begin{array}{r}
1\ \ 2\ \ 5 \\
\times\ \ 1\ \ \square \\
\hline
6\ \ 2\ \ 5 \\
\square\ \square\ \square\ \square \\
\hline
1\ \ y\ \ 7\ \ 58
\end{array}
$$

41. In the multiplication problem, what is the value of y?

   A. 2

   B. 5

   C. 7

   D. 8

42. Two siblings invent a unit for measuring length called a "gab." They measure their parents' living room to have a width of 10 gabs. If the length of the living room is twice the width and the perimeter is 90 feet, how many feet are equal to 1 gab?

   A. 0.67 foot

   B. 1.5 feet

   C. 3.0 feet

   D. 4.5 feet

43. To multiply the numbers 1.3 and 2.8, Joe rounded each to the nearest whole number and multiplied. By how much did Joe's estimate differ from the actual product?

   A. 0.64

   B. 1.64

   C. 4.40

   D. 6.40

44. A bag of marbles contains only red and green marbles. If a marble is randomly selected, the probability it is red is 9 percent. What is the probability a randomly selected marble is green?

A. 8.1%

B. 9.9%

C. 18%

D. 91%

45. In the triangle pictured here, which of the following methods can be used to find the value of x?

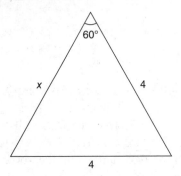

A. Since the given angle is 60 degrees and 60 is 1/3 of 180, x must be three times as large as the side opposite the given angle. Therefore, the value of x is $3 \times 4 = 12$.

B. Since the two given sides have length 4, by the Pythagorean theorem, the remaining side must have a length of $\sqrt{4^2 + 4^2}$ units, which would be the value of x.

C. The remaining angles in the triangle must sum to 120, which is twice 60. Therefore, x must be $2 \times 4 = 8$ units long.

D. Since the given angle is 60 degrees and the corresponding side has a length of 4, the angle opposite the other side of length 4 also is 60 degrees. Therefore, the triangle is equilateral, and the value of x is 4.

46. The area of a right triangle is 24 square units. If the length of the shortest leg is 6, what is the length of the hypotenuse?

A. 4

B. 8

C. 10

D. 14

47. Which of the following equations would represent a line with a slope of 0?

A. $y = 0.5x$

B. $y = 5$

C. $x = 7$

D. $x = 0$

48. The algebraic expression $(x + 2)^2 - 2x$ is equivalent to _____.

A. $x^2 + 2x + 4$

B. $x^2 + 4x - 4$

C. $x^2 - 4$

D. $x^2 - 2$

49. In the drawing shown here, the area of square *A* is 16 square units, and the area of square *B* is 64 square units. What is the perimeter of the shape pictured?

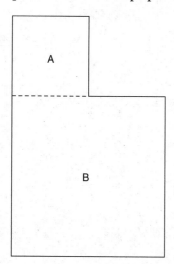

A. 12

B. 24

C. 40

D. 70

50. If the circle pictured here represents 1 unit, which of the following fractions represents the fraction of the circle that is shaded?

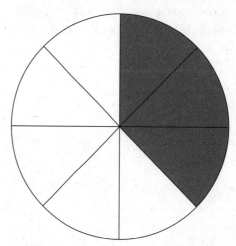

A. $\dfrac{12}{32}$

B. $\dfrac{3}{5}$

C. $\dfrac{6}{15}$

D. $\dfrac{1}{2}$

51. In the graph shown here, t represents time, and y represents the distance driven on a single day by a family on a trip. Which of the following statements best describes the relationship shown in the graph?

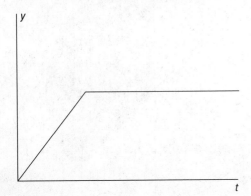

A. The family drove at a constant rate for the entire day.

B. The family drove quickly at first and then at a constant rate for the remainder of the day.

C. The family drove slowly at first and then drove at an increasing rate for the remainder of the day.

D. The family drove at a constant rate at first and then stopped for the remainder of the day.

52. Which of the following percentages is equivalent to $\dfrac{2}{1,000}$?

A. 0.002%

B. 0.02%

C. 0.2%

D. 2%

Constructed-Response Assignment 1

Use the diagram shown here and the information after it to complete the exercise that follows them.

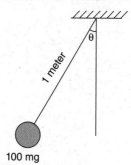

1 meter

θ

100 mg

A physicist measures the period of a pendulum at street level by swinging it at a small angle, q. He then takes the pendulum to the top of a tall building and measures the period again, using the same angle, noting that the period at the top of the building is 0.5 percent longer.

Using your knowledge of physics:

▶ Discuss why the pendulum's period is longer at the top of the building.
▶ Aside from the reason you already discussed, discuss two other factors that can lengthen the pendulum's period.
▶ Holding all other variables constant, describe the pendulum's period if the ball were composed of copper, and its period if the ball were composed of granite.

Constructed-Response Sheet—Assignment 1

_____

_____

_____

_____

_____

_____

_____

Constructed-Response Assignment 2

Use the diagram shown here and the information after it to complete the following exercise.

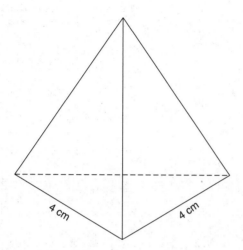

4 cm   4 cm

This pyramid is an equilateral tetrahedron. Using paint that can cover 10 cm² per milliliter, how much paint does it take to cover the entire surface of the pyramid?

Constructed-Response Sheet—Assignment 2

_____

_____

_____

_____

_____

_____

_____

_____

_____

Constructed-Response Assignment 3

Complete the following exercise.

In a particular breed of mouse, the A gene controls tail length, with a dominant gene resulting in a long tail and a recessive gene resulting in a short tail. The B gene controls coat color, with a dominant gene resulting in a brown coat and a recessive gene resulting in a white coat.

A male mouse with the genotype Aa aB has 28 offspring with a female of genotype ab Ab.

Using your knowledge of statistics and biology:

▶ Discuss how to estimate the number of short-tailed offspring.
▶ Determine how many of the 28 offspring will display both of their mother's tail *and* coat phenotypes, and how many will display both of their father's phenotypes.
▶ Describe what proportion of the offspring can produce a short-tailed white offspring of their own, should they reproduce with a mouse displaying both of those recessive characteristics.

Constructed-Response Sheet—Assignment 3

_____

_____

_____

_____

_____

_____

_____

_____

_____

Constructed-Response Assignment 4

Use the diagram shown here and the information after it to complete the following exercise.

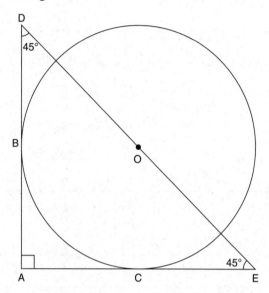

The circle with a center at *O* has an area of 10 cm².

Using your knowledge of algebra and geometry:

▶ Determine the area of the triangle, assuming that line *DE* is perfectly bisected at point *O*.
▶ Assuming that *DE* is NOT bisected at point *O*, what is the product of the lengths of lines *BD* and *CE*?

Constructed-Response Sheet—Assignment 4

_____

_____

_____

_____

_____

_____

SUBTEST III

PHYSICAL EDUCATION, HUMAN DEVELOPMENT, AND VISUAL AND PERFORMING ARTS

Multiple-Choice Answer Sheet

Physical Education

QUESTION NUMBER	YOUR RESPONSE
1	
2	
3	
4	
5	
6	
7	
8	
9	
10	
11	
12	
13	

Human Development

QUESTION NUMBER	YOUR RESPONSE
14	
15	
16	
17	
18	
19	
20	
21	
22	
23	
24	
25	
26	

Visual and Performing Arts

QUESTION NUMBER	YOUR RESPONSE
27	
28	
29	
30	
31	
32	
33	
34	
35	
36	
37	
38	
39	

Multiple-Choice Questions

1. Which of the following is a nonlocomotor skill?

   A. Kicking

   B. Sliding

   C. Twisting

   D. Walking

2. Which is the costliest health problem in the United States?

   A. Prescription medication abuse

   B. Alcohol, tobacco, and drug abuse

   C. Cardiovascular disease

   D. Diabetes

3. A physical education teacher plans activities that encourage his students to work together and build strong interpersonal relationships. Which approach is he using?

   A. Self-actualization approach

   B. Relationship-based approach

   C. Social responsibility approach

   D. Ecological integration approach

A kindergarten physical education class includes the following sequence of events:

- ▶ Students receive instruction on the activities they will participate in that day.
- ▶ They rotate through three stations, which include alternating running and galloping laps around the playground, hula hoops, and bouncing a ball to a partner.
- ▶ After completing each activity, the students regroup and practice breathing exercises.
- ▶ The teacher leads a discussion about the rotations and working with partners.

4. Which component should be added to the lesson?

   A. Students should engage in calisthenics before the initial instruction.

   B. Students should kick the ball with a partner in addition to bouncing it.

   C. Students should walk at a moderate pace while doing breathing exercises.

   D. Students should participate in a team sport during one of the activity rotations.

5. An activity requires students to extend body parts away from the center of their body. Which type of movement is this an example of?

   A. Bending

   B. Sliding

   C. Stretching

   D. Turning

6. Physical fitness has many health benefits, including decreased risk of future coronary problems, such as plaque being deposited on the walls of the arteries. What is this condition?

    A. Arteriosclerosis

    B. Congestive heart failure

    C. Coronary thrombosis

    D. Heart attack

7. Which statement accurately relates socioeconomic status (SES) and physical fitness?

    A. SES level does not affect the physical fitness of students.

    B. Students from a lower SES need lower expectations in PE class.

    C. Lower-SES students are more physically fit than higher-SES students.

    D. Higher-SES students are more likely to be involved in physical activities.

8. Which of the following is NOT an example of a weight-bearing activity?

    A. Tennis

    B. Walking

    C. Bicycle riding

    D. Aerobic dancing

9. Stability movements _____.

    A. are actions that are vital for the body to be able to maintain balance while moving

    B. are produced by contracting the skeletal muscles and increase the expenditure of energy

    C. use a device or the weight of the body as resistance to enhance strength and endurance

    D. are actions that are organized and occur around the axis of the body

10. Which of the following items must be included in an Individual Education Program (IEP)?

    A. Present level of performance

    B. Current grade in physical education

    C. Number of students in the child's class

    D. Physical education goals for nondisabled peers

11. Which manipulative skill does a child generally develop before learning to throw?

    A. Bouncing

    B. Kicking

    C. Skipping

    D. Striking

12. Students in a middle-school physical education class are instructed on how to calculate target heart rate. Following this, the students alternate walking, jogging, and running for a period of 15 minutes, monitoring their heart rate throughout the activity. Their goal is to maintain 70 to 85 percent of their maximum heart rate. Which of the FITT guidelines should be altered to improve the activity?

    A. Frequency

    B. Intensity

    C. Time

    D. Type

13. The development of motor skills in children involves both gross-motor and fine-motor areas. Which of the following is NOT a gross-motor area?

    A. Arms

    B. Legs

    C. Neck

    D. Toes

14. Which of the following statements is true of negative reinforcement?

    A. Students escape punishment by repeating a desired behavior.

    B. Students are rewarded for repeating a desired behavior.

    C. Students are not reinforced for undesired behaviors.

    D. Students are punished for undesired behaviors.

15. According to Jean Piaget, at what age do children begin to demonstrate the ability to reason effectively and think about concepts in fully symbolic terms?

    A. 18 months

    B. 7 years

    C. 12 years

    D. 16 years

16. Which of the following statements is true regarding low self-esteem, anxiety, and tension?

    A. Most students do not face any of these conditions.

    B. The majority of students suffer from these conditions.

    C. These factors cause students to have difficulty in school.

    D. These factors often work together to motivate students to be successful.

17. A teacher is planning to introduce a new game to a group of students who have mild mental handicaps. Which is the best strategy to use?

    A. Explain the game a few times.

    B. Have students practice the game repeatedly.

    C. Take students' turns for them if they are struggling.

    D. Tell students all of the skills involved in the game.

18. Which of the following methods is most appropriate when teaching diverse students?

   A. Lower expectations for students who do not speak English as their primary language.

   B. Encourage competitiveness among students from families with high socioeconomic status.

   C. Decrease the amount of structure for students from low-SES situations.

   D. Include context clues to help Limited English Proficiency (LEP) students understand instruction.

19. A student is well liked by her classmates and teachers, and she consistently earns high grades in most subjects. These successful social and academic experiences create a feeling of competence. This is an example of which stage of Erikson's development theory?

   A. Identity versus identity confusion

   B. Identity versus inferiority

   C. Initiative versus guilt

   D. Intimacy versus isolation

20. Which of the following is a true statement regarding play?

   A. Games with rules play are generally replaced by organized sports by adolescence.

   B. Rough-and-tumble play is most popular during the early teen years.

   C. Sensorimotor skills are developed through imaginative play.

   D. Constructive play involves the repetition of behaviors.

21. What percent of children and adolescents typically follow all of the recommended guidelines for diet and nutrition?

   A. 1 percent

   B. 3 percent

   C. 5 percent

   D. 9 percent

22. Over several weeks, a teacher notices that a second-grade student has seemed sad and often displays signs of anger toward his classmates. During this same period, the child has wet himself on a few occasions. He also has cut himself with scissors and stabbed himself with a pencil, although he reported that these were accidents. These occurrences could be signs of _____.

   A. emotional maltreatment

   B. physical neglect

   C. physical abuse

   D. sexual abuse

23. The tendency of a child to completely focus on one object or idea at a time while completely disregarding all others is _____.

   A. animism

   B. centration

   C. egocentrism

   D. seriation

24. According to Kohlberg's stages of moral development, which would be an example of conventional morality?

    A. Understanding that justice is always more important than law or social norms

    B. Actions that reflect a sense of respect for rules, rather than a desire to please others

    C. Behavior that results from a fear of punishment, rather than from a sense of conscience

    D. Belief that the needs of society may be more important than the needs of individuals

25. A student demonstrates strong interpersonal abilities as defined by Gardner's theory of multiple intelligences. Which type of class project might the student be most successful at completing?

    A. Building a model of a landmark

    B. Writing a poem about an activity

    C. Performing an interpretive dance

    D. Interviewing a sports personality

26. Which of the following statements is true about the physical development of children?

    A. Fourteen-year-old girls tend to experience greater growth spurts than boys of the same age.

    B. Children grow faster between the ages of two and six than during any other period.

    C. Twelve-year-old girls tend to be taller and weigh slightly more than their male classmates.

    D. Children experience an increase in the amount of fatty tissue between ages two and six.

27. Which art form naturally employs a linear perspective?

    A. Collages

    B. Paintings

    C. Photographs

    D. Prints

28. Which of the following practices occurred before the church attempted to restrict pagan dancing?

    A. Dance celebrated special events, and fertility dances celebrated the changing of the seasons.

    B. Dance evolved to incorporate freedom of movement and appreciation of individuals.

    C. The movement of ballet from France to Italy led to the beginning of court dancing.

    D. The minuet gained popularity as a formal aristocratic form of dance.

29. According to the key content standards for visual and performing arts, which method could best be used to teach kindergarten students about creative expression used in dance?

    A. Have students use movement to reflect various experiences that evoke emotions.

    B. Have students use pantomime or improvisation to retell familiar fairy tales.

    C. Ask students to name and perform traditional dances from various countries.

    D. Explain the basic features of different types of dances.

30. In music, a word naming the volume or intensity of a tone is _____.

    A. dynamics

    B. motif

    C. pitch

    D. timbre

31. An artist displays an oil painting she created using mostly tones of yellow. Which is true about the colors she used in the piece?

    A. The yellow tones appear to expand the size of the piece and create a cold mood.

    B. The yellow tones appear to contract the size of the piece and create a cold mood.

    C. The yellow tones appear to expand the size of the piece and create a warm mood.

    D. The yellow tones appear to contract the size of the piece and create a warm mood.

32. Which type of dance allows students to use movement to express their emotions and allows students of all ability levels to participate?

    A. Folk dance

    B. Social dance

    C. Modern dance

    D. Cultural dance

33. Which of the following notes is included in a D-major scale?

    A. C-sharp

    B. D-sharp

    C. F-flat

    D. G-flat

34. In dance, *accent* refers to _____.

    A. the underlying beat

    B. the plan for the performance

    C. a strong gesture or movement

    D. a dance that follows a story

35. During which time period did acting begin to mimic real life more closely and begin to deal with ordinary people more often?

    A. Medieval era

    B. Renaissance

    C. Eighteenth century

    D. Nineteenth century

36. Which statement accurately describes the positions of instruments in a symphony orchestra, from the perspective of the conductor?

    A. Double basses are on the conductor's right, behind the clarinets.

    B. Percussion instruments are on the conductor's left, behind the violins.

    C. Trumpets are in front of the conductor, seated in front of the bassoons.

    D. French horns are in front of the conductor, seated in front of the tubas.

37. During which period was notated rhythm added to musical notation?

    A. Baroque era

    B. Classical era

    C. Medieval era

    D. Renaissance era

38. Which value of color is also called chroma?

    A. Hue

    B. Saturation

    C. Shade

    D. Value

39. Form and shape are examples of which element of dance?

    A. Space

    B. Time

    C. Levels

    D. Force

Constructed-Response Assignment 1

Complete the exercise that follows.

A physical educator uses the FITT principles of fitness with her students.

Using your knowledge of exercise physiology, health, and physical fitness:

▶ List and briefly explain the four components of the FITT guidelines; and
▶ Give an example of an activity or duration for each FITT component that would be appropriate for an upper-elementary student.

Constructed-Response Sheet—Assignment 1

_____

_____

_____

_____

_____

_____

_____

_____

_____

_____

_____

_____

_____

_____

Constructed-Response Assignment 2

Complete the exercise that follows.

Psychologist Jean Piaget outlined four stages of cognitive development.

Using your knowledge of cognitive development:

▶ List and briefly discuss Piaget's four stages of cognitive development; and
▶ Give one example of how an understanding of these stages should influence educators.

Constructed-Response Sheet—Assignment 2

_____

_____

_____

_____

_____

_____

_____

_____

_____

_____

_____

_____

_____

_____

_____

Constructed-Response Assignment 3

Complete the exercise that follows.

Many distinct forms of dance have developed over the centuries.

Using your knowledge of visual and performing arts:

▶ Compare and contrast ballet and modern dance; and
▶ Include the time periods during which each of these dance forms was developed.

Constructed-Response Sheet—Assignment 3

_____

_____

_____

_____

_____

_____

_____

_____

_____

_____

_____

_____

_____

_____

CHAPTER 13

Practice Test 2 Results

Domain Answer Sheets

As with the diagnostic test, on the following pages you'll find Domain Answer Sheets that will help you evaluate your answers. The first two columns show the correct answer for each question. Use the other two columns to indicate whether you answered a specific question correctly. After the columns, there is a space where you can enter the total number of questions you answered correctly for that particular domain. After the Domain Answer Sheets, you'll have the chance to look over explanations for each question, which will help clarify which topics you've mastered and those you may need to review more.

SUBTEST I:
DOMAIN ANSWER SHEET

READING, LANGUAGE, AND LITERATURE

QUESTION NUMBER	CORRECT ANSWER	YOUR ANSWER Correct?	Incorrect?
1	B		
2	A		
3	A		
4	D		
5	C		
6	D		
7	C		
8	B		
9	C		
10	D		
11	A		
12	B		
13	B		
14	B		
15	C		
16	C		
17	A		
18	D		
19	B		
20	C		
21	B		
22	A		
23	A		
24	A		
25	C		
26	A		

You answered _____ out of 26 questions correctly.

SUBTEST I:
DOMAIN ANSWER SHEET

HISTORY AND SOCIAL SCIENCE

QUESTION NUMBER	CORRECT ANSWER	YOUR ANSWER Correct?	Incorrect?
27	B		
28	B		
29	C		
30	B		
31	B		
32	D		
33	D		
34	C		
35	B		
36	C		
37	B		
38	B		
39	A		
40	B		
41	D		
42	A		
43	C		
44	B		
45	D		
46	C		
47	B		
48	C		
49	A		
50	B		
51	C		
52	D		

You answered _____ out of 26 questions correctly.

SUBTEST II: DOMAIN ANSWER SHEET

SCIENCE

QUESTION NUMBER	CORRECT ANSWER	YOUR ANSWER	
		Correct?	Incorrect?
1	D		
2	B		
3	C		
4	D		
5	C		
6	C		
7	C		
8	A		
9	C		
10	A		
11	B		
12	A		
13	D		
14	B		
15	A		
16	A		
17	C		
18	A		
19	C		
20	C		
21	B		
22	C		
23	D		
24	A		
25	D		
26	A		

You answered _____ out of 26 questions correctly.

SUBTEST II: DOMAIN ANSWER SHEET

MATHEMATICS

QUESTION NUMBER	CORRECT ANSWER	YOUR ANSWER	
		Correct?	Incorrect?
27	A		
28	B		
29	B		
30	C		
31	C		
32	D		
33	A		
34	B		
35	A		
36	B		
37	C		
38	A		
39	C		
40	B		
41	D		
42	B		
43	A		
44	D		
45	D		
46	C		
47	B		
48	A		
49	C		
50	A		
51	D		
52	C		

You answered _____ out of 26 questions correctly.

SUBTEST III:
DOMAIN ANSWER SHEET
PHYSICAL EDUCATION

QUESTION NUMBER	CORRECT ANSWER	YOUR ANSWER	
		Correct?	Incorrect?
1	C		
2	B		
3	C		
4	A		
5	C		
6	A		
7	D		
8	C		
9	A		
10	A		
11	D		
12	C		
13	D		

You answered _____ out of 13 questions correctly.

SUBTEST III:
DOMAIN ANSWER SHEET
HUMAN DEVELOPMENT

QUESTION NUMBER	CORRECT ANSWER	YOUR ANSWER	
		Correct?	Incorrect?
14	A		
15	C		
16	C		
17	B		
18	D		
19	B		
20	A		
21	A		
22	D		
23	B		
24	B		
25	D		
26	C		

You answered _____ out of 13 questions correctly.

SUBTEST III:
DOMAIN ANSWER SHEET

VISUAL AND PERFORMING ARTS

QUESTION NUMBER	CORRECT ANSWER	YOUR ANSWER	
		Correct?	Incorrect?
27	C		
28	A		
29	A		
30	A		
31	C		
32	C		
33	A		
34	C		
35	C		
36	B		
37	C		
38	B		
39	C		

You answered _____ out of 13 questions correctly.

Subtest I Explanations

READING, LANGUAGE, AND LITERATURE; HISTORY AND SOCIAL SCIENCE

1. B The *oa* vowel pattern is associated with the long-*o* sound in words such as *boat, float,* and *coat.* There are very few exceptions to this rule. Choices A, C, and D are associated with multiple pronunciations: the *oo* in *drook* is found in *hoop, book,* and *roof*; the *ow* in *drow* is found in *cow, tow,* and *bow*; the *ou* in *sough* is found in *rough, though,* and *through.*

2. A The correct order moves from semantics (the structure, meaning, and context of language) to the basic building blocks of sounds (phonemes). Syntax (the structure of the sentence) comes after semantics. Morphemes come before phonemes. They are sound or sound combinations that create meaning and words.

3. A This is what a child typically is able to do during the transitional stage of spelling. Choice B occurs in the conventional stage of spelling. Choice C is typical of the semiphonetic stage of spelling. Choice D is associated with the phonetic stage of spelling.

4. D A child's oral vocabulary is an important factor in learning to read. Even though a child might attempt to sound out the word *crow,* he would not understand a word that is not in his speaking or listening vocabulary.

5. C This scaffolding tool helps support a child's ability to acquire language. Choices A and B are incorrect because this tool would not affect morphemic awareness or improve oral vocabulary. Choice D also is incorrect because in this example it only supports knowledge of one letter, and does not aid the child in sounding out words.

6. D Observing the child in creative play will tell a teacher the child's zone of proximal development (ZPD), since children engaged in undirected play naturally play at the boundaries of what they are capable of doing. Choices A, B, and C are not correct because they do not help assess a child's ZPD.

7. C While all of the choices can help children enhance their vocabularies, the best way is by having the child read independently. Reading aloud to children (choice A) can help alert them to new words, but it is not the most effective way to enhance vocabulary. Choices B and D also can be helpful, but not as helpful as choice C.

8. B Words and roots in Spanish and those in English are similar because the two languages are related, whereas English is not related to Polish. All languages have a logical syntax, so choice C is incorrect. The cultural conventions regarding language are different in every country, so choice D is incorrect.

9. C Discussing the meaning of key vocabulary in a difficult chapter is an effective prereading exercise. A discussion of vocabulary helps promote comprehension by making the important words and concepts clearer. This helps focus attention on the main ideas of the chapter. The other exercises would not lead to a better understanding of the text.

10. D The word *complement* means something that completes or makes up a whole. The word *compliment* means an expression of praise or admiration. Choice D is the only sentence that is correct. Choice A confuses *compliment* with *complement.* Choices B and C confuse *complement* with *compliment.*

11. A Choice A is a compound sentence because it contains two independent clauses. Choice B contains a relative clause. Choices C and D are complex sentences containing a main clause and a subordinate clause.

12. B Choice B creates a logical flow of ideas in the passage. Choices A, C, and D would not make sense.

13. B Choice B eliminates the duplication in the sentence by deleting "because of this," and it puts the uses of a camel's skin into a more logical order. Choice A is written in an awkward manner. Choice C unnecessarily adds an extra *often.* Choice D is awkward and less direct than the original sentence 7.

14. **B** This choice is the best topic sentence because it relates to what the passage is mostly about. Sentence 1 (choice A) gives an opinion about the gray whale but is not the main idea of the paragraph. Choice C relates more information about the main idea. Choice D also gives supporting information about the main topic.

15. **C** An overview of the issue and why it is important is an excellent way to start a persuasive essay. Choices A and B would most likely be found in the middle of the essay. Choice D would most likely come at the end of the essay.

16. **C** Because neither the news commentator nor the writer of general material knows his or her audience, both are most likely to use the conventions of Standard English. Choice A is incorrect because both could convey a feeling of excitement but need not do so. Choice B is not correct because idioms are useful when a person knows who the audience is. While allowing audience input (choice D) might be something a television personality would do, generally neither a news commentator nor a writer has audience input until after having been on the air or published the material that was written.

17. **A** This is the most effective way to keep an audience interested in an oral presentation. Choice B is not a good alternative because it would make the audience uncomfortable. Choice C is not effective; a higher-pitched voice is less likely to be agreeable to a listener than a lower-pitched voice. Choice D might temporarily keep the audience's attention, but only if the presentation were interesting.

18. **D** Sentence 8 most strongly suggests that the intent of the letter is persuasive, since it asks the reader to join with the group to oppose an initiative to impose school uniforms. Choice A gives background information, as does choice B. Choice C is not persuasive in nature.

19. **B** Choice B is the best option because it treats a measurable and important possible outcome of requiring school uniforms, and the answer to this question could help support arguments for or against the "usefulness" of uniforms. Choices A, C, and D do not specifically relate to the "usefulness" of school uniforms..

20. **C** Choice C is what a fairy tale generally includes. Choice A would apply to a play or dramatic piece. Choice B would be associated with a tragic play or story. Choice D would be consistent with an allegory.

21. **B** This is what a fable always includes: a message or moral about life. There may be elements of magic (choice A), but this is not typical of a fable. Magic is more typical of a fairy tale. Dialogue does not suggest that something is or is not a fable, so choice C is not correct. Although this fable does have a happy ending (choice D), this is not necessarily typical of a fable.

22. **A** This is the style element that is most like a fable. Usually fables have simple plots; they are seldom very long, so choice B is incorrect. Characters in a fable could be in opposition to one another (choice C), but not necessarily. This fable does not talk about creation (choice D); that would be more the style of a myth.

23. **A** All of the images stress the joy the poet feels toward the city he sees in the early-morning light. Choices B and C are not issues for the poet. The poet does not show any ambivalence toward the city (choice D).

24. **A** Choice A best supports the theme of the poem. Choice B is not correct because the poet is emotional, not philosophical. Choice C does not play into the theme of the poem at all. Although the city is quiet, there is no suggestion that the city is not peaceful (choice D).

25. **C** The road suggests a person's desire to see and experience new things. Choice A is not correct, since the poem says it is "bonny" at home and that the "heart" may be sad about leaving. There is no suggestion that the narrator wants to be alone (choice B) or break off relationships (choice D).

26. **A** The poet seems to be suggesting that there is no easy answer, and sometimes hard choices have to be made. Choice B is not what the poem suggests; the narrator decides to leave home. Choice C does not relate to the poem, because the poet makes no mention of doing good deeds. Choice D is the opposite of the poem's theme.

27. **B** After the death of the prophet Muhammad in 632 CE, Islam expanded rapidly, led by followers faithful to the concept of jihad through military conquest and conversion of nonbelievers, until they were defeated at Poitiers in southwest France in 732 CE. Neither the Ottoman Empire (choice A) nor the Phoenician Empire (choice C) occupied what is present-day Spain. The Han Dynasty was in China, so choice D is incorrect.

28. **B** The philosophy of Confucius emphasized the importance of productive members of society, so farmers held a status just under the samurai, higher than merchants, who were the lowest caste. Choice A is incorrect because samurai warriors made up less than 10 percent of Japan's population. The samurai protected the lords; the shogun was the military commander of the country, making choice C incorrect. Contrary to choice D, samurai sword makers were part of the artisan class, below farmers, along with potters and printmakers.

29. **C** Archaeologists have found no evidence of writing in their excavations. The Kush produced large quantities of gold and iron, which they exported to many countries, but not copper, so choice A is not correct. Choice B is incorrect because the Kush people were black Africans, so they did not look like Egyptians, who were lighter skinned. Contrary to choice D, Phoenicians, not Kush, are known for building ships and making long sea voyages.

30. **B** A poem about Aeneas, son of Anchises and the goddess Aphrodite, *The Aeneid* links Rome to the legends of Troy. Homer mentions Aeneas in *The Iliad*, and Virgil expands the theme into an origin myth. Choice A is incorrect because "Hymn to Aphrodite," a lyric poem by Sappho, is not a source. The Seven Sages were a group of early sixth-century BCE philosophers and statesmen named by the Greeks, making choice C incorrect. *The Birds* is a comedy about birds building a city in the sky to control communications between men and the gods; it also is not mentioned by Virgil, so choice D is incorrect.

31. **B** A general and a statesman, Marius made many changes to the Roman legion. Because of his reforms, the legions ultimately became more loyal to their generals than to the state, which eventually led to the fall of the republic. Tiberius Gracchus pushed through many agrarian reforms and was killed by Roman senators who feared his power, so choice A is incorrect. The First Punic War (choice C), a struggle between Rome and Carthage for control of the western Mediterranean, took place before Marius was born. Marcus Aurelius led the fight against Germanic tribes in 160 CE, so choice D is incorrect.

32. **D** At the Council of Clermont in 1195, Pope Urban II gave a speech urging the people to rescue the Holy Land, which resulted in the first crusade. The language of the excerpt strongly suggests the purpose of the speech. The Eastern Holy Roman Empire had nothing to do with the attack on Jerusalem (choice A). The pope did not demand that the invaders leave the city (choice B); he urged Europe to attack them. While the pope would certainly want the faithful to entrust themselves to God, that was not the intent of his speech, so choice C is incorrect.

33. **D** Dating from 1780 BCE and written by Hammurabi, the sixth Babylonian king, the code lays out laws dictating proper behavior and is seen as an early version of the concept of justice and rights. The Hippocratic Oath (choice A) is an oath that physicians swear to uphold and is commonly believed to have been written by Hippocrates. The Augsburg Confession (choice B) was written in 1530 by Martin Luther; it was a manifesto of the Protestant religion. The Magna Carta (choice C) was an agreement between King John and the barons to protect feudal rights.

34. **C** Vespucci left Portugal in 1501, explored the coast of Brazil, and returned to Lisbon the following year. Henry the Navigator (choice A) sailed along the western bulge of Africa in 1430; it was Bartholomeu Dias who discovered the Cape of Good Hope in 1487. Cortés (choice B) defeated the Aztecs in Mexico in a bloody battle in 1521 at Tenochtitlan; it was Juan Ponce de León who in 1513 landed near what is today Daytona

Beach, Florida, looking for the Fountain of Youth. Christopher Columbus, not Magellan, discovered Dominica in the West Indies on his second voyage in 1493, so choice D is incorrect. Magellan, who left Spain in 1519, discovered the Strait of Magellan at the southern tip of South America.

35. **B** The 1600s saw the publication of the works of Galileo, Copernicus, and Isaac Newton, all of which caused a revolution in scientific thought and transformed the age. The Protestant Reformation (choice A) began in 1517 with the publication of Luther's Ninety-Five Theses. Sir Francis Drake sailed the *Golden Hind*, becoming the first man to circumnavigate the globe, in 1580, which means choice C is incorrect. The Crimean War (choice D), pitting the Russian Empire against an alliance of the French, British, and Ottoman Empires, started in 1853.

36. **C** Women's rights, along with the issue of slavery, were omitted from the Declaration of the Rights of Man and of the Citizen, a document approved by the French National Assembly in 1789. The principle of sovereignty (choice A) is Article 3 of the declaration. Law as the expression of general will (choice B) is in Article 6. Freedom of communication (choice D) was included in Article 11.

37. **B** The excerpt from Pinckney's Treaty between Spain and the United States, ratified by Congress in 1796, has an amicable tone and demonstrates the friendship between the two countries. It gave the Americans the right to navigate the Mississippi River and resolved border disputes between the two countries. The tone is not conciliatory or forgiving (choice A), nor is it flattering (choice C) or obsequious (choice D), both of which indicate a tone of deference.

38. **B** The landmark case *Marbury v. Madison* in 1803 established the precedent that the Supreme Court has the authority to review acts of Congress and to determine if they are unconstitutional and therefore void. Contrary to choice A, the Supreme Court does not have original jurisdiction to issue a writ of mandamus, and Marbury's claim to a federal judgeship, which was the basis of the

case, was denied. Congress has the authority to establish circuit courts and district courts, as written in the Judiciary Act of 1789, so choice C is incorrect. The Supreme Court's jurisdiction cannot be expanded by Congress (choice D) beyond what is specified in Article III of the Constitution.

39. **A** In the early 1800s, the Prophet advocated a return to the ancestral lifestyle and a rejection of the American colonists. He preached that the white men could not be trusted, so he would not have favored being assimilated into their society (choice B). There is no indication he ever advocated moving west of the Mississippi, so choice C is incorrect. Contrary to choice D, he did not redefine the borders of the Indiana Territory, but instead demanded that Governor Harrison give back the three million acres the Indians had ceded at the Treaty of Fort Wayne in 1809.

40. **B** Written in 1828 by Vice President John Calhoun, the document protested the Tariff of 1828 and warned that, if it was not repealed, South Carolina would secede. Choice A is incorrect because it was the Compromise of 1850 that addressed keeping free states and slave states in balance in the new territories. Northern abolitionists often mailed to southern addresses literature denouncing slavery, but this was not what the *South Carolina Exposition and Protest* addressed, so choice C is incorrect. Choice D is unrelated: South Carolinian Preston Brooks caned Senator Sumner on the floor of the Senate in 1856 and was considered a hero in his state.

41. **D** What is now called the Mormon Trail was the 1,300-mile trail on which Young led his travelers to escape threats of violence and religious persecution in Illinois after more than 200 Mormon homes were burned in one month. Choice A is not correct; rather, when Joseph Smith had a vision in Fayette, New York, in 1827, he transcribed the Book of Mormon. When they arrived in Utah, the Mormons did start farming, but nobody specifically told them about farming land, so choice B is incorrect. The Wilmot Proviso (choice C) was an amendment to a bill that

would exclude slavery in lands acquired from Mexico during the Mexican-American War.

42. **A** South Carolina, Florida, Georgia, Alabama, Mississippi, Louisiana, and Texas seceded from the Union before the Civil War started. Region B, representing Arkansas, Missouri, Kentucky, Tennessee, North Carolina, and Virginia, seceded after the attack on Fort Sumter on April 12, 1861. It is not the land the Pawnee gave, which is in present-day Nebraska and northern Kansas. Region C is the land purchased from Mexico by the Gadsden Purchase in 1854, so choice C is not correct. Land was purchased from France in the Louisiana Purchase of 1803, but the region outlined in Region D was transferred in a treaty with Great Britain in 1846, making choice D incorrect.

43. **C** At Potsdam on July 26, 1945, the Allies issued an ultimatum to Japan: they must surrender or face "prompt and utter destruction." Japan ignored the demand, and U.S. President Harry Truman gave the order to drop the bombs on August 6 and August 9, 1945. None of the other choices is true.

44. **B** The Alliance for Progress was proposed by President Kennedy in 1961 to improve economic cooperation between the United States and South America. Over the next 10 years, the program saw numerous successes, including a reduction in adult illiteracy, construction of health clinics, and the start of land reform. In 1961 a CIA-trained group of Cuban exiles invaded Cuba at the Bay of Pigs to overthrow Fidel Castro. The mission failed and was a major foreign-affairs setback for Kennedy, so choice A is not correct. The Voting Rights Act was legislation enacted in 1965 by President Johnson, who succeeded Kennedy after JFK's assassination, which makes choice C incorrect. The U-2 incident (choice D), in which an American spy plane was shot down over the Soviet Union, occurred in 1960 before Kennedy was elected.

45. **D** The Native American tribes of Southern California gathered wild plants and acorns, fished the abundant streams and the ocean, and hunted. Contrary to choice A, they did not make soapstone carvings as did tribes in the northern part of the state. Nor did they domesticate animals (choice B); they did not need a lot of clothes, because of the climate. They did not cultivate the land, because of unpredictable precipitation and frequent droughts, so choice C is incorrect.

46. **A** In 1821, New Spain won its independence from Spain after a long war. The new country of Mexico promptly declared Baja and Alta California Mexican territories. Cattle ranches were established (choice B) when Spain established a pueblo government, called the Viceroyalty of New Spain, with Mexico City as the capital. Administrative governors gave out parcels of land as gifts. Choice C is incorrect because the citizens of Los Angeles revolted when Manuel Micheltorena was appointed governor. He surrendered in the Battle of La Providencia in 1848 and was the last governor to rule from Mexico City. Cattle herds began to grow rapidly (choice D) when the former mission lands were secularized.

47. **B** Hiring Chinese workers was very unpopular in California. With the discovery of silver in Nevada in 1865, the Irish, who had built all the railroads in the east, left to prospect for silver. Of every 1,000 men hired, 900 left. Choice A is not correct because the Chinese had no knowledge of railroad building; however, they did learn quickly. The Chinese were compulsive gamblers and played fan tan, a game similar to roulette, every night, and they smoked opium regularly, which means choice C is incorrect. Choice D also is incorrect: except for the difficulty of ascending the Sierra Nevada, the work went quickly, and once the Great Plains were reached, workers laid 10 miles of track per day.

48. **C** Driven by federal spending of $35 billion between 1941 and 1946, many specialized aircraft parts and supply companies were established in Southern California. Choice A is incorrect because the millionaire Howard Hughes established his aircraft company in 1932, long before World War II. Norman Rockwell created the famous image of Rosie the Riveter (choice B) for a cover of the *Saturday Evening Post* in 1943. The image honored women who were working in factories all around the country but was not an

effect of World War II on the aircraft industry in California; the tribute was nationwide. Choice D cannot be correct because Boeing developed the Boeing Model 1 in Seattle in 1916. It was made of wood with wire bracing.

49. **A** The California Supreme Court ruled in 1983 in favor of the Mono Lake Committee, a group of environmentalists, and the National Audubon Society, who together brought litigation against the Los Angeles Department of Water and Power because water levels had fallen so much. The court ruled the department had violated the public trust doctrine. Eventually, water levels returned to normal. Choice B is wrong: Mono Lake has no outlet and as a result is saline; saline levels increased significantly as a result of the diversion, affecting existing aquaculture. Completed in 1913, the Los Angeles aqueduct, another aqueduct, ran 233 miles from the Owens River to Los Angeles. Farmers in the Owens Valley dynamited sections in 1923 to protest the lack of water as a result of the City of Los Angeles's action, so choice C is incorrect. Aquifers in Owens Valley, far from Mono Lake, dried up; after many years of litigation, Los Angeles rewatered the river, so choice D also is incorrect.

50. **B** Reagan allowed police to use force during a demonstration at People's Park, on a day that became known as Bloody Thursday when more than 150 people were wounded and one was killed. A state of emergency was declared, and the governor sent in more than 2,500 troops. The governor was not referring to events outside the state: the My Lai Massacre (choice A) occurred when U.S. troops killed more than 300 civilians in the Vietnamese village of My Lai, and antiwar demonstrators clashed with police during the Democratic National Convention in Chicago (choice C). The shooting at Kent State (choice D), in which the Ohio National Guard killed four students, happened a month after Reagan's speech.

51. **C** Overwhelmingly approved in 1994 by a majority of 59 percent, the proposition was the first time a state had passed legislation related to immigration. In 1997, federal judge Mariana Pfaelzer found the law to be unconstitutional, which greatly energized Latino voters, increasing Latino voter turnout. Proposition 187 was never brought before the U.S. Supreme Court, so choice A is incorrect. Republicans did not court Latinos; on the contrary, the proposition, backed by Republican Governor Pete Wilson, caused a backlash against the party, so choice B is incorrect. There is no evidence that the Latino population increased as a result of the law being declared unconstitutional (choice D).

52. **D** Silicon Valley, a high-tech business corridor, attracted 40 percent of U.S. venture capital in 2009, according to a report from the National Venture Capital Association. It goes through a boom and bust cycle: 1 million employed in 2000, 850,000 in 2004, and 915,000 in 2007. Many of the engineers and programmers who work there are from India and China, so nearly half the population speaks another language besides English, and the area is responsible for almost half the patents issued each year. The San Fernando Valley includes half of the city of Los Angeles, as well as Burbank and Glendale. It is a center of the motion picture industry, so choice A is incorrect. The San Francisco Bay Area is known for its financial district and tourism, making choice B wrong. Sacramento is the capital of the state and has more politicians than businesses, so choice C is not correct.

Constructed-Response Assignments—Sample Responses

1. The author creates a sense of mystery in the passage though her choice of language, as well as the description of the scene. The description of the two people having different thoughts and a "low voice" rising in the night create a powerful image that makes the reader realize the two are at odds.

   The words of the song and the description of the man singing heighten the sense of mystery. The words "he sang in a passionate, vibrating baritone" lend a sense of sensuality to the scene. The writer goes on to tell how the voice "seemed to come from the dark shadows" of the garden, which produces an even greater sense of the mysterious.

Use of such words as "his voice lingering caressingly" and "the verse dying away softly" create further sensuality, in addition to mystery. Finally, the voice disappears, and the writer brings the reader back to reality.

2. Creative learning methods and playmates are two tools that greatly facilitate language acquisition during the early to middle childhood period.

Creative learning methods that teachers develop allow the child to acquire more language skills because children are encouraged to develop their mental capacities. For instance, children who are given age-specific activities develop the ability to retain information such as the fact that plurals are formed by adding -s. They also learn to develop patterns in language and use mnemonics through recitation of words and rules such as "i before e." This also helps them understand exceptions: "except after c." As a result, they learn the ways that they learn best, or through metacognition.

Playmates greatly assist in language acquisition, since playmates talk to each other, play games, and say rhymes, all of which increase the grasp of words and language. As children grow, they become more interested in finding out about their friends, and this leads to question asking and conversations. Children realize they want to express themselves, especially their emotions, more clearly. Teachers can play a part by encouraging friends to read together and by playing word games.

3. Signed in 1215, the Magna Carta was an agreement between King John and English barons to protect feudal rights. The barons, having grown weary of the heavy taxation imposed by the king to finance his wars in France, finally rebelled and convinced the king to meet with them at Runnymede, a water meadow along the River Thames.

The Magna Carta placed limits on the power of the king and made him subject to the law. Its two most famous clauses declared that no person can be imprisoned except by the judgment of his peers and the law of the land, and that justice cannot be delayed, denied, or sold.

These clauses led Sir Edward Coke, one of the greatest jurists of the Elizabethan era, to write that the Magna Carta was "declaratory of the principal grounds of the fundamental laws of England." Coke went on to write the major English constitutional document, the Petition of Right, in 1628.

The Magna Carta was instrumental in the creation of England's Parliament. The Magna Carta influenced the American Declaration of Independence in 1776, and the concept that the law is supreme was drafted into the U.S. Constitution. The United Nations Universal Declaration of Human Rights in 1948 also is rooted in the Magna Carta.

4. During the early years of the twentieth century, large numbers of African Americans migrated from the rural South to the cities of the North, a large majority of them to New York's Harlem district. Social changes had taken place in the African American communities after the abolition of slavery. African Americans in the South had no rights, could not vote, and had limited economic opportunities.

The First World War created industrial economic opportunities in the cities of the North, which brought even more African Americans to urban areas, particularly New York City. As a result, the African Americans from the South mingled with others of African descent from the Caribbean in Harlem.

From this melting pot, the Harlem Renaissance emerged. Writers, artists, and performers began to blossom. Musicians worked together, developing a new sound called jazz. The popularity of jazz spread through the country. The names of Duke Ellington, Count Basie, Billie Holiday, Louis Armstrong, and other musicians became household words. Activists and writers including Langston Hughes and W. E. B. Du Bois united with playwrights like Eugene O'Neill. Actors such as Paul Robeson were critically acclaimed.

The Harlem Renaissance profoundly changed how white Americans viewed African Americans. It demonstrated the importance of African American culture. Whites began to collaborate with African Americans to transform a society still largely segregated. The Harlem Renaissance had repercussions on race relations in America for many years to come.

Subtest II Explanations

SCIENCE, MATHEMATICS

1. **D** Barometers are used to measure the barometric (air) pressure.
2. **B** Since the larvae harm the grasshopper, this relationship is an example of parasitism.
3. **C** The charring of the vegetable represents a change in matter at the molecular level. Therefore, this is an example of a chemical change.
4. **D** The lithosphere of the earth includes the crust, which consists of large and small plates that move over large time scales.
5. **C** Photosynthesis occurs in the chloroplasts of plant cells.
6. **C** If the ball is released, gravity will act on it, causing it to roll down the incline. Additionally, the ball will increase in speed as it gains momentum.
7. **C** Since Mercury and Venus are the planets closest to the sun, they will be located near the sun in the sky. This would make them most visible in the early hours of evening and morning.
8. **A** The atomic number of an element represents the number of protons in a single atom of that element.
9. **C** If the density of an object is greater than the density of water, the object will sink in water. In this case, since the rock sinks and the candle does not, the rock must have a higher density than the candle.
10. **A** The equatorial diameter of Saturn is approximately 74,897.6 miles. All of the other planets listed have markedly smaller diameters.
11. **B** Gametes are formed through meiosis.

12. **A** In any given row of the periodic table, elements are listed according to atomic number from left to right.
13. **D** The point within the crust where the earthquake occurs is referred to as the focus, while the point directly above this on the surface is referred to as the epicenter.
14. **B** The air temperature has no effect on the height of a tide.
15. **A** The grasses create their own energy through photosynthesis, making them the primary producers of the described ecosystem.
16. **A** All of the atoms of the same element have the same number of protons in their nuclei, but the number of neutrons may differ.
17. **C** Differences in barometric pressure across a small area cause high winds.
18. **A** By definition, metamorphic rocks are rocks formed under exactly the conditions described.
19. **C** Acceleration is the rate of change in the velocity of an object.
20. **C** The most likely explanation is one that helps the dolphins in their own survival. Of the explanations, only answer choice C is based purely on this motive.
21. **B** Heat transfer by convection occurs when heat is transferred through the movement of fluids, such as the air heated by the radiator.
22. **C** A high pH represents a basic solution.
23. **D** Low barometric pressure is associated with large storm systems. The lower the barometric pressure, the stronger the hurricane.

24. **A** By definition, the prime meridian is the line that is defined to have 0 degrees of longitude.

25. **D** The ice cube is going from a solid state directly to a gaseous state. This is an example of sublimation.

26. **A** Overall, ice at the poles does not absorb carbon dioxide.

27. **A** Since the line is perpendicular, the slope is $\frac{1}{3}$. Given the y-intercept, the equation of the line is $y = \frac{1}{3}x + 6$. Only answer choice A represents a point that satisfies this equation.

28. **B** If x represents the cost of the baseball bat and y represents the cost of the baseball, then we can set up the following system of equations:

$$x + y = 15.5$$
$$x = y + 11.5$$

Solving for y yields $(y + 11.5) + y = 15.5$, so $y = 2$.

29. **B** Distributing the 2 on the left yields the equation $2x + 10 = 24$, which is equivalent to $2x = 14$.

30. **C** The line rises from left to right, which indicates a positive slope. Additionally, the graph crosses the x-axis to the left of the y-axis, indicating a negative x-intercept.

31. **C** The median is the middle value of a set of ordered numbers. When the numbers are placed in order (0, 1, 1, 4, 7), it is easy to see that 1 is the middle value.

32. **D** To answer the question stated in choice D, it would be necessary to multiply 25,000 by 3/4.

33. **A** The triangle given is a right triangle, which means the Pythagorean theorem applies. Use this to find the height:

$$(3x)^2 + \text{height}^2 = (5x)^2$$
$$\text{height}^2 = 16x^2$$
$$\text{height} = 4x$$

The area of any triangle is found using the formula $A = \frac{1}{2}(\text{base})(\text{height})$, which in this case is $\frac{1}{2}(4x)(3x) = 6x^2$.

34. **B** This data set has a large outlier of 81, which will skew the average (the mean, choice A) to the right. Therefore, the median is a better measure to summarize the center of the data set. None of the numbers is repeated, so mode is an inappropriate measure.

35. **A** Because 20 feet represents 1/5 of 100 feet, the scale drawing of the antenna should be 1/5 of 1 inch, or 0.2 inch.

36. **B** The space between 0 and 1 is divided into three segments, so the dividing lines must represent 1/3 and 2/3, respectively. This means that point A is less than 1/3, so it is not a candidate for x. Also, 3/8 = 0.375, which is slightly more than 1/3 but less than 1/2, ruling out points C and D. That leaves only B as a possible candidate for x.

37. **C** Expressing the information in the problem mathematically, 0.10(100) = 10 of the problems are word problems, and ½(10) = 5, so 5 problems would require two equations.

38. **A** The probability an item is both blue and type Y is 0. This is the definition of two mutually exclusive events.

39. **C** Prime factorizations consist only of powers of prime numbers, and 4 is not prime.

40. **B** The total commission would be $0.02s$, and the 500 is a fixed amount (so the term will have no variable). Therefore, the total pay is $0.02s + 500$.

41. **D** By finding the two numbers we are multiplying, we can easily find y. The first number below the line is 625. This can only be the case if the blank above the line is 5, meaning this multiplication problem is 625 × 15. Working out the problem, the y is 8.

42. **B** If the width is w, the perimeter can be expressed as $2w + 2w + w + w = 90$, which simplifies to $6w = 90$. Solving for w, we find that the width of the room is 15 feet. If 15 feet = 10 gabs, then 1 gab must be 15/10 = 1.5 feet.

43. **A** Joe would find a product of 1 × 3 = 3, which is 0.64 less than 1.3 × 2.8.

44. **D** The bag contains only red and green marbles, meaning the complement to the event "the selected marble is green" is "the selected marble is red." Complementary events have probabilities that add to 1.

45. D The only fact that will work for finding the value of x is that any side opposite a 60-degree angle will have a measure of 4 in this triangle. The Pythagorean theorem (choice B) does not apply, since the triangle is not a right triangle, and for answer choices A and C, the ratios using the angles and the sides do not hold.

46. C The area of the triangle is calculated using the formula $\frac{1}{2}(\text{base})(\text{height}) = 24$. Using the fact that one of the sides is 6, the other leg must be 8, because $\frac{1}{2}(6)(8) = 24$. Finally, since the triangle is a right triangle, the hypotenuse can be found using the Pythagorean theorem:

$$6^2 + 8^2 = c^2$$
$$100 = c^2$$
$$10 = c$$

47. B A line of the form "$y = \text{constant}$" is a horizontal line. All horizontal lines have a slope of 0.

48. A Use FOIL to simplify the expression $(x + 2)^2$, which is equivalent to $(x + 2)(x + 2)$:

$$(x + 2)^2 - 2x$$
$$= x^2 + 4x + 4 - 2x$$
$$= x^2 + 2x + 4$$

49. C Both figures are squares, so the length of any side of A is $\sqrt{16} = 4$, and the length of any side of B is $\sqrt{64} = 8$. Therefore, the perimeter is $8 + 8 + 8 + 8 + 4 + 4 = 40$.

50. A Three of eight segments are shaded, so any fraction equivalent to 3/8 will be represented by the picture.

51. D The graph starts out with a steady increase in distance as time progresses, and then distance does not increase anymore, indicating the family no longer was driving.

52. C $\dfrac{2}{1,000} = \dfrac{0.2}{100} = 0.2\%.$

Constructed-Response Assignments—Sample Responses

1. When a pendulum swings at a small angle, its period obeys the equation $T \approx 2p\sqrt{L/g}$, where T = the period, L = length of the pendulum, and g = acceleration of gravity. The only one of these variables that could have changed between the bottom of the building and its top is the force of gravity, g. When objects move farther from the earth's center of mass, the force of gravity acting upon them decreases. At the top of a tall building, that decrease is very small but measurable.

    As suggested by the formula in the first paragraph, it is possible to increase a pendulum's period by lengthening the string that it swings from. Alternatively, swinging a pendulum at a large angle (for example, 85°) causes the pendulum to swing with a longer period that can no longer be accurately described by the formula. For smaller pendulums, the period is much the same with each swing, but with very large pendulums, the period increases, making the formula inaccurate.

    The composition of the material that swings at the end of a pendulum does not affect its period.

2. To know how much paint to use to cover the entire surface of the tetrahedron, we must find the surface area. An equilateral tetrahedron has four faces, each of which is an equilateral triangle so the surface area will be four times the area of one of these triangular faces.

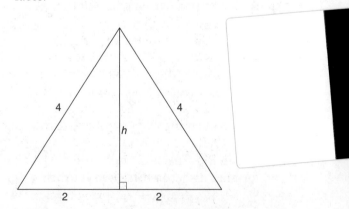

To find the area of one of the faces, we will use the formula $A = \frac{1}{2}bh$ where the base has a length of 4 and the height is indicated in this figure. As we can see, the height is the leg of a right triangle with sides h, and 2, and a hypotenuse of 4. Using the Pythagorean theorem, $2^2 + h^2 = 4^2$ or $h^2 = 4^2 - 2^2 = 16 - 4 = 12$. Finally, using the square root property, $h = \sqrt{12} = 2\sqrt{3}$ and the area of the triangle is $\frac{1}{2}(4)(2\sqrt{3}) = 4\sqrt{3}$.

Now that we have the area of one face of the tetrahedron, we can say the surface area of the entire tetrahedron is $4 \times 4\sqrt{3} = 16\sqrt{3}$. Since the paint can cover 10 square cm per mL, we will need $\frac{16\sqrt{3}}{10} = \frac{8\sqrt{3}}{5}$ mL to paint the entire surface of the tetrahedron. Simplifying and rounding to the nearest hundredth, we'd need 2.77 mL of paint.

3. Draw a Punnett square for this exercise.

		Male	
		Aa	aB
Female	ab	Aa Bb	aa Bb
	Ab	AA Bb	Aa Bb

To estimate the number of short-tailed offspring, notice that the Punnett square predicts that 25 percent of the mouse offspring will have short tails (genotypes aa):

28 × 0.25 = 7 short-tailed offspring

According to the Punnett square, none of the offspring will display their mother's white-coat phenotype, although all of the offspring will carry that recessive gene (b). Of the 28 offspring, 75 percent will display both a long tail and a brown coat (genotype Aa Bb or AA Bb). That is, 21 mice will likely resemble their father in these two characteristics.

Short-tailed white offspring display both recessive phenotypes, so these mice must carry genotype aa bb. For one of the mice represented in the Punnett square to produce white, short-tailed offspring, it must carry at least one recessive gene of each type. Of the 28 offspring, 75 percent are expected to be capable of producing white, short-tailed offspring.

4. If point O bisects line DE, then triangle ADE is an isosceles right triangle. The length of each of its sides is equal to 2 times the circle's radius, so substitute the radius for the triangle's sides when computing its area: $\frac{1}{2}(2r \times 2r)$.

Find the circle's radius by solving for r in the formula for the circle's area, πr^2:

$10 \text{ cm}^2 = \pi r^2$
$3.18 \text{ cm}^2 = r^2$
$1.78 \text{ cm} = r$

Now solve to find the triangle's area:

$\frac{1}{2}(2 \times 1.78 \text{ cm})(2 \times 1.78 \text{ cm}) = 6.33 \text{ cm}^2$

To determine the product of lines BD and CE, first connect point C with point O, making a line perpendicular to AE. Connect point B with point O in a similar fashion. Whether or not line DE is bisected at point O, triangles BDO and COE remain similar:

$$\frac{BD}{CO} = \frac{BO}{CE}$$
$$BO = CO = r$$

$$BD \times CE = r^2$$

$$BD \times CE = 3.18 \text{ cm}^2$$

Subtest III Explanations

PHYSICAL EDUCATION, HUMAN DEVELOPMENT, AND VISUAL AND PERFORMING ARTS

1. **C** Locomotor skills involve movement from one location to another, while nonlocomotor skills involve movement of the body without changing locations. Manipulative skills involve causing another object to move.

2. **B** The single costliest health problem in the United States is tobacco and alcohol abuse.

3. **C** The emphasis of the social responsibility approach is teaching students to work together and build strong interpersonal relationships. The self-actualization approach (choice A) matches the students' interests and motivation to the curriculum. The ecological integration approach (choice D) focuses on teaching PE as a way to prepare students for future successful group participation.

4. **A** Physical fitness activities should always begin with warm-up exercises involving the muscle groups that students will use throughout the class period, in order to prevent injury. This should be followed by instruction, the main physical activity, a cooldown activity, and a wrap-up discussion of the day's events.

5. **C** Stretching muscles involves extending parts of the body away from the center. Bending (choice A) involves using joints to bring body parts together; turning (choice D) involves rotation around the vertical axis of the body. Stretching, turning, and bending are nonlocomotor activities. Sliding (choice B) is a locomotor activity that involves a sideways galloping movement.

6. **A** This condition is arteriosclerosis. Congestive heart failure (choice B) occurs when the heart is not strong enough to supply enough blood to the rest of the body. Coronary thrombosis (choice C) occurs when a coronary artery is blocked by a blood clot.

7. **D** Students from higher-SES families are more likely to be involved in physical activities and sports than their lower-SES peers. Thus, students from lower-SES families are less physically fit.

8. **C** Weight-bearing exercises require one's feet or legs to carry one's own weight. Bike riding places the weight of the person on the equipment.

9. **A** Balance and equilibrium are important to the performance of any motor skills. Movements such as arm movement while walking, or lowering the center of gravity when stopping quickly allow the body to maintain balance.

10. **A** Federal law requires a number of things to be included in an IEP, including the student's present level of performance, long-term goal(s), and short-term objectives. The present level of performance should clearly indicate the specific skills the student is able to perform. For the physical education teacher, this should indicate specific strengths and weaknesses in motor, sports, and fitness skills.

11. **D** The order in which manipulative skills are generally developed is pull, push, lift, strike (choice D), throw, kick (choice B), and bounce (choice A). Skipping (choice C) is a locomotor skill rather than a manipulative skill.

12. **C** FITT guidelines suggest a minimum of 8 to 10 minutes of aerobic activity; however, the ideal duration should be at least 20 minutes out of an hour-long activity.

13. **D** Gross-motor areas include the arms (choice A), legs (choice B), and neck (choice C). Fine-motor areas include the fingers and toes (choice D). Gross-motor skills generally develop before fine-motor skills.

14. **A** Skinner's operant conditioning approach includes negative reinforcement, which allows students to escape punishment by repeating desired behaviors; positive reinforcement, which rewards desired behaviors; extinction, which does not reinforce undesired behaviors; and punishment, which punishes undesired behaviors.

15. **C** Piaget's stages of cognitive development include sensorimotor, preoperational, concrete operational, and formal operational. The ability to reason effectively and abstractly, think about concepts in fully symbolic terms, and develop concepts without concrete materials is demonstrated in the formal operational stage, which generally occurs beginning at age 12.

16. **C** Students' success in school can be affected by many factors. Anxiety, tension, and low self-esteem can have a negative impact on school performance.

17. **B** When instructing these students, select a few of the most important skills, and focus on these. These students need to learn through concrete experiences, with plenty of time and repeated opportunities for practice. Students should be given the opportunity to do as much as possible for themselves, even if they need extra time to accomplish the task.

18. **D** Limited English Proficiency (LEP) students did not learn English as their first language. To understand instruction as well as possible, these students benefit from the use of context clues, use of simple words, and avoidance of expressions such as idioms and figurative language. Contrary to choice A, learning expectations for these students should be adapted rather than decreased. Curriculum adaptations for students representing various SES situations should be used as well. Those from low-SES families benefit from an increase in structure and encouragement, so choice C is not correct. Those from high-SES families benefit from a decrease in competitiveness and structure, so choice B is not correct.

19. **B** Erikson developed a model of eight psychosocial stages that people go through during their lifetime. Four of these stages occur during a child's years in school. Initiative versus guilt (choice C) occurs between the ages of four and five. This is when a sense of responsibility is developed, which increases the child's initiative; irresponsibility leads to feelings of guilt. The next stage, identity versus inferiority (choice B), occurs between the age of six and onset of puberty. During these years, successful experiences, both in school and socially, lead to a sense of competence; failure leads to a feeling of inadequacy. Identity versus identity confusion (choice A), the stage that occurs during adolescence, is when concerns over identity peak. During young adulthood, people experience intimacy versus isolation (choice D), during which time they find it easier to establish relationships with others if they have discovered their identity and gone through the earlier stages successfully.

20. **A** Functional play involves using not only sensorimotor skills to manipulate objects, but also the repetition of behaviors. During constructive play, children use these sensorimotor skills to manipulate the objects in order to create something. Imaginative play, or pretend, centers around make-believe or fantasy and develops the imagination. Rough-and-tumble play, such as tag and wrestling, begins during early childhood and is most popular with students during their middle childhood. Games with rules generally lose popularity with children around the age of 12, and these games are replaced by interest in organized sports.

21. **A** Poor nutrition is a problem in children and adolescents. Diet and nutrition are strongly influenced by the home environment. Children from low-SES families face the biggest nutritional challenges.

22. **D** Each of the answer choices is a type of child abuse, which under California law should be reported by teachers. Sadness and anger may be signs of any of the types of abuse; signs of sexual abuse include self-inflicted harm, wetting, trouble walking or sitting, and inappropriate sexual knowledge or behavior, based on the age of the child.

23. **B** Centration is a characteristic of children in Piaget's preoperational stage of cognitive development.

24. **B** Kohlberg's stages of moral development include preconventional morality, conventional morality, and postconventional morality. Those in the conventional morality stage show respect for authority, rules, and expectations, and they recognize the importance of the laws of society. Their sense

of right and wrong is based on these rules, rather than on what will please others.

25. **D** Those with strong interpersonal abilities are able to understand and interact with others well and demonstrate strong conversation skills. Often, people with strengths in this area become teachers, salespeople, or politicians, since these occupations involve interacting with others.

26. **C** During infancy, children experience the greatest amount of growth of any period. Between the ages of 2 and 6, the early childhood years, there is a decrease in the amount of fatty tissue. By the age of 12, girls are slightly taller and weigh a few pounds more than boys of the same age. Between the ages of 13 and 14, however, boys experience a growth spurt that causes them to pass the girls in the areas of height and weight.

27. **C** Linear perspective means that objects which are farther away are drawn or painted smaller than those which are intended to appear closer to the viewer. Photographs naturally display this technique.

28. **A** The church attempted to restrict dance during the Middle Ages. Before this, dance celebrated births, rites of passage, religious rituals, hunting, and fertility.

29. **A** Performing pantomimes and improvisations of familiar stories (choice B) teaches creative expression associated with theater, rather than dance. Choice C helps students identify dances from around the world but does not help them learn about creative expression. Explaining the features of dance (choice D) teaches aesthetic valuing.

30. **A** The dynamics of a piece of music can be loud or soft. In music, the term *forte* is used to describe loud sounds, and *piano* or *pianissimo* is used to describe soft sounds.

31. **C** Color influences the mood of a piece of art. Cold colors, such as blue, create a cold mood and appear to contract the size of the artwork, while warm colors, such as yellows, create a warm mood and appear to expand the size of the piece.

32. **C** The choreography of modern dance involves the subjective interpretation of feelings and moods. It is unstructured and includes freestyle movements, so students of all ability levels can participate.

33. **A** The D-major scale includes two sharps: C-sharp and F-sharp.

34. **C** A strong gesture or movement in dance is called an accent. The underlying beat (choice A) is the pulse. The plan for the dance performance (choice B) is choreography. A type of dance that follows a story (choice D) is narrative dance.

35. **C** The direction of playwrights was determined by economic and societal changes during the eighteenth century. Commercial theater began during this time, and the plays more commonly began to reflect real people and real life than they had during previous eras.

36. **B** The harp and percussion instruments are behind the violins, which are to the conductor's left. French horns are behind the clarinets; trumpets are behind the bassoons. In front of the clarinets and bassoons are the flutes and oboes, respectively; violas are in front of these, nearest to the conductor. Double basses are behind the cellos, to the conductor's right.

37. **C** Before the end of the twelfth century, musical notation included only the pitch of the notes to be played. Notated rhythm was then added.

38. **B** The properties of color are hue, value, and saturation. Saturation, which describes the brightness or dullness of a color, is also called chroma.

39. **C** Form and shape, direction, level, range, pathway, and focus are all under the element of levels. Words describing the form and shape of dance include *angular*, *symmetrical*, and *asymmetrical*.

Constructed-Response Assignments—Sample Responses

1. The FITT principles of physical fitness are frequency, intensity, time, and type. Frequency is the number of times per week that the activity occurs. Intensity refers to

the difficulty level of the activity; it can be monitored by the student's cardiorespiratory rate. Time is how long the activity lasts, which depends on the type and intensity of the activity being performed. Type refers to the kind of activity.

Regarding frequency, upper-elementary students should perform cardiorespiratory endurance activities daily. Aerobic activities should be performed at an intensity level that allows students to still be able to talk fairly easily, which is at about 45 to 65 percent of their maximum heart rate. The time recommendation for flexibility exercises is that these students should hold each stretch for between 10 and 30 seconds, with about five stretches for each muscle group. The type of stretching these students should perform at school is slow, static stretching that involves all muscle groups.

2. The first of Piaget's stages of cognitive development is the sensorimotor stage, which occurs from birth to approximately 18 months to two years of age. During this time, infants demonstrate poor verbal and cognitive development but begin to understand the concept of object permanence. Young children use their senses to perceive the world, and behavior is based on responses to their surroundings.

Following this, children are in stage 2, which is Piaget's preoperational stage, until about the age of seven. During this time, children develop language and problem-solving abilities, have strong imaginations, and begin to think symbolically. However, their thinking is still egocentric, and they have difficulty developing concepts.

Stage 3, from ages 7 through 12, is the concrete operational stage, during which concepts become more logical and organized when children are working with concrete materials. Children in this stage are able to solve simple problems. Number conservation and other conservation skills are strengthened, although symbolic concepts and abstract thinking are not yet mastered.

The fourth stage, formal operational, occurs from age 12 through adulthood. At this point, adolescents are able to use abstract thinking and reasoning, and they are capable of solving complex problems and thinking hypothetically.

One way that educators can apply this information is to use concrete materials and manipulatives when teaching abstract concepts, such as math, to elementary school students. By middle school, students are able to master abstract mathematical concepts without using hands-on materials.

3. Ballet is a classical dance form that began in France during the European Renaissance period. It developed throughout the continent between the 1500s and 1800s. This structured dance form is highly technical and includes formal, conventional steps, body positions, and poses, as well as graceful movements, leaps, and spins. Often, a choreographed ballet tells a story or presents a theme. Many ballets are accompanied by classical music.

Modern dance, in contrast, did not begin until the 1900s. It is a type of freestyle, theatrical dance that is less formal and structured than ballet. It is based on original movements and the expression of feelings. The movements of modern dance are enhanced by the use of gravity and the dancers' body weight, whereas the movements in ballet are more elegant and graceful.

CHAPTER 14

Writing Skills Practice Test 2

Each of the constructed-response questions in the CSET Writing Skills section is graded on a scale of 1 to 4. At the end of each writing section, you'll find four sample responses for each question, with each sample response illustrating the level of work that would receive a score of 4 (highest), 3, 2, or 1 (lowest).

Expository Writing

Complete the exercise that follows.

You were asked to address the school board to explain why you think it is important to instill values in children. In an essay to be read by an audience of educated adults, tell why you think it is important to instill values in children and what values you feel are the most important.

1. Provide your answer in the the space allotted.

_____

_____

_____

_____

_____

_____

_____

_____

_____

_____

_____

_____

_____

_____

_____

_____

_____

_____

Expressive Writing

Complete the exercise that follows.

School plays an important part in children's development. One way that children can grow is by participating in class outings. In an essay to be read by an audience of educated adults, identify a class trip you have taken, and explain how it influenced you for the better.

2. Provide your answer in the space allotted.

_____

_____

_____

_____

_____

_____

_____

_____

_____

_____

_____

_____

_____

_____

_____

_____

_____

_____

Writing Skills Practice Test 2 Sample Answers

Expository Writing

Question 1 (Score: 4 points)

A good teacher should not just draw up lesson plans based on a syllabus; she should also teach the importance of good values. Values are essential beliefs that guide an individual's attitudes and actions. How an individual feels about what is right and what is wrong is a core principle of ethics. It is the model that will propel a person throughout life. And while values should be taught at home, I feel it is also vital to teach them in the classroom, because the classroom represents society to a child.

The concept of fair play, I believe, is a fundamental value to be taught to students, both in the classroom and in sports. Children who are taught to be fair become fair adults. Students should be taught to have a sense of fellowship with their competitors. Just as a good sportsman will help a competitor up who has fallen, he will also offer help in the classroom to a classmate who is faltering.

On the playing field, a student should be taught to play fairly, even if her opponents are not. She should be a good loser as well as a good winner. Competitors should always shake hands with each other after a game is over. The game should always be played according to the rules. It is extremely valuable for children to learn that there are rules for games, for school, and for life.

It is important that a teacher establish a standard of decency and honesty that registers with each student. I strongly feel that a classroom with an atmosphere of camaraderie, understanding, and openness will be much more conducive to learning than one with a spirit of succeeding or winning at any cost. The value of fair play builds good character in all and goes hand in hand with courage and persistence. Learned in school, this will become a way of life for individuals, who will apply the concept in their adult lives.

Score Note: This essay earns a 4 because it is well-structured and its arguments are supported by specific detail. It directly addresses the prompt, and it is free of grammatical and punctuation errors.

Question 1 (Score: 3 points)

I believe values should be taught to children as well as the three Rs, and I think charity is an important value to be taught to children. Charity means the act of caring and giving in a large-hearted and generous way. The importance of charity is stressed in all of the world's major religions as well as by the great philosophers.

Our students should be taught a spirit of generosity toward other people and to perform acts of generosity. Children need to learn not to be selfish. People who are charitable think of other people before they think of themselves. There have been many famous people in history who are examples of charity. Mother Teresa is one that comes to mind. Students can be taught about these examples and the good works that they did. They can be used as role models in the classroom.

Along with charity comes the concept of social justice, which is also important to be taught. Our society needs to be aware of those who are less fortunate and who are in need, and that all human beings have rights.

Score Note: This essay earns a 3 because it is reasonably well-structured and free of glaring grammatical errors, but it does not fully address the prompt and includes some extraneous details. Note how often "charity" is mentioned; however, the writer does not make a strong case, using concrete examples, to explain why charity, in particular, is important to teach to students.

Question 1 (Score: 2 points)

Honesty is the best policy is the way the old saying goes. This means you should always tell the truth. Thats what I would teach children. People who lie are probably the same ones that steal and cheat on there tests. So I agree honesty is an important value to instill in children in the classroom.

It is good to set an example to others by showing you tell the truth all the time. Just look at Honest Abe—he went on to become a president. Honesty is the best policy and it is important that school children learn this. They will be better citizens. Being a good citizen is a good goal for teachers to think about. Also if you find something that isnt yours you should turn it in.

Score Note: This essay earns a 2 because, although it addresses the prompt, it has grammatical and construction errors. It is very short and poorly organized. The details given do not directly support the argument.

Question 1 (Score: 1 point)

I would take the children who is in school and teach them respect. By that I mean the value of respect like respecting your parents and doing what they tell you to do and the flag. Instiling respect for the teacher. Something that is excellent is respected.

Score Note: This response receives a 1 because it fails to satisfy the requirements of the prompt. Responses that do not directly answer the prompt will always receive low scores. Further, the essay is inappropriately short and offers no supporting detail.

Expressive Writing
Question 2 (Score: 4 points)

The most amazing class trip I ever took was when I was at school in Virginia, where my family lived when I was in middle school. Our class took a school bus to Jamestown, the first settlement in the New World. We were all very excited when we arrived and saw the re-creation of the original settlement, which was filled with people who were pretending to be the original settlers. The guide told us all about the life they had there in Jamestown and how hard it was to survive.

There were houses with thatched roofs and people making things the way they used to make them during the colonial period. There were children playing with toys that they had during this time period. The whole place was fascinating. There was also an Indian encampment, where visitors could see a re-created village with reed-covered houses. The pretend Native Americans also showed visitors how the Indians grew crops and many of their customs.

What was probably the best part were the three ships, replicas of the ships the Jamestown settlers came in. Visitors could go aboard, and I loved pretending I was a passenger. I looked at how small they were and wondered whether I would have been able to withstand a crossing of the Atlantic. These people seemed very brave to me.

The visit to Jamestown literally changed my life. I became very interested in American history. I loved reading about what life was like in all the colonies. Later on I was able to visit Plymouth and see where the Pilgrims first set foot at Plymouth Rock and to visit what they call Plimoth Plantation, where the Pilgrims' settlement is re-created. As a result of this interest, I ended up majoring in American history and later decided I wanted to become a teacher. So, many of my life decisions came about because of my class trip to Jamestown.

Score Note: This essay earns a 4 because it is well-structured and its arguments are supported by specific detail. As an expressive piece of writing, it is also effective because it clearly conveys the writer's excitement and enthusiasm. It directly and fully addresses the prompt, and it is free of grammatical and punctuation errors.

Question 2 (Score: 3 points)

My favorite class outing was to the Monterey Bay Aquarium because I have never seen so many different kinds of fish and other denizens of the ocean. It was great way to learn more about the life that lives below the sea. Its a big place and has many different exhibits.

I especially loved the penguins. They were so wonderful to watch, and the guide told us a lot about them, too. He said that when they flap their wings or bow their heads, they are saying how they are feeling. He told us that when they throw their heads back and wings out, it means they are happy. When they lean forward and open their beaks, it means to go away.

Another exhibit I liked had a huge number of anchovies. Being little fish, I never really realized until that moment what anchovies were. The guide also told us that where the aquarium was built was originally a cannery for anchovies and sardines.

I also liked the sea turtle exhibit and the touching pond, where you could put your hand in and feel plankton and other things from the ocean.

Visiting the aquarium at my young age made me realize how important the ocean and the creatures that live in it are to us.

Score Note: This essay earns a 3 because it is reasonably well-structured and directly addresses the prompt; however it does have some grammatical problems. Also, it focuses more on describing the aquarium that on explaining how the experience of visiting the aquarium changed the writer. That should be a main focus of the essay, but it is only mentioned at the very end, and very briefly.

Question 2 (Score: 2 points)

When I was in high school our choris went to Disney World in Florida. It was amazing. We got to sing in front of everyone. I really enjoy it. The newspaper in our town did a story about us. They said we were outstanding. We were not the only chorus to sing. But I think we were the best. The weather was not very good when we were there, but we went on rides and had a lot of fun. Actually, it was my birthday. That made it even better for me. I decide after that I would like to study music. This is what the trip did for me. It helped me find myself.

Score Note: This essay earns a 2 because it is inappropriately short, and it features spelling and grammatical errors. It also includes extraneous details that do not support the central argument.

Question 2 (Score: 1 point)

I went to a museum. It was a old car museum. We seed many kinds of cars. I think old cars are fun. We brought our lunches. I was in the sixth grade. But I remember everything. I like to see different kinds of cars on the road to. I have a Ford car now. It isn't very new. But it isn't as old as those cars were.

Score Note: This essay receives a score of 1 because it is inappropriately short, features spelling and grammatical mistakes, and does not address the prompt.

NOTES

NOTES

NOTES

NOTES

NOTES

NOTES